MERCE CUNNINGHAM

Select Other Works by Richard Kostelanetz

Books Authored

The Theatre of Mixed Means (1968)
Master Minds (1969)
Visual Language (1970)
In the Beginning (1971)
The End of Intelligent Writing (1974)
Openings & Closings (1975)
Portraits from Memory (1975)
Constructs (1975)
One Night Stood (1977)
Wordsand (1978)
Twenties in the Sixties (1979)
And So Forth (1979)
Metamorphosis in the Arts (1980)
The Old Poetries and the New (1981)
American Imaginations (1983)
The Old Fictions and the New (1987)
Conversing with Cage (1988)
On Innovative Music(ian)s (1989)
The New Poetries and Some Old
  (1991)
Politics in the African-American
  Novel (1991)
On Innovative Art(ist)s (1991)
Solos, Duets, Trios, & Choruses
  (1991)

Books Edited

On Contemporary Literature (1964,
  1969)
Twelve from the Sixties (1967)
The Young American Writers (1967)

Possibilities of Poetry (1970)
Imaged Words & Worded Images
  (1970)
Moholy-Nagy (1970, 1991)
John Cage (1970, 1991)
Seeing Through Shuck (1972)
Breakthrough Fictioneers (1973)
The Edge of Adaptation (1973)
Essaying Essays (1975)
Language & Structure (1975)
Younger Critics in North America
  (1976)
Esthetics Contemporary (1978,
  1989)
Assembling Assembling (1978)
Visual Literature Criticism (1979)
Text-Sound Texts (1980)
The Yale Gertrude Stein (1980)
Aural Literature Criticism (1981)
The Literature of SoHo (1981)
American Writing Today (1981,
  1991)
The Avant-Garde Tradition in
  Literature (1982)
Gertrude Stein Advanced (1989)

Books Co-authored & Edited

The New American Arts (1965)

Books Co-compiled & Introduced

Assembling (Twelve vols, 1970–
  1981)

MERCE CUNNINGHAM

Dancing in Space and Time

EDITED BY RICHARD KOSTELANETZ

Essays 1944–1992 by Jack Anderson, John Cage, Remy Charlip, Arlene Croce, Merce Cunningham, Nancy Dalva, Don Daniels, Edwin Denby, Barbara Frost, Jill Johnston, Kenneth King, Alastair Macaulay, Don McDonagh, Wilfrid Mellers, Frank O'Hara, Sybil Shearer, Marcia B. Siegel, Stephen Smoliar, Calvin Tomkins, David Vaughan, James Waring, and the Editor; Symposia including Carolyn Brown, Earle Brown, Remy Charlip, Douglas Dunn, Viola Farber, Steve Paxton, Valda Setterfield, Marianne Preger Simon, Gus Solomons jr, and David Vaughan.

a cappella books

Library of Congress Cataloging-in-Publication Data

Merce Cunningham : dancing in space and time : essays 1944–1992 / by Jack Anderson . . .
  [et al.] ; edited by Richard Kostelanetz.
       p.   cm.
    Includes bibliographical references.
    ISBN 1-55652-152-9 : $16.95
    1. Cunningham, Merce.   2. Dancers—United States—Biography.
3. Choreographers—United States—Biography.   4. Modern dance—United States—
History.   I. Anderson, Jack, 1922–   .
II. Kostelanetz, Richard.
GV1785.C85M48   1992
792.8'028'092—dc20

    [B]   92-16911
                                                                                  CIP

a cappella books, incorporated
an imprint of
Chicago Review Press, Incorporated

5 4 3 2 1
Printed in the United States of America

Editorial offices:
PO Box 380
Pennington, NJ 08534

Business/sales offices:
814 N. Franklin St.
Chicago, IL 60610

Cover photo: Merce Cunningham in *Fragments*.
© 1987 JoAnn Baker, courtesy Cunningham Dance Foundation.

ACKNOWLEDGMENTS

Jack Anderson, "Dances About Everything and Dances About Some Things." In *Choreography Observed*. Iowa City, IA: U. of Iowa Press, 1987. Copyright © 1975, 1987 by Jack Anderson.

Carolyn Brown, contributions to a symposium in *Ballet Review* (1987), by permission of the author.

Earle Brown, contributions to a symposium in *Ballet Review* (1985), by permission of the author.

John Cage, "Grace and Clarity." In *Silence*. Middletown, CT: Wesleyan U. Press, 1961. By permission of the publisher and the University Press of New England. Copyright © 1961 by John Cage.

Remy Charlip, "Composing by Chance." *Dance Magazine* (January 1954); contributions to a symposium in *Ballet Review* (1985), by permission of the author. Copyright © 1954/1992, 1985 by Remy Charlip.

Arlene Croce, "The Mercists." *The New Yorker* (3 April 1978), by permission of the author. Copyright © 1978 by Arlene Croce.

Merce Cunningham, "Space, Time and Dance." *Trans/Formation* I/3 (1952); "A Collaborative Process Between Music and Dance." *Tri-Quarterly* 54 (1982); reprinted by permission of the author. Copyright © 1952, 1982 by Merce Cunningham. "Diary of a Cunningham Dance." *The New York Times* (15 March 1981), copyright © 1981 by the New York Times Company, reprinted by permission of *The New York Times* and Merce Cunningham.

Nancy Dalva, "The Way of Merce." *Dance Ink* III/1 (Spring 1992). By permission of the author. Copyright © 1992 by Nancy Dalva.

Don Daniels, "Cunningham in Time," excerpted from "Boutique Items and Risky Business." *Ballet Review* XIII/2 (Summer 1985), by permission of the author. Copyright © 1985 by Don Daniels.

Edwin Denby, reviews reprinted from the *New York Herald Tribune* by permission of Rudy Burkhardt for the Estate of Edwin Denby.

Douglas Dunn, contributions to a symposium in *Ballet Review* (1987), by permission of the author.

Viola Farber, contributions to a symposium in *Ballet Review* (1987), by permission of the author.

Barbara Frost, "Merce Cunningham." *Vassar Brew* (1948), reprinted from the public domain.

Jill Johnston, reviews from *The Village Voice*, reprinted by permission of the author.

Kenneth King, "Space Dance and the Galactic Matrix," previously unpublished, by permission of the author. Copyright © 1991 by Kenneth King. Portions appeared in *Chicago Review* (1992).

Richard Kostelanetz, excerpt from "Artists' Self-Books." *Ballet Review* III/2 (1969), reprinted in *Twenties in the Sixties* (Brooklyn, NY: Assembling; Westport, CT: Greenwood Press, 1979), by permission of the author. Copyright © 1969, 1979 by Richard Kostelanetz. "Twenty Years of Merce Cunningham's Dance," revised from *Dance Magazine* (1982), by permission of the author. Copyright © 1982, 1992 by Richard Kostelanetz.

Alastair Macaulay, "The Merce Experience." *The New Yorker* (4 April 1988), by permission of the publisher. Copyright © 1988 by Alastair Macaulay.

Don McDonagh, "Merce Cunningham." In *Don McDonagh's Complete Guide to Modern Dance*. NY: Doubleday and Company, 1977, by permission of the author. Copyright © 1977 by Don McDonagh.

Wilfrid Mellers, "Tranquillity." *The New Statesman* (31 July 1964), by permission of the publisher.

Frank O'Hara. "Cunningham, Here and Now." *The Village Voice* (4 December 1957), reprinted from the public domain.

Steve Paxton, contributions to a symposium in *Ballet Review* (1987), by permission of the author.

Valda Setterfield, contributions to a symposium in *Ballet Review* (1987), by permission of the author.
Sybil Shearer, "Dance in Review." *Dance News* (March 1949), by permission of the author.
Marcia B. Siegel. "Come in, Earth. Are You There?" In *At the Vanishing Point* (NY: Saturday Review Press/E.P. Dutton, 1972), by permission of the author. Copyright © 1972 by Marcia B. Siegel.
Marianne Preger Simon, contributions to symposia in *Ballet Review* (1985, 1987), by permission of the author.
Stephen Smoliar, "Merce Cunningham in Brooklyn." *Ballet Review* III/3 (1970), by permission of the author. Copyright © 1970 by Stephen Smoliar.
Gus Solomons jr, contributions to a symposium in *Ballet Review* (1987), by permission of the author.
Calvin Tomkins, text for an exhibition by Merce Cunningham (Multiples, 1974), by permission of the author.
David Vaughan, "Merce Cunningham's *Walkaround Time*." In *Art and Dance* (Boston: Institute of Contemporary Art, 1982); "Retrospect and Prospect." *Performing Arts Journal* (Winter 1979); "Locale: The Collaboration of Merce Cunningham and Charles Atlas." *Millennium Film Journal* 10/11 (Fall–Winter 1981/82); contributions to symposia in *Ballet Review* (1985, 1987); all by permission of the author. Copyright © 1982, 1979, 1981, 1985, 1987 by David Vaughan.
James Waring, "Merce Cunningham: Maker of Dances." *The Village Voice* (2 January 1957), by permission of David Vaughan for the Estate of James Waring.

Every effort has been made to identify the sources of original publication of these essays and make full acknowledgment of their use. If any error or omission has occurred, it will be corrected in future editions, provided that appropriate notification is submitted in writing to the publisher or editor.

CONTENTS

Especially for Kenneth King

Dance encodes not explicit hand signals as in Hawaiian or Balinese forms, but rather the intricate formal movements of the human body. In the hands of modern choreographers the dance becomes a form almost as abstract as nonobjective films, yet, however, firmly planted in the human figure which serves as its focus and counterpoint. It is removed from, yet dominated by, actual physical humans, differentiated as to sex, and meaningful as a play of human forms against one another and with respect to the field of the dance floor and whatever props or lights are used.
                                        —Robert E. Mueller, The Science of Art *(1967)*

For the early modern dance, emotional motivation had been essential; it was at once the cause and the aim of movement invention. With the new choreographers, emotional motivation has been deliberately eliminated from the scheme of composition, while other factors—dance, mathematics, musical, or pictorial structure—have taken its place.
                    —Selma Jeanne Cohen, "Introduction," The Modern Dance *(1966)*

Instead of this universe of "signification" (psychological, social, functional), we must try, then, to construct a world both more solid, more immediate. Let it be first of all by their presence *that objects and gestures establish themselves, and let this presence continue to prevail over whatever explicatory theory that may try to enclose them in a system of reference, whether emotional, sociological, Freudian, or metaphysical.*
                            —Alain Robbe-Grillet, *"A Future for the Novel" (1956)*

The esthetics of dancing—that is, a sort of algebra by which the impression a performance makes can be readily itemized, estimated, and communicated to a reader—is vague and clumsy. The dance critic's wits have to be all the sharper; he has to use esthetic household wrinkles and esthetic common sense to help out. And he has to pull his objectivity out of his hat. . . . A dance critic's education includes dance experience, musical and pictorial experience, a sense of what art in general is about, and what people are really like.   —Edwin Denby, Looking at the Dance *(1949)*

PREFACE

One day as I was sitting for a long time outdoors in our wooded dance-deck, I became aware of light on a tree, a red berry that fell at my side, a fog horn in the distance, and children shouting; and I wondered if they were really in trouble or just playing. These chance relationships, each independent of the other, seemed beautiful to me.—Anna Halprin, in *The Theatre of Mixed Means* (1968)

Many of us Merce Cunningham aficionados have long awaited a critical monograph on his work, by common consent one of the most extraordinary achievements in modern dance, not to mention the contemporary arts in general. Rumors have circulated about the forthcoming appearance of one or another volume, all of which I look forward to reading. However, until such a book appears, it seems appropriate to publish an anthology of writings from my fellow critics, as well as Cunningham himself. It also seems appropriate to showcase American dance critics by illuminating a major contemporary subject in a variety of intelligent ways. We tend to forget nowadays that dance was perhaps the last traditional art to develop serious criticism in America. Not too long ago, dance criticism was thought unlikely, not only because performances were necessarily transient and unavailable in any other medium (unlike plays that appear in books or operas that appear on recordings), but also because its principal language is not words but movements. Not too long ago, the only visible "dance critics" were newspaper reviewers scarcely predisposed to Cunningham, if they acknowledged his work at all (mostly because, if rumor is to be believed, it was customarily presented off-Broadway).

I can recall an evening over two decades ago, after a Twyla Tharp performance at the Brooklyn Academy of Music, when Arlene Croce, then a struggling freelance critic, invited several of us over to her house nearby. If I remember correctly, the critics included Don McDonagh, George Dorris, Jack Anderson, David Vaughan, George Jackson (who then as now doubled as a research biologist), and Edwin Denby, our senior by a good many years. Croce had just founded *Ballet Review*, whose principal purpose was publishing extended critical considerations similar to those found in the best American literary journals—criticism written by experienced observers unconstrained by editorial concessions to audience and length, among other vulgarities. The people gathered in her parlor thought that dance criticism should be more ambitious, initially more extended and more serious, than that found in newspaper reviews. Whenever Denby spoke in his soft voice, the others would hush, so palpable was his authority. It seems apparent now that I was witnessing the beginnings of the more serious American dance criticism represented here, so it is scarcely surprising to find now that more contributions to this book come from *Ballet Review* than anywhere else. Except for historic documents originally published prior to 1965 (at the beginning of Cunningham's regular New York seasons), this book contains criticism, not reviews; the two are not the same.

I am grateful to Jill Johnston who insisted three decades ago that I see Cunningham's work, to Arlene Croce for founding *Ballet Review*, to David Vaughan for guiding me through the clippings he has collected as the Cunningham Company's veteran archivist and for sharing his bibliography of Cunningham criticism and chronology of Cunningham's choreography, to Anne Del Castillo for copyediting the manuscript and editorial advice, to Andrew Benker and Nicole Hinrichs for proofreading assistance, and finally to the contributors for granting me permission to reprint their materials.

The biggest problem for me has been, in truth, determining in what order the essays should appear. I tried various thematic schemes, in part to avoid redundancy, only to discover that because certain assumptions of Cunningham's dance were so unique to him critics would "discover" them over and over again. In the end, I resorted to a mostly chronological order that has the virtues (over, say, alphabetical order by contributors' names) of historical truth.

This book would have been dedicated to its subject, had he not already received another book of mine, *American Imaginations* (1985); it might have been dedicated to his longtime coconspirator, John Cage, had he too not received yet another book of mine, *Recyclings* (1984). And so it goes to Kenneth King, whose inspired essay prompted the vision of this anthology, though he insists, as he tells me, "It's all for Merce." For the past quarter century now, King has also been not only an adventurous choreographer but a loyal friend. Thanks, pal.

Richard Kostelanetz
New York
14 May 1991

Don McDonagh

MERCE CUNNINGHAM (1973)

Merce Cunningham was among the first to challenge the conventions of the founding generation of modern dance. His own career started on the West Coast. He was born in Centralia, Washington in 1919, and showed an early interest in dance instruction which was centered on popular forms, including tap, a style for which he retained a great fondness. At Cornish School of Fine and Applied Arts in Seattle, he continued his studies and became exposed to the musical ideas of John Cage, who was on its faculty in the late thirties. One summer, he attended the dance session at Mills College in Oakland, and danced in Lester Horton's *Conquest*. The following year, in 1939, the faculty of the Bennington College Summer School of the Dance, including Martha Graham, was resident at Mills College, and Cunningham was invited to join the Graham company in New York for the fall season. He was the second man to join her company.

He remained with the company until the mid-forties and created many roles, including the Revivalist in *Appalachian Spring*, the Acrobat in *Every Soul Is a Circus*, the Christ figure in *El Penitente*, and a sprightly solo "March" in *Letter to the World*. It was in this last role that great use was made of his nimble and high jump. He began to experiment with his own choreography at Bennington College, where he cochoreographed three works with Jean Erdman, a fellow member of the Graham company. He subsequently created solos for himself and formed an artistic alliance with John Cage as his musical director that persists to this day.

He formed his own company after leaving the Graham company and his work was increasingly marked by its new approach, which was not dependent on the accepted need for story, character, and dramatic mood. He was

1

interested in pure movement and its inherent possibilities. In 1947, he created a ballet, *The Seasons*, for Ballet Society, the precursor of the New York City Ballet, and during this time he also taught a modern dance class at its official school, the School of American Ballet. His first major season with an expanded company of his own took place in the early fifties at the Theatre De Lys, in Greenwich Village.

He undertook a world tour in 1964 that began in Europe and concluded in Japan. He introduced the idea of chance determination in which parts of a dance would be ordered according to random methods and even sequences of movements selected according to the toss of a coin. His method of dance composition in which the scenic designer, the composer, and the choreographer each worked independently of one another, knowing the climate of a dance but not its particulars, attracted advanced painters such as Robert Rauschenberg, Jasper Johns, Robert Morris, Andy Warhol, among others, and advanced composers Christian Wolff, Morton Feldman, Earle Brown, Gordon Mumma, and Conlon Nancarrow, to name but a few. Each of the three elements of a dance united by mood and duration came together as an entity after they had been completed separately.

The Cunningham Dance Studio has over the years attracted some of the most promising students in modern dance, and at its present location in Westbeth on Manhattan's lower West Side it serves also as a showcase for experimental dance, theater, and music.

Suite for Five in Space and Time

Choreography by Merce Cunningham. Music by John Cage. Costumes by Robert Rauschenberg. First performed at the University of Notre Dame, South Bend, IN, May 18, 1956, by Merce Cunningham, Carolyn Brown, Viola Farber, Remy Charlip, and Marianne Preger Simon.

One of the results of Cunningham's forward-looking career has been to open up creative possibilities for other choreographers. Many young choreographers have been quick to seize on the new freedom of stage space and the ideas of chance and random activity having a part in dance and to use these ideas naturally but without direct attribution to Cunningham's influence. One of those who admire his work profoundly is Twyla Tharp, who as a homage created a dance tribute to Cunningham, a set of variations based upon the trio in this piece. She called it *After "Suite."*

"At Random" begins the piece and is a quiet solo for a man who moves spiritedly after the initial silence and then bends forward to the ground. A woman follows with a similarly calm solo, "A Meander," in which she almost seems like a woman regarding herself in a mirror and striking poses as the lights go down. The trio for two women and a man is called "Transition" and finds one woman to the rear of the stage while the two others are forward, closer to the audience. The woman close to the audience runs off, and the woman upstage whips her arms around, and again the lights are dimmed. When they come up the man poses, leaning on the two women for support. They separate and act independently of one another.

"Stillness" is the second solo for the man who opened the piece. Again he is tranquil in his movement, doing no more than wandering easily around the stage. He is joined by the woman who did the second solo, and together they dance a duet, "Extended Moment," which incorporates gestures from each of their solos and contrasts them. He develops a jolly, humorous persona while she emphasizes the more meditative side of the duet. She leaves and he works through a strong, violent sequence in "Excursion," extends a hand out toward the audience, and bows his head. The whole company joins in the finale, "Meetings," where each passes along in his or her separate orbit for the most part, although there are meetings and momentary alliances, but then the women move to one side and are looking up as the men exit.

Cunningham, who tends not to be a wordy man, preferring to let his dancing speak for him, usually includes the following program note for performances of this work: "The events and sounds of this dance revolve around a quiet center, which, though silent and unmoving, is the source from which they happen." It makes one think of Elgar's *Enigma Variations*, which has a counterpart theme that is not heard but is a very real part of the work.

Collage III

Choreography by Merce Cunningham. Music by Pierre Schaeffer with the collaboration of Pierre Henry (excerpts from Symphonie pour un homme seul). *This solo first performed at the University of Pittsburgh, PA, May 21, 1958, by Merce Cunningham.*

Cunningham was introduced to the *musique concrète* of Pierre Schaeffer and Pierre Henry by Leonard Bernstein at a concert that the conductor was giving at Brandeis University in 1952. Bernstein chose excerpts from *Symphonie pour un homme seul*, which was composed directly on magnetic tape, and because of the novelty of the score he wanted to play it twice. Cunningham composed a solo for himself and then created a dance for his own highly trained company and the students of Brandeis who wished to participate which he titled *Excerpts from Symphonie pour un homme seul;* when it was performed in 1953, it was retitled *Collage*. The latter were given everyday gestures as their part of the dance so that they would not be intimidated and could participate fully in the event. He subsequently created another solo for himself, which he designated as *Collage III*.

He is dressed in street clothes, jacket, shirt, and trousers, and slowly circles, punctuating his walk with little jumps. He removes his jacket and then takes a balletic formal stance at the center of the stage, placing his feet tightly together. He opens his arms and legs outward with a strong, easy command of the technique, then swings his legs from side to side in a contrasting impish movement.

He then appears to be a man beset, scanning with his eyes rapidly around the empty space. He becomes more careful and almost guarded in his movements and then begins a rousing variation to counter the feeling of malaise, but then runs off shaking his head from side to side as if saying, ''No!''

One of the strongest dance technicians of his generation, Cunningham has never stressed the showy aspects of dance for their sake alone, but it is a distinct treat to see him as a soloist commanding the stage with his performing presence. The piece is a very personal one and very moving, as it explores the fate of a man alone with his craft and his tools of space, to be meaningfully traversed in a given time.

Antic Meet

Choreography by Merce Cunningham. Music by John Cage (Concert for Piano and Orchestra). *Scenery and costumes by Robert Rauschenberg. First performed at Connecticut College, New London, CT, August 14, 1958, by Merce Cunningham, Carolyn Brown, Viola Farber, Marilyn Wood, Judith Dunn, and Remy Charlip.*

Because of his formidable reputation as a serious, uncompromising, and advanced choreographer, many are surprised at the number of humorously light dances that Cunningham has created. This is one of his best.

Four women and two men enter. One man walks on a diagonal with his girl and looks enviously at her. He offers a bunch of flowers and she ignores him. He exits. A moment later, he returns with a bentwood chair strapped to his back. A door on wheels follows him across the stage. He opens it and there is his girl in a mammoth muumuu. He kneels and she sits in the chair and they banter as best they can. She leaves and he is alone and rubs his hands with glee and cavorts with three mini-skirted women. His girl returns and does catch-up movements to duplicate everything that they have done.

The man returns without the chair and does a series of large balletic forward kicks very rapidly with a smile, then leaves with his legs a bit twisted. Two women mime throwing things at one another and spin into a balletic mode of moving. They stop and relax into normal posture. One bends and the other braces herself on her as one might on a ballet practice barre. The two men cavort like burly dock hands wearing sweat shirts covered with tattoos. Both collapse as they shuffle away, and then one drags himself off only to return to retrieve his friend.

One woman wearing sunglasses is brought out and deposited, then the others enter with sunglasses and all do a round of elegant poses linked with sudden little turns. In the next episode, the first man desperately tries to put on a sweater which seems to have more than the usual number of sleeves but no hole to put one's head through. The women in voluminous white dresses circle and simper as he struggles. They cup their hands to their heads and leave and he finally does the same as well.

One woman sits at a table near the edge of the stage and the other man enters to remove it. She gets up and does a short, rapid sequence of small steps. The first man returns in white coveralls and launches into a soft-shoe routine with relaxed confidence and then wanders off. The four women return in their original costumes to parade in front, while the two men leap frantically in the background.

The dancers constantly look startled as they meet one another, almost as if they never expected to see another human being, and the piece develops as a wacky flirtation dance. The men are always being driven to some feat or another, and the women are studiously decorative. It has the zaniness of slapstick farce and a lovely warm ambience.

Night Wandering

Choreography by Merce Cunningham. Music by Bo Nilsson. Costumes by Nicola Cernovich; new costumes by Robert Rauschenberg, 1963. First performed at the Kungl Teâtern, Stockholm, Sweden, October 5, 1958, by Merce Cunningham and Carolyn Brown.

In Cunningham's long career, one of his most valued collaborators has been Carolyn Brown. In addition to being a superb technical dancer with elegant bearing and precisely articulated gestures, she also has an excellent visual memory and has functioned as the *régisseuse* of the company during her association with it. It is difficult to assess her exact contribution to the body of work that Cunningham has produced while she was in the company, but she has always been his most resilient and compliant dancer in picking up on his choreographic suggestions and fleshing them out to his satisfaction. Finding himself at an engagement in Stockholm and having to create a dance on short notice, he decided to make a duet for them. Three days is an awfully short time to complete a dance, but undoubtedly the task was facilitated greatly by her responsive intelligence.

The first thing that strikes one about the dance is its primitive costuming, which suggests early cave dwellers. He wears a rough, shaggy sleeveless vest and she a furry long garment also without sleeves. While the textures and the appearance of the costuming appear rough, the movement is lyrically smooth. The course of the piece reflects support on his part and dependence on hers. They run rapidly around at one point and then he pauses and she luxuriously stretches her body back to back with his, or at another point he arches his body upward and she reclines easily across him as he rocks back and forth.

The dance pairs two of the finest performers in the world, picking up and playing off each other's strength. He is the motive energy of the pair and she translates the power into exquisite pictures.

Crises

Choreography by Merce Cunningham. Music by Conlon Nancarrow. Costumes by Robert Rauschenberg. First performed at Connecticut College, New London, CT, August 19, 1960, by Merce Cunningham, Carolyn Brown, Viola Farber, Marilyn Wood, and Judith Dunn.

An unusual aspect of the dance derives from the elastic bands that the dancers wear around the waist or one arm. At times, one or another of the dancers will join another by slipping a hand through the band and effectively linking the two. In this situation they have to move together, but in others the dancers reflect each other without the linkage.

A man and a woman stand on opposite sides of the stage facing one another. He bows to her eccentrically, touching various parts of his body as he acknowledges her presence. She responds with an equally quirky *arabesque* and he approaches her, turning and rolling his head while keeping his torso quite still. Three women enter as he flexes his arms above his head. Two of the women are joined with an elastic band and they kneel and lie down as the third continues to move, only to return, striding deliberately. All perform individual variations and then exit.

One by one, the women return to run or stand and extend one leg. The man dashes out to grasp one leg then releases it to watch while kneeling. Two other women dance similarly before all leave. The three women return to course about in little semicircles, and the man returns to catch another woman, who is bending backward, and he assists her in a backward walk. He offers her his elastic band and she grasps it behind her head, and both whirl to the rear of the stage. Their duet begins with falls and displays an almost classical *adagio.* A slow passage of walks is punctuated by lifting the heels from the floor periodically and then developing into a series of turns. Two of the women join hands and leap up and down in unison.

The man makes a slow, crab-like crossing of the stage to the woman he first bowed to. He grasps her hand and one extended leg as she hops into the wings. All enter singly to perform solo variations of hops and form a rough circle in the center of the stage. The man returns to the center of the stage with one of his hands trapped beneath the elastic band around his own waist and turns frantically from one to another as if faced with an extremely difficult choice. He rejoins the first woman, and slides his arm beneath the band circling her upper arm and assists her in sliding off.

The crises all seem to be of a technical humorous nature, such as trying to find suitable ways to dance while linked. Cunningham has wedded both classically balanced, almost balletic movement with odd asymmetrical gestures. It is as if the dance existed at two levels at the same time: one showing polite reserve and then another pragmatic set of movements designed to solve particular problems and commenting wittily on the process. In *Changes: Notes on Choreography*, Cunningham wrote: "One of the special characteristics of this dance was due to Viola Farber [the first woman]. Her body often had the look of one part being in balance and the rest extremely off."

Aeon

Choreography by Merce Cunningham. Music by John Cage (Atlas Eclipticalis with Winter Music, *electronic version*). *Scenery and costumes by Robert Rauschenberg. First performed at* La Comédie Canadienne, *Montreal, Canada, August 5, 1961. First performed in the United States at Palmer Auditorium, Connecticut College, New London, CT, August 17, 1961, by Merce Cunningham, Carolyn Brown, Viola Farber, Judith Dunn, Marilyn Wood, Remy Charlip, Shareen Blair, Valda Setterfield, and Steve Paxton. First performed in New York City at Philharmonic Hall, August 13, 1963.*

The dance celebrates an epoch that is not placed in any time but almost seems to be the story of man and woman throughout time. The strict definition of "aeon" as given in the dictionary is that it denotes a long but indefinite period of time, usually thought of in thousands of years. The dance is full of elaborate stage effects including exploding flares, and a large smoking machine which travels across in the air while some of the dancers lie prone in the darkness. Because of its complexity, a shorter version and an even shorter touring version of the piece were prepared which did not contain all of the effects or the movement.

The piece opens with all the dancers onstage and two dazzling flares fire off. One man begins to move, then the dance is picked up by two women and the other men, and all are moving in place. The last two women to begin now switch places and six of the seven start skipping while the other eventually joins and all go off. The flash seems to announce some cataclysmic event such as the beginning of animate life. A brief duet has one man carrying a woman from place to place, pausing, and then they leave. All the women run around and are joined by the men wearing ruffled leggings. One of them makes an approach to one of the women, and it is like a comic version of an eighteenth-century gallant pressing his suit. Various men take turns in presenting themselves but leave, and the women leave as the smoking machine crosses the stage.

A man returns without the leggings and does a proud rooster-like dance and is joined by a woman. Together they dance a jazzy variation. Other groupings succeed them: two trios of a man and two women; first one group falls and then the other, and then they both collapse together. A single spotlight now illuminates the stage, and one man walks just outside of its glare. When the lights illuminate the rest of the stage, he joins one of the women who enter with three others and a man. All of the women leave as the third man enters, and these three walk, pausing from time to time to clasp a foot. A woman with a colorful cloak enters and is carried off by one of the exiting men, the last of whom duck-walks off, making gestures of combat like a Japanese warrior.

All return to dance a variation again in place as at the opening of the piece, whipping arms about, and then the men separate from the women. All leave except a man dancing alone, as another man and a women enter and cross, occasionally flashing stroboscopic lights from their wrists. Again there is a period of romantic ardor as a man in leggings dances, followed by a woman who rides out on the back of another man. The chap in leggings ties a string of tin cans to her, suggesting a honeymoon trip. She immediately has an argument with the man bearing her, and he leaves in a huff. The rapid-fire encounters continue until one man is left dancing with the women, and they leave and he leaves to conclude the piece.

This dance shows Cunningham's mastery of entrances and exits. He uses the disappearance and reappearance of his dancers with consummate artistry, always bringing an element of surprise to the dance. One can never anticipate precisely who or what will be the next to appear from the wings. In this case he gave us the battle of the sexes with wit, humor, and a dazzling array of technical stage machinery and fast costume changes.

Winterbranch

Choreography by Merce Cunningham. Music by La Monte Young (2 sounds, April 1960). Costumes by Robert Rauschenberg. First performed at the Wadsworth Atheneum, Hartford, CT, March 21, 1964, by Merce Cunningham, Carolyn Brown, Viola Farber, Barbara Lloyd, William Davis, and Steve Paxton.

This dance has been a puzzle and problem since it was first performed. It is a good dance, but it is difficult to enjoy at first viewing because of its unusual setting and musical accompaniment. At one performance, an outraged man seated near me shouted angrily that he wanted the lights turned out, which were shining across the audience and momentarily dazzling some. In subsequent performances, the lighting design was modified and various other of the stage elements were changed. The setting which I enjoyed the most was at the Brooklyn Academy of Music, and the description follows the details of that series of performances.

The stage area is in dusky shadow, and one perceives the dancers and the decor as one might peering around in early evening. One black curtain hangs straight and squarely down, while its mate is drawn up partially into a full, rich romantic curve: a suggestion of male and female. The dance commences in absolute silence and pencil-thin shafts of light cut through the gloom; someone crawls along the back of the stage in a sack. A woman stretches near the edge of the stage, and two men enter to carry her to the rear of the stage, where she again stretches. A man and a woman dance together and then topple to the ground. (There is a general feeling of energy running down as all of the people in the dance tend to go earthward at some point or another in the course of the piece.) He rises and assists her to her feet and she slides back and he drags her off. Another couple does a lackadaisical duet.

At this point, the sound begins. It consists of two sustained tones, one low pitched and the other high, and both are amplified greatly, and the dance picks up to a frenzied pace. All of the dancers wear sweat shirts and pants and have black smudges applied beneath their eyes; one man wears a black skullcap. The woman who stretched in the first part of the dance now reclines on a cloth, and two men grab the ends and drag her off. Three couples dance duets in which one of the partners falls and the other supports her. One girl arches backward with her arms above and to the side and begins to teeter, and her partner bends beneath her and catches her so that she slides off his back to the floor. One couple remains, as the other exits, to whirl and tumble rapidly. Others return, two men lift a woman; one supports the upper body as the other supports her legs. At the rear of the stage, a strange little machine with winking lights begins to make slow progress across the stage from the right to the left. It looks like a cartoon version of an official police car with its flashing red light on the top. The company masses and is covered with a large cloth by one woman and crawls off en masse as she does a slow bump and grind in the center. All return to lie prone as the performance ends.

Interpretations of the piece have ranged from a plea for racial understanding to an interpretation of a shipwreck. Reactions have been violent at times, warm at others, and quietly hostile at still others. The loudness of the score at times provokes anger and the intermittent flashing of the lights bothers others, but the mystery of the gloomy setting is probably most disquieting. It is a dance which provokes a sense of uneasiness. It is certainly not pretty in any conventional sense, but it has a sincerity and an integrity that make it one of Cunningham's most intriguing dances.

Variations V

Choreography by Merce Cunningham. Music by John Cage. Film by Stan VanDerBeek. Distortion of television images by Nam June Paik. Electronic devices by Billy Klüver and Robert Moog. First performed at Philharmonic Hall, New York, NY, July 23, 1965, by Merce Cunningham, Carolyn Brown, Barbara Lloyd, Sandra Neels, Albert Reid, Peter Saul, and Gus Solomons jr.

Always receptive to the new and newer, Cunningham has been in the forefront of those choreographers willing to use the latest in stage properties and decor. In this case, five magnetically sensitive poles are the pylons around which the dance develops. As the dancers pass near them, their bodies break electromagnetic fields which cause changes in the electronic score accompanying the dance and the slide projections and films which provide its background.

The dance contrasts slow, ordinary, paced gestures such as sitting and walking with high-velocity dancing. A man first walks across the stage alone carrying a plant in a small clay pot and places it down at the edge of the stage. Another man and a woman walk on as projections show a dance studio and a locomotive, and she promptly stands on her head as he raises and lowers her, tugging on her upraised legs. The first man returns to dance among the poles; his partner walks slowly on and places a pot with newspapers in it next to his plant. Their duet is followed by a series of solos for three men, while three women also do solo variations at another part of the stage. The films at one point show bicycles as the men do imaginary pedaling in the air.

Dancers enter and leave the performing area with zestful enthusiasm, in contrast with some of the slower walking paces of the earlier section. The first man sees his partner smash his flowerpot and replant the plant in her own pot, carefully arranging the leaves. He does a series of exercises on an electronically sensitive mat. The costumes of the dancers change as the dance moves along. The women appear at one time in fast sleek bathing suits and flesh-colored tights, then at another in street clothes. The pace accelerates as the dancers dash across from one side of the stage to the other, and then abruptly two of the men stop to sit and watch the others dance. Then all join in unwinding a long cord which is pulled into a large zigzag shape that they weave up and down, and then all dash off. There is a momentary pause, and then suddenly the first man returns, and this time he is riding a bicycle that has a small air horn attached to the handlebars. He wheels in and around all of the poles, breaking the magnetic fields and causing changes in sound and sight while tooting his little horn.

The dance has an ironic twist to it when one thinks of the simple act of walking which opened the dance and the unusual (onstage) act of bicycle riding to conclude the dance. In between, of course, there has been a great deal of easily recognizable "dance" movement, but Cunningham also draws our attention to other types of movement which can function equally well and humorously in a dance.

How to Pass, Kick, Fall and Run

Choreography by Merce Cunningham. Music by John Cage (reading from his book Silence, *later including readings from his* A Year from Monday).

First performed at the Harper Theatre, Chicago, IL, November 24, 1965, by
Merce Cunningham, Carolyn Brown, Barbara Lloyd, Sandra Neels, Valda
Setterfield, Albert Reid, Peter Saul, and Gus Solomons jr.

Playful is the word one thinks of in connection with this dance. There is, in addition to the playful frisky movement of the dancers themselves, a playful performance by John Cage, who reads anecdotal stories from his book *Silence*. This is the sound accompaniment to the dance and consists of one story per minute. Cage smokes, sips at a fine vintage champagne, and sometimes is joined by a second reader, David Vaughan. The stories are light and humorous in tone. The dance requires no special decor, and the costumes are very simple black tights and solid-color sweaters.

On a brightly illuminated clear stage, a man jumps on exuberantly, flings his arms outward to the side, and twirls. Two other men take up a stance that suggests Indian wrestling. A couple of women run between the men; another woman is lifted high. One feels as if there is an elaborate game of "tag" being played. The whole pacing of the first part is fast; women pick their way across the stage, looking carefully where they place their steps; a man and two women leap in short, bouncy jumps. Then there is a pause in the frantic activity.

Slower-phrased gestures replace the energetic ones, falls are performed by the various couples, and then all sit in a semi-circle. Runs begin and the first man repeats part of his opening solo, the group forms a large cluster which revolves upon itself, and then all scatter. The first man remains in the center, skittering and raising himself on the balls of his feet as the others move to opposite sides of the stage, and the curtain falls on a scene of activity.

Cunningham explained that the reason he created the dance was that he was a practical man of the theater and had to have a simple piece; simple in the sense of costuming, lack of decor, and necessity for special rehearsal time. It would, of course, be an easy piece to tour, but more than that it is an example of his puckish humor given an expansive and enjoyable outing.

Place

Choreography by Merce Cunningham. Music by Gordon Mumma (Mesa,
for Cybersonic Bandoneon). Scenery and costumes by Beverly Emmons.
First performed at the Foundation Maeght, Saint-Paul-de-Vence, France,
August 6, 1966, by Merce Cunningham, Carolyn Brown, Barbara Lloyd,
Sandra Neels, Valda Setterfield, Albert Reid, Peter Saul,
and Gus Solomons jr.

This is an odd title for a dance that seems to be about no particular place, but then it could be anyplace. It is also unusual in that it respects the traditional conceptions of theatrical space. The center of the stage is the most important part of it, and the most important actions occur there and the dance always develops forward toward the audience. Usually Cunningham allows his dances to transpire over the entire surface of the dance space, but in this one he chooses not to. The music has a menacing drone.

A man enters a totally deserted area and performs a short, cautious solo as if seeing strange territory for the first time. Suddenly he is joined by a woman, then three others; all are costumed in industrial-weight, transparent plastic subtly tinted blue, pink, green, and yellow. The others leave and he partners the first woman. They separate and he goes to the rear of the stage, where two small geodesic lights sit on a length of cloth. He lights the smaller of the two and rubs his shin reflectively as if meditating about an old hurt.

He kneels and slowly draws the cloth toward him. The others dance farther down the stage closer to the audience. He lights the second lamp. He stands and makes crisscross motions with his hands as if to ward off something, almost like a man brushing away annoying gnats or trying to get rid of troublesome thoughts. He is soberly clad in black, and the other men and women are in colored costumes. His second solo finds him still alone and isolated. The men and women change partners and carry through a rather cool series of duets like mating automatons. The man in black dances alone again, and, while the others involve themselves with one another, he tends the two lamps. The women drop one by one and are carried off by the men. When they have all left, the man in black walks forward to look around him at the deserted area. He returns to his solitary life, and this time he half slips into a plastic bag and wriggles, thrashing, along the floor. It is not clear whether he wants to be wholly in it or free from it, but the curtain descends as he is still thrashing.

The dance has a futuristic look in its see-through plastic costuming and geodesic lights and makes one feel very lonely and abandoned. The man tending his lights seems intent upon preserving something in the midst of this alien atmosphere, but, at the end, even he is driven to some display of emotional desperation as the last of the coolly distant inhabitants has left. He is not of like temperament and yet they both dwell in the same place virtually side by side, separated by an invisible wall of exclusion.

RainForest

Choreography by Merce Cunningham. Music by David Tudor. Scenery and costumes by Andy Warhol. First performed at the Upton Auditorium, Buffalo, NY, March 9, 1968, by Merce Cunningham, Carolyn Brown, Barbara Lloyd, Albert Reid, Sandra Neels, and Gus Solomons jr.

There is no rain to be seen or heard in the piece, and the "forest" is a cluster of inflated pillow shapes, but there is a strong feeling of a jungle setting in the choreography. Some of the silver pillows are filled with helium so that they float in the air above the dancers, and others are just tossed casually on the stage, to be moved by the breeze of the dancers passing. They provide a changing and playful backdrop to the somewhat animalistic dance. Just before the first performance, the designer Jasper Johns went around from dancer to dancer cutting little holes in the costumes so that the dancers would appear to be somewhat ragged in contrast to the smooth, shiny pillows.

Three figures are seen standing as the light slowly brightens. A man and a woman are close together and another man stands some distance away. All weave their arms and swirl in place. It appears as if they are stretching, suggesting the first movements of the day. The man and the woman now start to snake around one another; the movement is young, strong, almost rough. The first man leaves, and the one in the background moves forward to dance with the woman, after which they lie together.

A third man enters and together he and the other man push the lying woman to the edge of the stage. The man most recently arrived does a fast and assertive solo which attracts the woman, and they go off together. The second man stands and a second woman dashes on briskly and engages in an athletic romp with him, after which they go off together.

A third woman begins a proud, vital solo that attracts the attention of the first man who has returned. He joins her and creates the impression of a warrior, during which she leaves and he follows, to leave the stage bare of people but full of the slightly rocking and swaying pillows, serene as ever.

The dance is like a representation of life in a primitive society where relationships are simple and somewhat brutal. The suggestions of rooting and cavorting that are in the piece contrast wonderfully with the almost antiseptic decor, suggesting cave men in a computer era.

Changing Steps

Choreography by Merce Cunningham. Music by David Behrman, John Cage, Gordon Mumma, and David Tudor. Costumes by Charles Atlas. First performed as part of Event #65, Brooklyn Academy of Music, March 22, 1973, by Douglas Dunn, Meg Harper, Susana Hayman-Chaffey, Chris Komar, Robert Kovich, Barbara Lias, Brynar Mehl, Sandra Neels, Valda Setterfield, Julie Roess-Smith.

This exceptionally fine dance is a rarity in that it does not have a part for the choreographer himself. Ordinarily one expects to see him in each work, but this one was created for the members of his company and represents a beautiful and lean demonstration of Cunningham's style of movement as designed for others' talents, not just his own.

A man enters and performs a slow sequence of Adonis-like poses that are classically clean, and leaves after a few thrusts and leaps. A woman lyrically bends forward and backward, dancing lightly on the balls of her feet. A second woman dances a solo, entering the spot just vacated by the other. She turns and strikes balances and then exits. There is an utter simplicity in the way that the dancers execute the steps and then just leave without a hint of dramatic or emotional coloring to the dance.

A series of solo dances by men and women ensue, and then two men enter with a woman for a trio in which they cradle her in their arms. Two women and a man prance side to side in unison and separate to do solo variations, skittering and leaping off. Three women slide into splits and hold the position while two men leap across their outstretched legs like sword dancers avoiding sharp blades. They turn and assist the women up, and then all cluster into a cozy group huddle and collapse. The energy of the dance is high, and the physical look that the dancers have makes it appear as if almost the whole dance is being done on the tips of the toes.

A couple dances together, he presenting a strong, solid appearance while she does little fluttering foot movements. It is almost as if they are sketching out the movement for a duet rather than dancing it full out. A second couple almost appears like a pair of tap dancers doing a team routine, at the end of which he lifts her on his shoulder and carries her off. A man forms the secure center of a trio in which two women turn and depend on him. Each sinks to the floor from time to time but revives, and all exit, turning rapidly.

A man lies prone with his palms flat on the stage and rests his chin on them. A woman sits on his shoulders, and, as he rolls over, she cuddles comfortably close to him. They perform a romantic duet just rolling and then conclude by returning to the opening pose. Another couple flirtatiously romps across the area, running hand in hand back and forth. Another man enters to do an exaggerated version of ballroom dancing with his partner. A second girl tags along with them, inserting herself between them at one moment or just fluttering around at another, like a persistent little sister. She tires and dashes off to do her own solo variation but collapses. The couple has pity and includes her in the dance, and all exit together. Two couples enter and form a tight circle and create a miniature world of gestures, all working very closely to one another, passing and repassing one another in a highly compact area, bringing the dance to its triumphant finale.

It is the lean economy of the piece that gives it its extreme delight. One feels that the choreographer has taken every unnecessary or extraneous movement out of the work and kept only those absolutely essential steps required to accomplish his design. It is spare but not desiccated and has a taut richness that marks it as one of Cunningham's finest dances, almost a distillation of an entire aspect of his career.

Richard Kostelanetz

TWENTY YEARS OF MERCE CUNNINGHAM'S DANCE (1982)

Twenty years ago, it was not so easy to see Merce Cunningham dance, and the experience often involved incidental hazards. I remember a concert at [New York's] Philharmonic Hall, August 13, 1963, in a subscription series with Donald McKayle, Paul Taylor, and José Limón. The audience was incredibly aggressive. After every cacophonous crunch from the orchestra pit, several people in militant unison hit the aisles, creating a comic, continuous, distracting stream of exiting herds for the duration of the performance. Some *New York Times* reviewer advised that Cunningham would fare better without John Cage's music. Jill Johnston, then the dance critic of the *Village Voice*, took to her columns to reply that Cunningham without Cage would be like the Bible without God.

In those days, it is hard to believe now, Cunningham rarely performed in New York, the city in which he lived since 1939. One reason was that a set of performances at the end of 1953 went completely unreviewed. In another year, he was included in a putatively comprehensive series of contemporary choreographers, only to be excluded the next. My recollection is that the 1963 concert was his first New York recital in three years. In previous seasons, aficionados had to go somewhere else—Hempstead, Philadelphia, or New London—for their annual dose. During the mid-sixties, Cunningham's concerts would happen almost by surprise, here and there around New York, perhaps once a year.

The faithful audience for his work back then had a certain quality. Consisting of many familiar faces—artists, writers, and other performers—it was the sort of peer audience that Cunningham as well as Cage had from the beginning of their mature careers. John Gruen, in *The Party's Over Now* (1972), tells the story of the critic Harold Rosenberg screaming during the 1953 season that the show could not start because a certain painter had not yet arrived. "Everyone doubled up laughing," Gruen explained. "We all attended every event and everyone in the audience knew everyone else. 'There's a stranger in the third row,' Harold continued. 'Throw him out!' " Even a decade later, I was struck by the loyalty and quality of Cunningham's backers. By the mid-sixties, I recollect, painters such as Jasper Johns and Robert Rauschenberg were selling their works explicitly to finance Cunningham's performances in New York.

Back then, Cunningham himself was the key *issue* dividing the world of modern dance. What a person thought of his work would usually indicate what else he or she liked or disliked on the current dance scene, if not in contemporary art in general. (Remember that expressionism/antiexpression-ism was more of an issue then.) Like all artistic edges, his work inspired many private arguments comparable to the one between Jill Johnston and the *New York Times* reviewer.

I liked what I saw, and attended Cunningham's performances as often as I could. His dances were for me a revelation about the possibilities of nonex-pressionistic movement and, by extension, of nonexpressionistic mixed-means performance; about noncentered space and, analogously, uninflected time; about experiment that nonetheless respected grace; about surprises that were, yes, beautiful; and then about nonsynchronicity. What one dancer did had no definite connection to what the others were doing, while the music had no ostensible connection to the dance. There were abstract truths to be learned from his refusals both to suggest erotic themes or to give his women dancers movements that were generically different from those given to the men.

Even when Cunningham was in his early forties (and had outgrown his early reputation as a spectacular jumper), he was the strongest male dancer I had ever seen, while his principal partner at the time, Carolyn Brown, also stood out from the rest of the company (that, alas, invariably included at least one person who was visibly outclassed). The dance I liked best in those days was *Winterbranch* (1964), which I regarded as a masterpiece of terrifying theater, with its dark stage, its dancers in black sweatsuits and blackened faces, and its howling La Monte Young score. The other work I especially remember is *Variations V* (1965), which was likewise a mixed-means piece combining Cunningham's choreography with Stan VanDerBeek's films and a forest of sensitive vertical wands designed to stimulate sound generators. The conclusion had Cunningham on a bicycle, which I took to be a vivid epitome of his polemical assertion that *all* movements should be available to modern dance. Rich in kinetic activity and sensory stimulations, not to speak of esthetic implications, these pieces also drove viewers to exit the hall and reviewers to splenetic outbursts.

Two decades later, so much is different. What was initially a difficult career is now a fortunate one. Cunningham has annual two-week seasons in New York. His name fronts a foundation that regularly receives both federal and state grants. The stagecraft and administrative duties are no longer done by moonlighting dancers but by a whole crew of technicians and executives. His new works are respectfully reviewed in the same journals that once panned or ignored him. Presidential prizes are no doubt waiting around the corner.

The audiences for his work are different as well. The same David Tudor abrasiveness that once sent spectators to the exits move few in New York; the bright lamp directed into the City Center audience's faces is not taken as offensive by most. On the other hand, the audience has fewer artists (or at least fewer known to me), and then most of those few are professionally involved with Cunningham and Cage, mostly as collaborators. Are the rest of these spectators, I wonder, the same people who patronize the other attractions in the City Center season: Martha Graham, Paul Taylor, Dance Theater of Harlem, Alvin Ailey, The Joffrey Ballet, and Les Grands Ballets Canadiens? Might they be the children of those who, two decades before, would have idolized "Martha" and ignored Merce? Or those who walked out of his performance at Philharmonic Hall?

Cunningham's choreography has not changed as much as the times and the context. Before, as I said, I was most impressed by the scrupulous abstractness and disconnectedness. The parts of the dancers' bodies did not complement each other; the ties binding the dancers to each other were irregular; his choreography cultivated the idiosyncrasies of his performers. There was little resemblance to the traditional modern dance of Isadora Duncan, Graham, Limón, or whomever. The music proceeded utterly independent of the choreography. Given what I remember (and what Cunningham taught me), I now find that his dancers often move in unison, that their arms and legs often echo balletic conventions, that male/female distinctions are frequently emphasized, that the female dancers resemble one another in both appearance and competence, and that gauche movements are rare. At times I could swear the music was providing a patent platform for the dance. What changed? The company perhaps; my sense of innovation in dance (and art) for sure.

What I now find missing is the earlier audacity—the audacity of *How to Pass, Kick, Fall and Run* (1965), whose "music" is John Cage reading funny stories (and at times upstaging the group); the audacity of the conclusion of *Place* (1966), where Cunningham wraps himself in a plastic bag and rolls off stage with twitches and crackles; or the audacity of the interlude in *Walkaround Time* (1968) where the dancers don warmup clothes and amble leisurely about the stage. By my count, Cunningham's last audacious move for the stage was the presentation of an Event, which is a terribly ingenious conception initially designed for nonstandard performance spaces. Cunningham has always thought of his dances as having four fronts, or as being open on all sides. The proscenium theater, with only one front, was a convention to which he capitulated with particular backdrops for each piece. On tour, he often was offered gymnasiums or other comparable spaces in lieu of theaters; and since the backdrops could not be used, he was free to fill the performance space and time in another way.

Events are composed of earlier dances, either in whole or part, performed in continuous sequence for over an hour. They are unique self-anthologies drawn from an ample storehouse. Though different in detail, every Event has the same theme, which is the range and characteristics of Cunningham choreography. (It seems odd that no one else has appropriated this propitious structure. Perhaps their scrapbooks are not thick enough.) The first of the two Events at City Center included a sequence danced in black sweatsuits. Sure enough, it was *Winterbranch*, now in bright light (but, alas, without LaMonte Young's intimidating score). Both Events included a spectacular duet between Lise Friedman and Susan Emery; its source was *Aeon* (1961).

However, those two Events at City Center were fundamentally different from another one I saw five years before at the Barnard College gymnasium. Whereas the first of the two was performed in front of a backdrop of a huge bare wall and theatrical appliances, the second had a large white cloth (that looked to me like the scrim of *Inlets*). That cloth gave this second City Center Event a definite backside and thus a single front that was made even more definite by the proscenium structure of the space. What we saw this year was not a true Event, if you please, but a compromised one. Next time, please consider using Madison Square Garden, the 69th Regiment Armory, or the Sheep Meadow.

One friend of mine found eighty minutes too long to sit for a single dance, but that comment ignored a certain quality that this work has in common with Cage's music (and much else in avant-garde art)—it need not be seen from beginning to end, because it is a series of sequences that are essentially independent of one another (and yet complementary). Therefore, one can tune out and come back without feeling lost. (This is an interesting contemporary form—also present in *Finnegans Wake*, among other places—that scarcely anyone has written about.) My vision is that these Events really should be longer—indeed, as long as is physically tolerable—not only because some might feel a bit shortchanged after only eighty minutes of dance, but because the temporal dimensions of the piece should be such that spectators inclined to take a walk should not feel discouraged from doing so. That, indeed, is another reason for doing them in spaces more open than a proscenium theater.

What impresses me most about Cunningham are his apparently limitless resources for unobvious invention—inventions not only in dancers' movements but in stage compositions. Once he decided that all movements were open to dance, he proceeded down an apparently endless road. Every work contains something that even his most loyal fans had not seen before (and probably will not see again); even when he honors choreographic conventions, he disrupts them with surprising quirks. On top of that penchant for originality is an incomparable range, from the comic in his *Gallopade* (1981) to the somber in *Inlets* (1977), from the elegant in *Trails* (1982) to the messy in *Roadrunners* (1979), from the spacious in *Fielding Sixes* (1980) to the constrained in *Tango* (1978), which is a solo composition.

Indeed, it is perhaps in his solo choreography that Cunningham is now doing his most exploratory work, for he is discovering a new vocabulary of movements for an older dancer who must nearly always keep both feet on the floor. Since *Canfield* (1969), he has given himself (and, to my recollection, only himself) solos for his hands, often fluttering with the speed of a juggler's (and yet moving nothing). He frequently uses props, less as extensions in the Alwin Nikolais sense, than as foils and supports. In *Gallopade*, both he and the company play a lot on the floor.

Five years ago, his own performance reminded me of Gordie Howe, the legendary hockey player who had come out of retirement to be on the same team as his sons. Visibly a generation older than his teammates, yet able to do things they could not, Howe was both sympathetic and embarrassing in his desire to skate along with the kids. Nowadays, Cunningham puts more distance between himself and the group, if only in his choreography for himself. What might be more interesting would be a Cunningham piece for a company entirely of older dancers.

The other pioneering dimension of his current art is his work with film and videotape. While he is more fortunate than earlier choreographers in having survived into an age of media that can transcribe economically both sight and sound, Cunningham also realizes that they offer him the opportunity to create works that ultimately exist on screens. Working in collaboration with Charles Atlas, he has produced at least two films and one videotape that can be rented or purchased. Each is different in style from the others; each explores territory that is scarcely occupied. Of the three I saw, the most impressive was *Locale* (1979), in which the camera moves as the human eye cannot—in speed, to heights, from angles—making us profoundly aware of the limitations of the traditional theatrical view of dance. (Televised sports have made us similarly aware of the limitations of even the "best" stadium seat.) Indeed, *Locale* suggests that the choreographer might eventually be responsible not just for the movements of his dancers but for the "movements" of his audience.

Of the eleven works I saw this past season [1981], the strongest to my senses is *Inlets*, whose initial distinguishing mark is the white scrim that covers the proscenium from end to end and from top to bottom. For nearly the entire piece the scene is bathed in hazy light whose overall murkiness is reminiscent of *Winterbranch*. (But whereas the earlier work is black and strident, *Inlets* is fair and mellow.) The music is a John Cage composition that sounds electronic but is actually the amplified sound of water jostled in large conch shells. (Why do amplified natural noises sound more like other amplified sound than anything heard in nature?) The crowning touch of the Morris Graves decor is a silver medallion, several feet in diameter, that inches across the back of the stage, higher than the dancers. When it reaches the center, the stage is suddenly bathed in strong white light that visually obliterates the scrim until there is an equally sudden return to the initial murkiness. One quality that separates *Inlets* from other recent work and yet connects it to my earlier favorites is a fuller exploitation of theatrical resources.

Whenever Cunningham appears on stage nowadays, he gets an extra round of applause (as did Gordie Howe in his reborn years), but (as with Howe) one wonders whether these fans are honoring him in the present or appreciating his career which, as everyone knows by now, has had the classic avant-garde shape of early innovation that his elders dismissed, professional exclusion, sustained productivity in spite of public incomprehension and financial hardships, the development of a loyal nucleus of colleagues and then an expanding, loyal, proselytizing audience, and finally a breakthrough into popular acclaim.

The difference is that Cunningham two decades ago made us think about the possibilities of dance and of the theater. There was a spikey edge to his work and to its relationship to the audience. I find that challenging quality—that risk of unacceptability—still in much of John Cage's recent work, which is at times outrageous and can drive out audiences; I find a bit of that sort of edge in Cunningham's work with film and video. (There might be even more of such an edge in choreography for *objects,* the dance equivalent of electronic music, were he to think about doing it.)

At the root of his creative predicament is, paradoxically, his company—or, rather, the pragmatic and ultimately esthetic burdens of supporting his talented entourage, which is the professional convention that Cunningham shares with his more conservative colleagues; and now that the company is so strong, and so much larger than before, while invitations remain plentiful, he is even more beholden to it. Nonetheless, isn't it reasonable to speculate about what would happen to his art if he freed himself of that baggage?

John Cage

GRACE AND CLARITY (1944)

The strength that comes from firmly established art practices is not present in the modern dance today. Insecure, not having any clear direction, the modern dancer is willing to compromise and to accept influences from other more rooted art manners, enabling one to remark that certain dancers are either borrowing from or selling themselves to Broadway, others are learning from folk and Oriental arts, and many are either introducing into their work elements of the ballet, or, in an all-out effort, devoting themselves to it. Confronted with its history, its former power, its present insecurity, the realization is unavoidable that the strength the modern dance once had was not impersonal but was intimately connected with and ultimately dependent on the personalities and even the actual physical bodies of the individuals who imparted it.

The techniques of the modern dance were once orthodox. It did not enter a dancer's mind that they might be altered. To add to them was the sole privilege of the originators.

Intensive summer courses were the scenes of the new dispensations, reverently transmitted by the master-students. When the fanatically followed leaders began, and when they continued, to desert their own teachings (adapting chiefly balletish movements to their own rapidly-growing-less-rigorous techniques), a general and profound insecurity fell over the modern dance.

Where any strength now exists in the modern dance, it is, as before, in isolated personalities and physiques. In the case of the young, this is unfortunate; for, no matter how impressive and revelatory their expressed outlooks on life are, they are overshadowed, in the minds of audiences, and often,

21

understandably, in the dancers' own minds, by the more familiar, more respected, and more mature older personalities.

Personality is a flimsy thing on which to build an art. (This does not mean that it should not enter into an art, for, indeed, that is what is meant by the word *style*.) And the ballet is obviously not built on such an ephemeron, for, if it were, it would not at present thrive as it does, almost devoid of interesting personalities and certainly without the contribution of any individual's message or attitude toward life.

That the ballet *has* something seems reasonable to assume. That what it has is what the modern dance needs is here expressed as an opinion.

It is seriously to be doubted whether *tour jeté, entrechat six,* or *sur les pointes* (in general) are needed in the modern dance. Even the prettiness and fanciness of these movements would not seem to be requisite. Also, it is not true that the basis of the ballet lies in glittering costumes and sets, for many of the better ballets appear year after year in drab, weather-beaten accoutrements.

Ballets like *Les Sylphides, Swan Lake,* almost any *pas de deux* or *quatre,* and, currently, the exceptional *Danses Concertantes* have a strength and validity quite beyond and separate from the movements involved, whether or not they are done with style (expressed personality), the ornamented condition of the stage, quality of costumery, sound of the music, or any other particularities, including those of content. Nor does the secret lie in that mysterious quantity, form. (The forms of the ballet are mostly dull; symmetry is maintained practically without question.)

Good or bad, with or without meaning, well dressed or not, the ballet is always clear in its rhythmic structure. Phrases begin and end in such a way that *anyone* in the audience knows when they begin and end, and breathes accordingly. It may seem at first thought that rhythmic structure is not of primary importance. However, a dance, a poem, a piece of music (any of the time arts) occupies a length of time, and the manner in which this length of time is divided first into large parts and then into phrases (or built up from phrases to form eventual larger parts) is the work's very life structure. The ballet is in possession of a tradition of clarity of its rhythmic structure. Essential devices for bringing this about have been handed down generation after generation. These particular devices, again, are not to be borrowed from the ballet: they are private to it. But the function they fulfill is not private; it is, on the contrary, universal.

Oriental dancing, for instance, is clear in its phraseology. It has its own devices for obtaining it. Hot jazz is never unclear rhythmically. The poems of Gerard Manley Hopkins, with all their departure from tradition, enable the reader to breathe with them. The modern dance, on the other hand, is rarely clear.

When a modern dancer has followed music that was clear in its phrase structure, the dance has had a tendency to be clear. The widespread habit of choreographing the dance first, and obtaining music for it later, is not in itself here criticized. But the fact that modern choreographers have been concerned with things other than clarity of rhythmic structure has made the appearance of it, when the dance-first-music-later method was used, both accidental and isolated. This has led to a disregard of rhythmic structure even in the case of dancing to music already written, for, in a work like Martha Graham's *Deaths and Entrances,* an audience can know where it is in relation to the action only through repeated seeings and the belying action of memory. On the other hand, Martha Graham and Louis Horst together were able to make magnificently clear and moving works like their *Frontier,* which works, however, stand alarmingly alone in the history of the modern dance.

The will to compromise, mentioned above, and the admirable humility implied in the willingness to learn from other art manners is adolescent, but it is much closer to maturity than the childish blind following of leaders that was characteristic of the modern dance several years ago. If, in receiving influences from the outside, the modern dance is satisfied with copying, or adapting to itself, surface particularities (techniques, movements, devices of any kind), it will die before it reaches maturity; if, on the other hand, the common denominator of the completely developed time arts, the secret of art life, is discovered by the modern dance, Terpsichore will have a new and rich source of worshippers.

With clarity of rhythmic structure, *grace* forms a duality. Together they have a relation like that of body and soul. Clarity is cold, mathematical, inhuman, but basic and earthy. Grace is warm, incalculable, human, opposed to clarity, and like the air. Grace is not here used to mean prettiness; it is used to mean the play with and against the clarity of the rhythmic structure. The two are always present together in the best works of the time arts, endlessly, and life-givingly, opposed to each other.

"In the finest specimens of versification, there seems to be a perpetual conflict between the law of the verse and the freedom of the language, and each is incessantly, though insignificantly, violated for the purpose of giving effect to the other. The best poet is not he whose verses are the most easily scanned, and whose phraseology is the commonest in its materials, and the most direct in its arrangement; but rather he whose language combines the greatest imaginative accuracy with the most elaborate and sensible metrical organization, and who, in his verse, preserves everywhere the living sense of the metre, not so much by unvarying obedience to, as by innumerable small departures from, its *modulus*" (Coventry Patmore, *Prefatory Study on English Metrical Law,* 1879, pp. 12–13).

The "perpetual conflict" between clarity and grace is what makes hot jazz hot. The best performers continually anticipate or delay the phrase beginnings and endings. They also, in their performances, treat the beat or pulse, and indeed, the measure, with grace: putting more or fewer icti within the measure's limits than are expected (similar alterations of pitch and timbre are also customary), contracting or extending the duration of the unit. This, not syncopation, is what pleases the hep-cats.

Hindu music and dancing are replete with grace. This is possible because the rhythmic structure in Hindu time arts is highly systematized, has been so for many ages, and every Hindu who enjoys listening to music or looking at the dance is familiar with the laws of tala. Players, dancers, and audience enjoy hearing and seeing the laws of the rhythmic structure now observed and now ignored.

This is what occurs in a beautifully performed classic or neo-classic ballet. And it is what enables one to experience pleasure in such a performance, despite the fact that such works are relatively meaningless in our modern society. That one should, today, have to see *Swan Lake* or something equally empty of contemporary meaning in order to experience the pleasure of observing clarity and grace in the dance, is, on its face, lamentable. Modern society needs, as usual, and now desperately needs, a strong modern dance.

The opinion expressed here is that clarity of rhythmic structure with grace are essential to the time arts, that together they constitute an esthetic (that is, they lie under and beneath, over and above, physical and personal particularities), and that they rarely occur in the modern dance; that the latter has no esthetic (its strength having been and being the personal property of its originators and best exponents), that, in order for it to become strong and useful in society, mature in itself, the modern dance must clarify its rhythmic structure, then enliven it with grace, and so get itself a theory, the common, universal one about what is beautiful in a time art.

EARLY REVIEWS

Merce Cunningham (1948) by Barbara Frost

As the musician Louis Horst has said, very few people can really know Merce Cunningham. Just as the sequences of an especially fantastic nightmare elude our understanding in retrospect, so it is difficult to fasten on specific qualities in the personality of this young dancer that might enable us to present him in the usual "profile" syntax. To use another analogy, in contemporary philosophical terms, Merce Cunningham is always in process. The volatile, fluid nature of the artist can never be defined by collecting static fragments of movement from his dances or instances from his own life, connecting them with transition sentences, thus assembling a composite portrait of the artist. If he escapes our complete understanding, however, he does not defy our appreciation of what he gives. His nature being such as it is, Merce Cunningham is the most effectively equipped of his contemporaries to reach out and touch the sides of our natures that seldom find verbalization or physical articulation.

An awareness of his Irish-Slavic descent offers much insight into his work. His heritage offers explanation below and beyond the superficial level of appreciation. When we witness a finished dance of Cunningham's we are not particularly struck by its intensity. The music and the movement seem to evolve with a simultaneous facility. The groundwork for such an effect is, however, intense, slow, and precise. In his tireless choreographic revisions and patient trial upon discard and trial to find the precisely correct movement, we find perhaps the Slav. While this might be overly fine-drawn, the Irish temperament is more obvious to one who is familiar with his dancing.

Mysterious Adventure (1945) is an example of the influence of both traditions. Where the simple action of, in everyday activity, coming upon an extraordinary and inexplicable occurrence, could have been translated into ponderously complex dance vocabulary, Cunningham plays with the idea, tries to probe the adventure, concludes, not in broken desperation, but in almost humorous resignation that it is all beyond him.

The humor of his dancing cannot be called satirical. He not only makes fun of the adventure itself, but of the proportions of mysterious complexity most people would allow it to assume in their minds. Consequently he is at the same time too good natured and too fantastic to be called a satirist. For example, the adventure is represented by a surrealistic stage piece. In contrast to the neurotic contortions of the Graham dancers around similar Noguchi sets in *Dark Meadow*, Cunningham's interpretation is infinitely more appealing to our understanding in its near slapstick confusion. Where the comedy of human foibling might in this case appear empty or trite, it is saved by the above-mentioned care and work which translates his psychological ingenuity into unique dance movements.

Something of Cunningham's educational background is necessary to clarify the subject matter of his dances. Initially, perhaps, we should not say "subject matter," but rather, focal point, since he does not plan to convey a message. He is more "showing" than "saying." His interest in ideas was always and is now, curious and diverse. At the Cornish School of Acting in Seattle he studied acting for a year, becoming preoccupied with acting movements. To follow up this interest, he attended the Bennington summer session where he first met Martha Graham and joined her group. By this time, the emphasis had shifted to movement for dance and many can recall the roles created for Cunningham in that group, notably March in *Letter to the World* and the preacher in *Appalachian Spring*.

Perfection in movement now predominates in Cunningham's career as an independent dancer and teacher. His work with students is painstaking and cautious. For so young a dancer he has achieved remarkable success and recognition. But justifiably.

To attempt to pin down the old cliché, universality of appeal, is difficult but essential in Cunningham's case. The individual experience, if sensed, can hardly be adequately verbalized. What Cunningham illustrates almost consistently in his dances, are the variations, the wanderings, the conjectures, of the human mind on individual human experiences, usually commonplace. *The Open Road* (1947) is a very delightful example of this. The external experience being exactly indicated by the title, Cunningham lavished upon it all the whimsical imagination of the most confirmed vagabond. Consequently we are carried off the stage of reality with him into a realm of daydreams and fantasies which could (and do) totally take possession of an ordinary man walking down an ordinary road.

In *Root of an Unfocus* (1944), Cunningham has applied a similar technique to a more serious theme. The dance most nearly approaches a psychological study. With tightly-woven choreographic sequences, he dances the unsequential, disassociated flow of ideas in an unbalanced mind. The change of level and direction, the shifting movement of his head, emphasize the constantly changing focus characteristic of unstable mentality.

Cunningham's universality, then, would lie in his sense contact with human emotions and mentality. This appeal is not intellectualized. Whether the subject the artist wishes to embody in his movement is simple or complex, it is characteristic human experience. The experiences are translated to the spectator in Cunningham's own fantastical terms. Fantasy is this artist's medium as equally as is choreography, and in this medium the description of human experience becomes, for the Cunningham audience, a deftly treated view of experience, valid artistically and personally.

Two Reviews by Edwin Denby

I. Elegance in Isolation (1944)

At the small Humphrey-Weidman Studio in the darkness of Sixteenth Street, Merce Cunningham and John Cage presented a program of solo dances and of percussionist music last night which was of the greatest esthetic elegance. The audience, an intelligent one, enjoyed and applauded.

It was Mr. Cunningham's first solo recital, though he is well known to dance audiences as soloist in Martha Graham's company. His gifts as a lyric dancer are most remarkable. His build resembles that of the juvenile *saltimbanques* of the early Picasso canvases. As a dancer his instep and his knees are extraordinarily elastic and quick; his steps, runs, knee bends and leaps are brilliant in lightness and speed. His torso can turn on its vertical axis with great sensitivity, his shoulders are held lightly free and his head poises intelligently. The arms are light and long, they float, but do not often have an active look. These are all merits particularly suited to lyric expression.

As a dancer and as a choreographer of his own solos, Mr. Cunningham's sense of physical rhythm is subtle and clear. His dances are built on the rhythm of a body in movement, and on its irregular phrase lengths. And the perfection with which he can indicate the rise and fall of an impulse gives one an esthetic pleasure of exceptional delicacy. His compositions too were in no way derivative in their formal aspect, or in their gesture; they looked free and definite at the same time.

The effect of them is one of an excessively elegant sensuality. On the other hand—partly because they are solo dances, partly because they lack the vigorous presence of the body's deportment characteristic of academic ballet style—their effect is one of remoteness and isolation. This tone may well be due to the fact that Mr. Cunningham is still a young dancer, who is only beginning to discover his own dramatic resources. But I have never seen a first recital that combined such taste, such technical finish, such originality of dance material and so sure a manner of presentation.

Mr. Cage accompanied the six dances on "prepared" piano and his compositions for them were perfect as dance accompaniment. He also played six piano solos of his own, accompanied Juanita Hall in two songs (one to a text from *Finnegans Wake*), and directed his quartet *Amores,* which performed at the Modern Museum last year. The new pieces were applauded—as had been those heard last year—for the delicate sensuality of their odd timbres, for their rhythmic subtlety, and their willfully remote tenuousness of construction. His music, like Mr. Cunningham's dancing, has an effect of extreme elegance in isolation.

II. *Alone on Stage (1945)*

Merce Cunningham, a brilliant soloist in Martha Graham's company, and the most gifted of the young dancers who follow her, gave a solo recital last night at [New York's] Hunter College Playhouse. Though his first recital last year had been a distinct success with the audience, this second one was not. But Mr. Cunningham's quite exceptional merits as a dancer were as clear as ever and as interesting to a dance lover.

As a virtuoso in our modern school technique he is second only to Miss Graham herself. His face is always expressive. The elasticity, strength and quickness in the legs and feet, the variety of bearing in the torso and neck, the clarity of motion in arms and hands allow him very striking effects. Better still is the variety of drive and speed which phrases his dances; and best is the improvisatory naturalness of emphasis which keeps his gestures from ever looking stylized or formalistic.

With his physical elegance and originality of gesture Mr. Cunningham combines a rare good sense in what a man dancing alone on the stage may with some dignity seem to be occupied in doing. A man alone can suggest he is looking for something invisible, that he is trying out a trick, that he is having a bad time, or that he is just fooling. Cunningham's dances express these lyric possibilities with real imagination, and subtlety. The unhappy numbers have dignity and the joking ones have humor. One funny one, *Mysterious Adventure* (1945) with an absurd object on the stage (designed by David Hare) was long but alive all the time.

In short, Mr. Cunningham is an exceptionally gifted and exceptionally intelligent dancer. For dance enthusiasts whatever he does is a pleasure to watch. But the variations of solo lyric dancing he shows are not sharp enough themselves to attract the intelligent audience he is equipped to interest. He does not create on stage different objective characters, but rather lyric variations of his own character. His genre, which hovers between lyric and character, is one that expresses itself best in comic numbers, in which the divided personality is a virtue.

A virtuoso like Mr. Cunningham is a rarity, and his ability is of the greatest value to modern-school dancing. For the moment, he shines best however in group compositions, where his character contrasts with that of other dancers. His solo-recitals, impeccable as they are in taste, are not yet bold enough in expression to communicate to a general audience. But he has all the possibilities of becoming a great dancer, and we need as many of those as we can get.

Dance in Review (1949) by Sybil Shearer

I remember Merce when he was a boy; now he is a young man, and it seems to me he is one of those rare beings who keep changing and developing so that not only he but his audience can look forward to a long and vitally interesting career, if all goes well. I say this because I have not seen him for several years and already notice a change, and feel sorry at having had to miss any of this process.

As a boy he had an elfin quality, and a lightness. Now he also has solidity. At first his dancing probably reflected the obvious in his personality, but now he has begun to go below the surface in a way that leads one to believe that, as he goes inward further and further, he will emerge more and more until he may stand revealed in a way that will need no translation.

Of course, it is just possible that this can never happen to an artist until the world develops a bit on its own. In any case, today one has to transport oneself into Cunningham's world as though you were listening to the language of the animals or the insects. I like his work best because it is pure, and once you have made the transition into his world, you can see that.

The audience—all the people on Chicago's north shore who have any interest in the arts, and who for the most part had never seen him before—was, from all reports, prepared to accept something unusual and really opened up for the occasion.

In the first number, *A Diversion* (1948), we looked at him as a phenomenon as he introduced his style, personality, and the range of his movement. He moved much more than I thought he did from the last time I saw him, and he used his arms more. He was strong and clear cut.

The second dance, *Root of an Unfocus* (1944), was a high point emotionally, and I felt chills of repulsion and attraction mounting and tacking until I wanted to get in there and dance too.

In *Tossed as It Is Untroubled* (1944), there was a settling into the concert, a feeling that we now knew at whom we were looking. *Totem Ancestor* (1942) left most of the people I talked to breathless with its spectacular leaping and falling.

But in *Mysterious Adventure* (1945) we were drawn into the warm hypnotic flow and were carried on and on way past the end of the performance, not only by the dance itself, but also by the marvelously integrated accompaniment by John Cage and lighting by Helen Morrison.

Each of Merce Cunningham's dances has a very precise structure, and moved on by itself like a locomotive into which he climbed and rode until the next stop. This, too, gave his dancing the hypnotic quality which was pointed up even more by the broken quality of the dance that I composed for him (called *A Woman's Version of a Man's World*) in which he was definitely on his two feet struggling with and navigating for himself.

In retrospect, this contrast served to bring up again the magnificent fact that it is not the instrument we are moved by so much as the mind behind it, and the better the instrument, the more the mind is revealed. It was amazing to me to see my thinking revealed by his instrument, and how completely he was able to change for the occasion.

Yes, the audience was fully aware that in witnessing the work of Merce Cunningham and John Cage they were dealing with artists. It seemed that, almost to a man, they were swept in and moved in a way that does not happen every day.

Merce Cunningham: Maker of Dances (1957) by James Waring

New Yorkers will have their first chance in two years to see the work of Merce Cunningham, Villager and well-known modern dancer, when on Saturday evening, January 12, he brings his company into the Brooklyn Academy of Music. During the interregnum, Mr. Cunningham and his group—Carolyn Brown, Viola Farber, Karen Kanner, Marianne Preger [Simon], Remy Charlip, and Bruce King, with David Tudor, pianist, and John Cage, musical director— have been concerned with a series of American tours reaching as far west as California. Teaching and performing since 1945 at Black Mountain College, the Brandeis University Arts Festival, the Palacio de Bellas Artes in Mexico City, and in his own studio on Sixth Avenue near 10th Street, Mr. Cunningham's principal work has been the making of new dances in a style eloquently his own.

One element in the formation of a choreographer's style is the way he dances. Mr. Cunningham's roles as soloist with the Martha Graham company from 1939 to 1945 seemed to show a kind of fierce vitality held in restraint, a quality which has persisted since that time.

Unlike Miss Graham's work, if Mr. Cunningham's dances have "stories," they perhaps take place beyond the scenery, out of view of the audience, like Erik Satie's ballet which was to be performed entirely offstage. What the spectator encounters is the second ripple after the dropping of the stone, not the event itself in explicit flesh. Something has happened, because something is felt. This art is one of feeling, not of meaning, like the instructions in a model-airplane kit. The grammar is the meaning, Cunningham likes to say, quoting Gertrude Stein.

The quality of energetic life in containment has been visible since such early solos as *Totem Ancestor* (1942) and *Root of an Unfocus* (1944) and persists in *Lavish Escapade* (1956). Recently this energy has modified to the andante of the white and tender *Nocturnes*, (1956) set to five night-music pieces by Satie and dressed in appropriate white nightclothes by Bob Rauschenberg. *Nocturnes* will have its New York premiere at the Brooklyn Academy concert.

Merce Cunningham's choreography moves in a peculiar kind of counterpoint alongside the work of musical director John Cage, one of the most forward-looking of today's composers. Asked what he thought music should do for the dance, Mr. Cunningham answered: "Leave it alone." Perhaps it is that his dances do not need anything done for them except to be looked at. It is true that audiences often prefer their meat soaked in sauce. However, Mr. Cage's music is the opposite of sauce—not decoration, or to hang on a tree, but a thing which stands and moves on its own feet and breathes independently of the dancers.

To throw light on Merce Cunningham's choreographic method is to risk blindness from the dazzling return of that light from the polished surface. If the "chance dances" were dictated by slips of paper drawn from a hat, that hat was the one which produces rabbits, doves, and silk kerchiefs. *Minutiae* (1954), made from witnessed movements of passersby beneath his window, is Mr. Cunningham's singular transmogrification of the prosaic into prose. The grammar has become the meaning: seeing is believing. If looking becomes seeing, beggars will fly.

Cunningham, Here and Now (1957)
by Frank O'Hara

What a shame it is that Merce Cunningham does not have a repertory season each year! He is a great dancer, has an exceptional company, and his choreography is always rewarding. *Labyrinthian Dances* (1957; to Hauer), first on the program and a premiere, seemed to be one of his most important choreographic works, but I think it would have become clearer in subsequent performances.

Throughout the evening Mr. Cunningham, whether solo or in ensemble, displayed those qualities of lyrical power and delicacy of taste which make him unique. In *Springweather and People* (1955; to Earle Brown), an ambitious and perhaps over-elaborated work but danced marvelously, he provided his company with some extraordinary passages for their individual talents, particularly those of Carolyn Brown and Remy Charlip.

The major event of the program, *Nocturnes* (1956; to Satie), was distinguished in every aspect. Miss Brown indicated her gifts a couple of years ago in performing *Amores* (1949) with Mr. Cunningham, and she has continually grown in stature; in *Nocturnes* Viola Farber and Mr. Charlip also move to the fore, and I must also mention John Cage's performance of the Satie, which can only be indicated as "ideal" or "inevitable."

Sets and costumes by Bob Rauschenberg displayed a verve and unerring taste which one could only expect from him. The lighting for the Cunningham recital was by Nicola Cernovich, who has no small part in the general success.

Two Reviews (1960–63) by Jill Johnston

1960

With three works new to New York, Merce Cunningham appeared at the Phoenix Theatre the evening of February 16. The only dance "old" to New York was *Changeling,* performed November 1957, his solo in bright red. But one performance two years and four months ago does not make it so old; it would in fact take a number of performances to make a Cunningham dance seem very old, and even then it would probably seem old only because of the number of times it had been performed, not because it had grown tiresome through familiarity.

There is much to see in a dance by Cunningham. *Summerspace* (1958) and *Rune* (1959) are teeming with the ever-shifting patterns and designs that he creates in his dances for group. Imagine sitting in a room where two large and complicated paintings are on exhibition; but instead of reposing in their conventional stationary positions, they are passed slowly through the room, in one door and out the other, and that is all you see of them. You would probably retain the impression of the dominant color tones, the general shape and texture, and the pervasive "mood." But you would feel like returning to the room to examine all the details and the way everything fits together.

Well, *Rune* is a very large and complicated dance. It would be good to see it again soon. It is a Grand dance, statuesque, and almost heroic. It contains some typically swift and dazzling passages, but the dominant tone is a rich, slow brown. By contrast, *Summerspace* is light and resilient, a "lyric dance," the program says. It is bounding and spacious with air. And it has the quality of the speckled backdrop and costumes—something like the dappled play of light and shadow caused by the sun when it glints through leaves.

Antic Meet (1958) is not so difficult to see at one sitting, perhaps because each incident has a special character and makes an indelible impression—indelibly funny. What a superb joke, these episodic "take-offs" on the dance, with inserted nonsense! It is not really so important that the dance is mostly a spoof of various kinds of dancing; the idea provides a good excuse for a wonderful collection of absurdities. And except for two or three numbers, you can't be too certain what is a take-off on what. Anyway, it does include: a delicate ballet farce between two girls called "Sports and Diversions #1"; another "Sports and Diversions #2" in which the two men romp around in a kind of athletic competition, ending with Mr. Cunningham in a raccoon coat, dragging off a defeated Mr. Charlip; a mechanically efficient solo by Viola Farber carrying an umbrella with a spray of lights under it, which could be a nightclub act; a wonderful "Social" for everybody in dark eyeglasses with a femme-fatale ending (you might miss it, but Marilyn Wood puts a death grip on Mr. Charlip as they exit); "Room for Two," a bedroom farce, I believe, which includes a door, a nightgown (on Carolyn Brown), and a chair strapped on a back; Mr. Cunningham as Bacchus in a big sweater with several arms, dancing with several cohorts (including Judith Dunn)—a number which someone tells me is a take-off on Martha Graham; a charming soft-shoe dance by Mr. Cunningham, whimsically understated; and an "Opener" and "Exodus" which *could* be a spoof by Mr. Cunningham on himself . . . ?

1963

During the intermission at José Limón's recent concert in [New York's] Philharmonic Hall someone observed that Limón's art is for middlebrows. The observer meant that his dances are easy to grasp. In "The Traitor" there is a bad man and a kind of saint, and nobody could doubt the issue. Moreover, the embodiment of good and evil in the figures of Christ and Judas could hardly escape any Western spectator, since the symbolism is explicit and complete. Limón has never been a subtle artist. If you don't get it the first time he'll hammer it out a few more times. The dance distortions never veer far from the broad representational gesture. The choral movements emphasize the solo drama. The narrative proceeds in logical sequence. So altogether the audience is permitted to feel quite comfortable. That must account for the packed house at Philharmonic Hall.

By contrast, the audience the previous week for Merce Cunningham, although substantial enough, was far from packed. I learned from *The New York Times* that more people would turn up if they didn't have to hear John Cage's music. The implication in the *Times* was that Cunningham himself is okay but that he ought to get rid of Cage if he wants to appeal to the outlying districts. That's like asking Limón to throw down the Bible, although nobody would suggest it, because the Bible is a big drawing card in the outlying districts. I don't mean to equate Cage with the Bible. What I'm saying is that the collaboration of Cage and Cunningham makes perfect sense and that it is as difficult to conceive of Cunningham without Cage's music (and direction) as it is to imagine Limón without his literature.

In any event, Cage is not the only deterrent in this matter of popularity. Cunningham's dances are still beyond the general public because he doesn't give the public anything literal to hold on to. His dances are all about movement, and what you see in them that relates to your common experience is your own business and not his.

The dance world is embarrassingly backward. Cunningham should pack

Philharmonic Hall for a week at least. He has no peer in the dance as a consummate artist. Moreover, he continues to be abreast, if not in advance, of all recent developments. Working through movement ("I don't look in a book, I make a step") as he does, Cunningham belongs to that great shift of focus—from representation to the concentration on materials—which is *so* central to the revolution in art in this century. The pure aspect of ballet is a long established fact. Yet it is still the story aspect of the ballet that interests the public at large. Moreover, until recently, with such works by George Balanchine as *Agon* and *Episodes,* the pure movement of ballet has always been invested with the general connotation of grandness and of romantic aspiration.

It is not so hard to think of Limón as a modern ballet dancer. The attitudes are the same. The difference lies in vocabulary, and choreographic method—both new to dance, but not so unfamiliar in the painting and music of, say, the 17th century. Limón's anachronism is no special issue. I can have a fine time in the museums. I think *The Moor's Pavane* is a great dance. And there are moments of high pictorial beauty in *The Traitor.* Judas and Jesus aside, a scene like the Last Supper, with its sensual shift of forms in a gold light—heads and hands inclining up and down or across the sheet (table) as the sheet is manipulated into horizontal, diagonal, or vertical positions—makes an exquisite moving picture. And there is an exciting passage for the six men as they speed through the space in pairs with a twisting, jumping phrase in a contrapuntal, fugal pattern.

The problem of *The Traitor* as a whole is its story. When the story becomes obtrusive you stop looking at the dance. Since I couldn't care less about the "message"—and I'm not sure that Limón cares either—the passages of torment are like bagsful of hot air. This is modern dance at its rhetorical worst. A few well-known movements from a personal style are contrived to "express" a profound emotion. And what could be more profound than suffering? If there must be suffering, let it be original, and then if I can't suffer too, I can enjoy the dancing. The plot of *The Moor's Pavane* holds up because the expression is contained by the beautiful rondo form of the dance. Since Limón is a grand and tragic figure, the problem has always been a matter of finding the proper vehicle, in form and content, for that image. And even when it works the image may still seem hopeless to those living in 1963. The aristocracy is dead and corn flakes are profound for breakfast.

When Cunningham walks out on stage and looks at the audience he comes as a man. There is no image beyond that of his physical presence. Limón never looks at anybody because he has a lot on his mind. He's more than a man, and that makes it hard to look at other men. I don't care much, except that I'm living in 1963 and I like the facts of life. That is the only basis for my preference. But that's saying a great deal, for it is Cunningham's magic as a performer to make his art so lively. Freed of ideas and pretensions he can make that mere step. And the next step is such an involvement in the possibilities of movement that there is no end to it and the result is one amazing dance after another.

The curious thing about this kind of dancing is that emotion is created by motion rather than the reverse, which is the traditional view in modern dance. But since there is no specified emotion, I believe that what you feel in the movement is the impact of a total action. Each movement means only itself and it moves you by its pure existence, by being so much itself. It is Cunningham's magic as a performer to make every action a unique and complete experience. The gesture is the performer; the performer is the gesture. In response or in motion the quality and the man appear indivisibly, with the concentrated potency of complete confidence in the fact of a movement or the fact of a silence.

Aeon (1961) is a staggering dance because it's bursting with such facts. On the huge stage of Philharmonic Hall it looked like the universe. From the profusion of sounds and movement qualities and spatial changes every conceivable condition of the physical world is suggested. The clarity of line, the slow extensions, the fast detail, the complex coordinations, the air and the ground, the waiting the no waiting, the great vacancies, the coming and going, the sudden unison or the sudden dispersion and isolation, the brief or extended encounters. *Aeon* keeps moving in my imagination as a world of sound and movement that is like our world without limits, for it is pure process and although each moment is like no other moment it cannot stop anywhere.

Tranquillity (1964) by Wilfrid Mellers

A musician of exquisite aural sensitivity, John Cage has become gradually less concerned to compose sounds into "significant" order, more concerned to effect composure within the mind by accepting sounds for what they are, in the silence that surrounds them. At the furthest swing of the pendulum from Europe's post-Renaissance obsession with the will, he would free us from past and future, inviting us to enter an autonomous Now. Similarly, Robert Rauschenberg at one time painted completely white or completely black canvases, invoking the space, the nothingness within which we may perceive afresh the astonishingly disparate objects (introduced bodily into his later work) of the visible world. For Cage learning-to-hear, for Rauschenberg learning-to-see, are separate from action but not independent of it, since life must be lived in time. This is why "any relevant action is theatrical," and is also why Cage and Rauschenberg have collaborated with the dancer Merce Cunningham to complement their aural and visual images with movement in time and space.

This movement, however, like hearing and seeing, has no before and after. There is no expressionist purpose, only a "purposeful purposelessness," in the relationship between movement, sound, and image. Thus in *Suite for*

Five (1956) the actions—now gay, now anguished, now grotesque—are as diverse as nature herself; yet in being purged of causation they are purged too of the nag of memory and the tug of desire. This they achieve *through* their lack of relationship to Cage's music, which is even more devoid of progression or motor-rhythm than is Japanese temple music. The softly reverberative sounds of the prepared piano—occurring at chronometric points dictated by chance operations, and separated by immense silences—really do cause one to listen anew: while Rauschenberg's almost-blank costumes and decor help one to see the actions with unblinkered eyes.

Crises (1960), as the title suggests, is less abstract, more dramatic, though the erotic implications of these actions between a man and four women evade climax. The music is Conlon Nancarrow's celebrated studies for three player-pianos. The fantastic complexity of the polyrhythms, which machines can negotiate when human beings couldn't, transmutes the sexy and nostalgic flavour of jazz and pop into loony hysteria. Yet the sounds preserve, in their mechanisation, a disembodied detachment, and this communicates itself to the actions. For all the sleaziness of the atmosphere and the violence of the gestures, we are released from our more inchoate appetites in simply accepting them. Even they can take their place with "the permanent emotions of Indian tradition"; and Merce Cunningham's [untitled] *Solo* (1953) to Christian Wolff's pianistic explosions goes still further, for it induces a therapeutic calm from the neurotic twitch and spastic shiver that (at least since *West Side Story*) we've come to recognise as gestures typical of our world and time.

Story (1963), with background noises derived from the audible universe by Toshi Ichiyanagi, is the least abstract of these ballets. Here Rauschenberg comes into his own, for there is a setting (a television studio), and the dancers, inspiring one another to variously indeterminate activities, bring in an assortment of Rauschenbergian "objects." The ballet consists of "happenings," executed, however, by dancers of great technical skills. While the result is dadaistically hilarious, it's by no means only that. The pathos of the clown figures reminded me of Satie's *Parade,* for which Cunningham could and should do a superb new choreography. It's a pity that the large and on the whole enthusiastic audience decided in advance that this piece was to be an unmitigated hoot; though it's only fair to add that they remained rapt during the longest and stillest silences of *Suite for Five*.

Merce Cunningham

SPACE, TIME AND DANCE (1952)

The dance is an art in space and time.
The object of the dancer is to obliterate that.

The classical ballet, by maintaining the image of the Renaissance perspective in stage thought, kept a linear form of space. The modern American dance, stemming from German expressionism and the personal feelings of the various American pioneers, made space into a series of lumps, or often just static hills on the stage with actually no relation to the larger space of the stage area, but simply forms that by their connection in time made a shape. Some of the space-thought coming from a German dance opened the space out, and left a momentary feeling of connection with it, but too often the space was not visible enough because the physical action was all of a lightness, like sky without earth, or heaven without hell.

The fortunate thing in dancing is that space and time cannot be disconnected, and everyone can see and understand that. A body still is taking up just as much space and time as a body moving. The result is that neither the one nor the other—moving or being still—is more or less important, except it's nice to see a dancer moving. But the moving becomes more clear if the space and time around the moving are one of its opposites—stillness. Aside from the personal skill and clarity of the individual dancer, there are certain things that make clear to a spectator what the dancer is doing. In the ballet, the various steps that lead to the larger movements or poses have, by usage and by their momentum, become common ground upon which the spectator can lead his eyes and his feelings into the resulting action. This also helps define the rhythm, in fact more often than not does define it. In the modern dance, the tendency or the wish has been to get rid of these "unnecessary and balletic" movements, at the same time wanting the same result in the size and vigor of the movement as the balletic action, and this has often left the dancer and the spectator slightly short.

To quibble with that on the other side: one of the best discoveries the modern dance has made use of is the gravity of the body in weight, that is, as opposite from denying (and thus affirming) gravity by ascent into the air, the weight of the body in going with gravity, down. The word "heavy" connotes something incorrect, since what is meant is not the heaviness of a bag of cement falling, although we've all been spectators of that too, but the heaviness of a living body falling with full intent of eventual rise. This is not a fetish or a use of heaviness as an accent against a predominantly light quality, but a thing in itself. By its nature this kind of moving would make the space seem a series of unconnected spots, along with the lack of clear-connecting movements in the modern dance.

A prevalent feeling among many painters that lets them make a space in which anything can happen is a feeling dancers may have too. Imitating the way nature makes a space and puts lots of things in it, heavy and light, little and big, all unrelated, yet each affecting all the others.

About the formal methods of choreography—some due to the conviction that a communication of one order or another is necessary; others to the feeling that mind follows heart, that is, form follows content; some due to the feeling that the musical form is the most logical to follow—the most curious to me is the general feeling in the modern dance that nineteenth-century forms stemming from earlier pre-classical forms are the only formal actions advisable, or even possible to take. This seems a flat contradiction of the modern dance— agreeing with the thought of discovering new or allegedly new movement for contemporary reasons, the using of psychology as a tremendous elastic basis for content, and wishing to be expressive of the "times" (although how can one be expressive of anything else)—but not feeling the need for a different basis upon which to put this expression, in fact being mainly content to indicate that either the old forms are good enough, or further that the old forms are the only possible forms. These consist mainly of theme and variation, and associated devices—repetition, inversion, development, and manipulation. There is also a tendency to imply a crisis to which one goes and then in some way retreats from. Now I can't see that crisis any longer means a climax, unless we are willing to grant that every breath of wind has a climax (which I am), but then that obliterates climax, being a surfeit of such. And since our lives, both by nature by the newspapers are so full of crisis that one is no longer aware of it, then it is clear that life goes on regardless, and further that each thing can be and is separate from each and every other, viz: the continuity of the newspaper headlines. Climax is for those who are swept by New Year's Eve.

More freeing into *space* than the theme and manipulation "holdup" would be a formal structure based on *time*. Now time can be an awful lot of bother with the ordinary pinch-penny counting that has to go on with it, but if one can think of the structure as a space of time in which anything can happen in any sequence of movement event, and any length of stillness can take place, then the counting is an aid towards freedom, rather than a discipline towards mechanization. A use of time-structure also frees the music into space, making the connection between the dance and the music one of individual autonomy connected at structural points. The result is the dance is free to act as it chooses, as is the music. The music doesn't have to work itself to death to underline the dance, or the dance create havoc in trying to be as flashy as the music.

For me, it seems enough that dancing is a spiritual exercise in physical form, and that what is seen, is what it is. And I do not believe it is possible to be "too simple." What the dancer does is the most realistic of all possible things, and to pretend that a man standing on a hill could be doing everything except just standing is simply divorce—divorce from life, from the sun coming up and going down, from clouds in front of the sun, from the rain that comes from the clouds and sends you into the drugstore for a cup of coffee, from each thing that succeeds each thing. Dancing is a visible action of life.

Remy Charlip

COMPOSING BY CHANCE
(1954)

Merce Cunningham's suite, *Sixteen Dances for Soloist and Company of Three* (1951) when last performed at the Alvin Theatre, produced a lively, controversial reaction. Programmed between the familiar *Appalachian Spring* of Martha Graham and *The Moor's Pavane* of José Limón, the response was immediate. After each of the sixteen dances there were boos and applause, cheers and hisses. The dances were simply titled, "Solo," "Duet," "Trio," or "Quartet," and followed one another without any apparent story or thematic coherence. The music, movement, and costumes, as well as the continuity, were unfamiliar.

One of the ideas that prompted these dances is to be found in the traditional Hindu theory of the *rasas* or permanent emotions. The *rasas* number nine. Four are white: the Erotic, the Heroic, the Mirthful, and the Wondrous. Four are black: Fear, the Odious, Anger, and Sorrow. The ninth, neither white nor black, but essential to both, and often described as special to the performer's art, is Tranquillity. The aspect of impermanence or sentimentality has been attributed to other emotional qualities than those given above.

Using this as a starting point, Mr. Cunningham choreographed a continuity of individual dances, a dance using a permanent emotion to be followed by one using an impermanent emotion. This, of course, was a structural idea, and need not interfere with anyone's own direct emotional response to each dance. For example, dance number 9, a solo, in which Mr. Cunningham wears a huge colorful coat, and makes use of vocal sounds, shouts, groans, and grunts, there seems, to this writer, to be an emphasis on the Heroic, with the Mirthful and the Odious also present; whereas, Mr. Cunningham used as a starting point only the Odious. Reactions are naturally various. Some see this dance as a hunter frightened by his hunt, others as an exuberant drunk on a binge.

The music and the costumes have a formal arrangement, which allows for a single change for each dance. In the music, John Cage started with a specific set of sixty-four sounds for the first dance, and for each pair of dances replaced eight sounds with eight others, until at the end there was a completely new set of sounds. The first piece started with harsh and sharp sounds, and in the last piece there were long and resounding sounds. The costumes were treated in a similar manner, with dark and warm colors in the beginning, and with one costume change for each dance, ending in cool, light colors in order to contribute to the final, serene effect.

Mr. Cunningham's arrangement of the sequence of dances was based on the conviction that it is possible for anything to follow anything else, and that the actual order of events can be chanced rather than chosen, the resultant experience being free and discovered, rather than bound and remembered.

The chance method of choreography can clearly be seen in a later work which will have its New York premiere on December 29th called *Suite by Chance*. It is a long dance in four movements to music for magnetic tape by Christian Wolff. For this dance, a large series of charts was made: a chart numbering body movements of various kinds (phrases and positions, in movement and in stillness); a chart numbering lengths of time (so that a phrase or position could be done in a long or short duration, or, in the case of the impossibility of lengthening the time of a movement, as, for instance, a single step, it could be repeated for the length of time given); a chart numbering directions in space (floor plans).

These charts, which defined the physical limits within which the continuity would take place, were not made by chance. But from them, with a method similar to one used in a lottery, the actual continuity was found. That is, a sequence of movements for a single dancer was determined by means of chance from the numbered movements in the chart; space, direction, and lengths of time were found in the other charts. At important structural points in the music, the number of dancers on stage, exits and entrances, unison or individual movements of dancers were all decided by tossing coins. In this way, a dancer may be standing still one moment, leaping or spinning the next. There are familiar and unfamiliar movements, but what is continuously unfamiliar is the continuity, freed as it is from usual cause and effect relations. Due to the chance method, some of the movements listed in the charts were used more than once in different space and directions and for different lengths of time, and, on the other hand, many movements, to be found in the charts, do not appear at all in the final choreography.

For each new dance a new set of charts is made listing movements that Mr. Cunningham is interested in using at the time of composing.

Excerpts from Symphonie pour un homme seul (Pierre Schaeffer) was commissioned by and presented at the first Brandeis University Creative Arts Festival in June 1952. The music, by Pierre Schaeffer, is for magnetic tape, sometimes called "musique concrète." The measurement of magnetic-tape music is in inches, that is, spatial, rather than metric beats in time, as generally in music. The elimination of a fixed beat presents a new situation for the dancer with regard to his relationship to the music. By employing chance means in the choreography, the presence of consistent metric beat is largely eliminated in the dancing, since the tempo is changing so often that the sense of a particular tempo disappears. (It is interesting to note that in Japanese Classical Court music, such an absence of fixed beat has been called "sky tempo.") In this piece, since the music is made up of strange sounds, sounds not traditionally identified as musical, the use of chance continuity helps to avoid the tendency one might have had to imitate or interpret the sounds with body movements. The dance has a life of its own, with high and low moments which do not necessarily coincide with the high and low moments of the music.

At the Brandeis Festival, the music was to be played twice because of its very unusual and unfamiliar character (this occasion was the first performance in America of any example of musique concrète). Wishing to introduce variety, Mr. Cunningham choreographed two versions, both by chance methods, but by two different organizations of dance elements. The first version is a solo, without dramatic focus. The second is with company, and presents a continuity of dance movements and pantomimic events of such commonplace nature as washing hands and filing nails; both the movements and the mime events receive their continuity by chance. This work is now called *Collage*, and is presented with both versions, that is, the solo, and immediately following, the ensemble version.

The two most recent works by Mr. Cunningham which make use of chance elements in their choreography (some of them do not, for example *Banjo* [1953], *Rag-Time Parade* [1950], and *Septet* [1953]) are both solos. The first, called *Solo Suite in Space and Time* (1956), with music by John Cage, is a long dance in five parts. Spots or slight imperfections in the texture of an ordinary sheet of white paper (seen by holding the paper in front of a bright light) were numbered, and from these "found" arrangements came the space and lengths of time of each dance. The spots on another piece of paper, similarly numbered, gave the sequence of the movement. In this dance, the lengths of time of the individual movements and phrases were literally made in inches.

The choreographic idea special to the composition of the chance dance, *Solo* (1953), to music by Christian Wolff, was the possibility of a movement superimposed over another movement. A by-chance-found leg or torso movement could be added to a by-chance-found arm or head movement. This added to the richness and complexity of the resultant rhythmic and movement structures.

Experiments with chance have been made by musicians, poets, painters, and sculptors, surrealists and dadaists, well-known among whom are Marcel Duchamp, Jean Arp, Max Ernst, and Kurt Schwitters. Now in the field of higher mathematics and physics, the "laws" of probability and chance are also being seriously investigated and are influential in nuclear-fission research. In psychoanalysis, the term "synchronicity," the subject of recent lectures by Jung in Switzerland, denotes a similar concern. For the dancer of today these stimuli freshly felt and used in accord with contemporary necessity open up a wide and fertile field of action. Not only do they free the choreographer from habitual ideas and the compulsions of personal likes and dislikes, but they present endless possibilities of movement in space-time that introduce one, whether on the stage or in the audience, to a world beyond the imagination.

Calvin Tomkins

ON COLLABORATION (1974)

You have to love dancing to stick to it. It gives nothing back, no manuscripts to store away, no paintings to show on the walls and maybe hang in museums, no poems to be printed and sold, nothing but that single fleeting moment when you feel alive.

Merce Cunningham

Twenty years ago, when Merce Cunningham's first company was still evolving from an occasional association into a seasoned performing unit, Cunningham asked Robert Rauschenberg to design a set for a new dance called *Minutiae* (1954). It was not the first time Cunningham had collaborated with a visual artist—Isamu Noguchi had done the set for *The Seasons*, a Cunningham ballet commissioned in 1947 by Lincoln Kirstein's newly-formed Ballet Society; David Hare had designed a costume for a Cunningham solo dance in 1945 (it proved too heavy to wear); and Remy Charlip had done the costumes for a number of Cunningham's early dances. But in commissioning Rauschenberg, Cunningham had in mind a different sort of working arrangement.

"The dance was not finished," Cunningham recalls. "I said to Bob, 'I don't want you to decorate a dance, but to make something that we could use *in* a dance.' He made an object, and beautiful as it was it wouldn't work, because it needed a pipe to hang on. So he made a second one through which we walked, huddled, and climbed. It was very fragile, with lots of lace, and comic strips, and a little hanging mirror. It was like an object in nature which hadn't been named." This was the beginning of an association that lasted for eleven years, during which Rauschenberg made the sets or costumes (or both)

44

for twenty-four Cunningham dances, and also toured with the company as its lighting designer. It now appears inevitable that Cunningham, who over the years has commissioned scores for his dances by most of the leading avant-garde composers, should also have wanted to work with artists such as Rauschenberg, Jasper Johns, Frank Stella, Andy Warhol, Robert Morris, and Bruce Nauman. Far more than any other choreographer in our time, Cunningham has pursued the difficult goal of a true synthesis of the arts, and the manner of his doing so, I believe, has a bearing not only on his own remarkable career but on the development of twentieth-century art.

It is necessary to remember that for Cunningham, collaboration never implies the subordination of one art to another. It was Cunningham and John Cage, since 1953 the musical director of the Cunningham company, who first broke with the tradition that the music in a dance performance had to support the dance (or, conversely, that the dance should "interpret" the music). Cunningham and Cage have always proceeded on the basis that music and dance are two separate activities taking place within the same time sequence, and, in a Cunningham dance, neither depends upon the other. The same process applies to the artists who design sets for Cunningham. Consultations between artist and choreographer determine a few general guidelines, such as the dimensions of the stage, and sometimes the kinds of movement to be expected, but after that the artist goes off to his studio and makes the set while Cunningham makes the dance, and usually the two come together only during the final rehearsals.

Curiously enough, this seemingly "blind" form of collaboration does not engender catastrophes. The Cunningham dancers move with their customary precision through the brilliant maze of Stella's stretched canvas strips (in *Scramble* [1967]), or among Warhol's floating silver pillows (in *RainForest* [1968]); they are no more put off by Morris's moving column of light (*Canfield* [1969]) or by Nauman's phalanx of electric fans (*Tread* [1970]) than they are by the electronic and "found" sounds of Cage, Morton Feldman, Christian Wolff, Toshi Ichiyanagi, or La Monte Young. Movement, music, and decor coexist in the same stage space and the same performance time, and the result—what is the result? Not a melding of these elements into a unified spectacle, not that at all. It is closer in feeling to collage, in which disparate elements are brought together without becoming fused. We, the spectators, are invited to pay attention on three levels simultaneously, to hold in mind three separate forms and all the subtle reverberations among them. The result is as complex, as demanding, and as full of surprises as anything in our experience. If we are sufficiently alert, it can also be indistinguishable from "that single fleeting moment when you feel alive."

In its early years, the Cunningham company's New York performances attracted more painters and sculptors than musicians or dancers. A benefit sale of paintings by New York artists helped to make possible the company's first world tour in 1964; two years later, when the company was invited to take part in the Paris International Dance Festival and the State Department refused to pay a nickel toward its travel expenses (Cunningham was still too "controversial"), the trip was financed through the sale of a painting donated for that purpose by Joan Miró. The fact that so many contemporary artists have admired Cunningham's work to the point of supporting it financially may suggest that they also sensed in it a certain affinity to their own. Certainly Cunningham's feeling that dance movement could be presented for its own sake—not to express ideas or emotions or to tell stories—has its clear parallel in Rauschenberg's wish to work as a sort of "collaborator" with his materials, as well as with the efforts of Morris Louis, Ellsworth Kelly, and others to liberate color from any nonchromatic reference. The "all-over" paintings of Jackson Pollock and others of his generation had helped Cunningham to arrive at his own method of making dances in which there is no single center of interest ("Any part of the stage is interesting, can be used," as Cunningham says). And in their use of chance methods to go beyond self-expression, Cunningham and Cage went much further along the road travelled earlier by the surrealists and to a certain extent by the abstract expressionists. The surrealists saw chance as a means of allowing the subconscious mind to assert itself directly in art. For Cage and Cunningham, on the other hand, chance offered a possible means to outdistance the self entirely—subconscious and all—and to get into a new field of human awareness in which every part of the terrain was unfamiliar.

The new set of demands that work of this kind made and makes upon the spectator was prefigured, of course, in the life and work of Marcel Duchamp, who still enrages traditionalist critics by emerging, ever more clearly since his death, as the most influential artist of the century. It was Duchamp, speaking as a "mere artist" in 1957, who proposed that the artist should be seen as a "mediumistic being" who performed only one part of the creative process, and that it was up to the spectator to decipher and interpret the work's inner qualifications, relate them to his own experience, and thus complete the creative cycle. Every dance by Cunningham invites this sort of participation, and in recent years his audiences have proved more and more willing to accept the compliment thus paid them. Each person is free to interpret each dance as he sees fit, or not to interpret it at all. A work such as *Winterbranch* (1964), for example, with its random patterns of light and darkness on stage and its falling movements, has impressed various people as being "about" nuclear war, concentration camps, or Vietnam—it once struck the wife of a sea captain as being about shipwreck. *Walkaround Time* (1968), the hour-long piece that Cunningham made in homage to Duchamp, and for which Jasper Johns designed a set derived from Duchamp's *Large Glass* in Philadelphia, has seemed to this observer a strikingly different dance each time he has seen it. Cunningham himself does not think that his dances are "about" anything, but he is willing to accept the fact that others may find specific ways to interpret them. As he wrote some years ago, "If the dancer dances—which is not the same as having theories about dancing or wishing to dance or trying to dance or remembering in his body someone else's dance—but if the dancer *dances*, everything is there. The meaning is there if that's what you want."

Cage once expressed the idea that at certain periods, one of the arts does the talking while the others listen. During the fifties and the early sixties in New York, he said, painting clearly was doing the talking. Is it possible now that dance has become the main speaker? The proliferation of modern dance and ballet companies not only in New York but throughout the country, the rapid growth in the audience—according to a recent Ford Foundation report, dance now outdraws rock music on college campuses—and the overflowing classes at schools such as Cunningham's all point to some such conclusion. One might also note the number of contemporary artists and composers who seem drawn today in the direction of "performance" or "process" pieces that depend to a large extent on movement and gesture of one kind or another, and the recent developments in theater—Peter Brook's international experiments, for example, or Robert Wilson's spectacles in extended time—whose real roots are in the dance and the body's natural expressiveness. How much these developments owe to Cunningham is anyone's guess (Brook and Wilson have both acknowledged their enthusiasm for his work). What is certain in any case is that for more than twenty years, the immense creative energy generated first by Cunningham, Cage, and Rauschenberg working together, and after 1966 by Cunningham, Cage, and Jasper Johns (who became the company's artistic advisor in that year) has been among the strongest forces at work in the arts, here and abroad, and that it shows no sign of losing momentum.

Cunningham's influence is all indirect, like that of Zen master who goes on doing what he does. "I don't think I've ever demanded particular things," he said the other day, referring to his work with visual artists. "My ideas about dancing are all so flexible, and working with artists has made them more so. I could just as well tell people to go and dance in a field, with or without a tree—it would be nice if there were a tree, but not essential. So many people think that decor should emphasize something, or define it, or frame it somehow, but life doesn't work that way, and I don't either. I grew up with this business of dance movements meaning something specific, but it always seemed to me that a movement could mean a lot of different things, and that it didn't make much sense to act like a dictator."

Not one center but a multiplicity of centers, connected and equal in value. Cunningham and Cage are there in that expanding field of awareness (with or without a tree) and we are there with them, if we are lucky. This is the new situation. And as Cage would say, it is simply delightful.

A Symposium with Earle Brown, Remy Charlip,
Marianne Preger Simon, David Vaughan

THE FORMING
OF AN ESTHETIC:
MERCE CUNNINGHAM
AND JOHN CAGE (1985)

DAVID VAUGHAN: The first music that John Cage wrote according to chance operations was *Music of Changes* in 1951. Christian Wolff had given him a copy of the *I Ching,* and John became interested in the possibility of using chance operations in composing. And Merce decided to extend them into his choreographic processes. The first piece in which he used chance operations was a long work called *Sixteen Dances for Soloist and Company of Three* in the same year, 1951. The chance element was chiefly in the arrangement of the order of the dances, though there was a quartet, the last dance but one in the piece, of which the whole choreography was done by chance.

Two influential events occurred during the summer of 1952. Firstly, Merce was invited to make two pieces for a Festival of the Creative Arts at Brandeis University. One was *Les Noces,* to the Stravinsky score, which he choreographed more or less in the conventional way. Merce was also asked to make choreography for *Symphonie pour un homme seul,* to the musique concrète tape

---

The text is an edited transcript of a panel discussion heard 16 June 1984 at a Dance Critics Association Conference at The Kitchen in New York. The transcript was prepared under the auspices of Dance Research Foundation, Inc.

score by Pierre Schaeffer and Pierre Henry. This was the first time such tape music would be heard in the United States. For dancers, Merce had those who were working with him in New York and were, therefore, accustomed to his way of choreographing, but he would also be using students who didn't have a lot of technique or experience. Merce decided that he would make a piece in which he would use gestures from daily life and just ordinary movement— walking, ambient movement—but also popular dance movements, in addition to movements he devised.

All this was put together by chance methods. His first reason for choosing to use this kind of movement was that it was movement that untrained dancers could do. Also there was the question of how to set the piece to the music. John Cage and Merce Cunningham had been making pieces for quite a few years in which they worked with a common rhythmic structure: dance and music came together at certain points but otherwise pursued an independent course. But the *Symphonie* was the first piece, I think I am right in saying, in which Merce decided simply to make a dance of the same length of time as the music and just put the two things together.

The second event happened later that summer, when he was teaching at Black Mountain College in North Carolina. John Cage put on the famous theater piece, the prototype of the Happenings and other kinds of performance art that came later, in which Merce Cunningham danced, slides of paintings by Robert Rauschenberg were projected onto the walls. John Cage read a lecture, Charles Olson and M. C. Richards read their poetry, David Tudor played the piano, and Nicholas Cernovich showed films. All of this evolved from John's reading of Antonin Artaud and also from his study of Buddhism with Suzuki.

Earle Brown, the composer, remembers that period well.

EARLE BROWN: My then wife, Carolyn Brown, and I first met Merce and John in Denver in the spring of 1951. I was teaching arranging and composition there; Carolyn was dancing with Jane McLean, who was an ex-Graham dancer, I believe. Jane McLean was choreographing for her own company in Denver, and Carolyn was working with it.

John and Merce came through on a countrywide tour, Merce giving master classes and John playing his *Sonatas* and *Interludes for Prepared Piano*. From a pianist who worked with Jane McLean, I'd heard stories about how strange John Cage was: weird and off the wall and all that. But I didn't know very much about Cage's music. I went to the concert of the *Sonatas and Interludes*, and, although they weren't like any music I wrote or would want to write, I thought they were extraordinary.

At a party later, John and Carolyn and I—Carolyn had majored in philosophy at Wheaton College, graduating with honors, and John was high on Zen Buddhism and other Oriental philosophies (she was high just on philosophy, nothing else)—had a long conversation. In fact, Carolyn, John, and I had such a vibrant meeting and conversation that we sort of dominated the evening, which made everybody else at the party rather angry.

Then there was a master class at Jane McLean's, and I remember seeing Merce's eyes watching Carolyn do diagonals from one corner of the studio to another. I don't think he expected to meet a dancer like Carolyn in Denver, but to this day I can see Merce looking up as if he were saying, "Where did *that* come from?"

So it was a good meeting, for Merce and Carolyn as dancers and for John and me as composers. And we had marvelous conversations at two or three parties on different nights.

Then John saw my music. I sent some early work, *Three Pieces for Piano,* which I wrote in 1951, to John in New York, and he gave them to David Tudor, and that led to the first performance of any music of mine in New York. That was at the Cherry Lane Theater, under the auspices of the Living Theater, later in 1951.

After the Brandeis festival and the Black Mountain summer of '52, Carolyn and I moved to New York. John had invited me to work with him and David Tudor on what John called *Project for Music for Magnetic Tape.* I believe he was inspired to start that kind of project after hearing the Schaeffer-Henry *Symphonie* at Brandeis. Anyway, John invited me, and Merce was quite obviously pleased to have Carolyn arrive too. This must have been about September 1952. And there began an extraordinary kind of friendship and collaboration: learning, arguing—John and myself especially arguing. Carolyn began taking classes with Merce, and also at Juilliard, and soon after joined the Cunningham company.

MARIANNE SIMON: The company coalesced at Black Mountain the following summer.

BROWN: The first piece of mine that Merce used, I wrote for him. He used two other of my pieces, but the work I wrote for him was *Indices* for chamber orchestra, seventeen or eighteen instruments, and *Springweather and People* (1955) was danced to it. Didn't it have costumes and scenery by Remy?

REMY CHARLIP: No scenery, just costumes. I conceived it, and it was a collaboration of several people.

BROWN: I remember there were big parachutes. Looped.

CHARLIP: It was fan-pleated silk.

BROWN: The music and the dance were twenty-nine minutes long. That's a lot of music. *Why* I did it is important. I was writing a piece for Merce in order to pay for Carolyn's dance classes, because we had no money. John and David and I were getting forty dollars a week each, working on the tape music project, so we didn't have much extra money. I knew way in front that I would have only one hour of rehearsal for a piece twenty-nine minutes long. That means twice through, if you're lucky.

The other two works of mine that Merce used, but which I didn't write for him, were from a collection called *Folio*, composed between 1952 and 1954. He set *Galaxy* (1956) on *Four Systems*. I believe that was the first time Merce had done an open-form dance, in the sense of spontaneous performance.

I was not at all interested in composing by chance. I was far more interested in spontaneity and immediacy and directness. I usually wrote all of my material subjectively (and that's a long story), making what I called mobile scores, mobile musical pieces, which Europeans later called "open-form." That means the music can begin anywhere and go from that point to any other point within my composed materials. *Four Systems* was a graphic piece which, as a matter of fact, I wrote backstage at the Brooklyn Academy of Music, where Merce's company was performing. Merce, I guess, said, "We're having a party for David Tudor's birthday tonight at the studio," which was then on Sheridan Square in the Village. John and I glanced at each other. Neither of us had remembered that it was David's birthday; we didn't have any presents for him. So John and I looked around backstage. I found a scrap of cardboard big enough to sketch a little music on. John found some cardboard, too, or some kind of paper, and he punched holes in it, by chance, I suppose. Under any conditions he always had three pennies to flip, except in Chinese restaurants, when he usually *chose* his menu.

Anyway, John punched out a piece which was his first music for carillon, I believe. I called my piece *Four Systems*. And those were the birthday presents we gave David Tudor at the studio party that night. David performed my piece long before Merce choreographed to it.

That is how the music for *Galaxy* came to be. I'd like to know if it was the first—and only—time Merce choreographed an open-form work. Four people were in it: Carolyn, Viola Farber, Marianne, and Remy. Their material was choreographed but, as in my music, they could enter at any time they wanted. I believe it was the first spontaneous—

CHARLIP: I don't remember doing anything spontaneous in Merce's dances. Maybe the entrances were. The piece itself was set.

BROWN: In form?

CHARLIP: Yes. I mean, there was always that big argument about spontaneity.

BROWN: But if the entrances are not fixed, how can the form be fixed?

CHARLIP: Well, I remember going through my whole solo, the length of time that it was. I don't remember changing the order of what I did.

BROWN: But they could overlap in different ways?

CHARLIP: I guess so.

VAUGHAN: Each person had a solo. Didn't Merce, essentially, make four solos that were performed at the same time?

CHARLIP: We were the four elements. I was Fire. Marianne was Earth. Carolyn was Air. I made the costumes for it, and Carolyn had mesh hose on

her arms and over her back, and I put feathers in the mesh at each performance. They flew off in the course of the dancing. Viola was Water. She had
a costume with a lot of belly buttons on it.

BROWN: As I remember, Merce said something to me about whether it was
open-form or whatever. I asked why he had not worked that way before or
later, and he said, "In music you can have instruments come in at different
times, highly spontaneously. You can cue in a brass section on top of strings,
or not, or winds and brass and strings. But with dancers you can get killed
cueing like that. They run into each other unless everybody knows where the
other person is going to be at what time; you know, they can really break
bones." Merce was concerned about this, and I think it scared him in relation
to that piece.

The other work of mine he used—it's a graphic score, really—was a solo
for Carolyn, which he choreographed for her to do in Venice at the *Teatre La
Fenice* in 1960, with a costume by Bob Rauschenberg. It was called *Hands Birds*,
which is the poem in its entirety by Mary Caroline Richards. Merce used my
December 1952, a version for two pianos. I'm sure it was David and John
playing two pianos. Or one piano, four hands. But it's a graphic score, so they
had to improvise, which they were not wont to do very often. John didn't
agree with improvisation, which interested me a lot; and I didn't really agree
with him very much on composing by chance. Although I didn't disagree with
him, it just didn't interest me to do it.

VAUGHAN: Remy Charlip both danced with the group and designed a lot
of its costumes in those days. Can you tell us more about the early dances?

CHARLIP: First, I'll quote from Judith Malina's published diary. "2 March
1955: To Merce's advanced class with Remy. Merce teaches coordination rather
than precision. John Cage is a sight at an old player piano, chopping out bits
of Chopin and simple one-two-three-four rhythms for two solid hours! He did
it with great humor and suggested I come again because 'sometimes the music
is even worse!' "

Actually, John and Merce used to have a lot of trouble together because
John couldn't keep a beat and couldn't follow the phrasing of the dancing.
I believe that, in a way, was how indeterminacy was born. His music was
always delightful and charming but often had nothing to do with what we
were doing.

I'll tell you how I got to know Merce and work with him. I was an art
student in 1946 at Cooper Union and was lying on the floor with a fellow
student. She was a dancer. When my knees were up, my back touched the
floor, but when I let them slide down and straighten out, my lower back did
not touch the floor; and, therefore, she said that I could never be a dancer.
Probably, that was the reason I started to want to be a dancer.

She gave me a book by Carlo Blasis, and one of the things it said was
"Study with a master." And she decided for me that Merce was the master. In

March 1948 she took me to the City Center to see his *The Seasons* that the now New York City Ballet did, with music by John Cage and sets by Isamu Noguchi. Then later, in December 1949, she took me to see Merce dance *Two Step*, again at the City Center. And it was the first time I was ever aware that Merce was doing something different, besides being just such an extraordinary dancer. That awareness happened when I saw him leaping across the stage on a diagonal entrance in *Two Step*. He covered half the stage in that one leap. And the audience gasped in a collective intake of breath; everybody went "Aaaaah!" upon Merce's entrance.

Merce and John were very friendly with Lou Harrison, whom I was living with, and we used to go to dinner together; that is how I actually met Merce. At that time John was eating with his right hand only. He was influenced by some Indian beliefs which say that you're supposed to use the left hand for other activities and the right hand for eating. But nobody, I realized, paid any attention to him in the restaurant. And from that I realized that it was possible to do almost anything, and nobody really notices what you do, or cares, particularly in New York.

In May 1950, I went with Lou to the 92nd Street "Y" to see a program for which he had written some music, Merce's *The Open Road* (1947). And Merce did a piece called *Root of an Unfocus* (1944). In the first half of the dance, the music was just banging away. It was John's piece. Merce was crawling all over the floor and carrying on, totally disassociated. But about three-quarters of the way through, suddenly they came together. That is, the music and the dance came together. Suddenly a joining happened. It was absolutely riveting. At the time I didn't know what had happened, why it was so strange. But when I saw the dance again, that's what I realized it was. So already there was for me a beginning, an understanding of what structure could be in relation to music and dance.

I think one of the reasons that both John and Merce didn't like improvisation—at least, this is what they said—is that they felt that in improvisation you always head toward what you know, but with chance you have the possibility of doing something you never could have thought of, such as your head going in one direction while your body must move in another.

In *Symphonie pour un homme seul*, there were gestures like we were washing our hands and then wiping them off or drying them. Lots of different ordinary moves—as if we were showering or eating or combing our hair—were put with movements that were not literally recognizable: someone would sort of shoot an arm out or just put it forward or turn and twist, and it didn't have anything to do with real-life activity. There were several kinds of dance movements, actual gestures, and activities.

SIMON: And when we washed our hands we stood on one foot.

CHARLIP: We danced to unusual sounds. Lou Harrison did a piece where he used unusual instruments. I went up to a Bronx automobile graveyard with him to get brake drums. It was a sight, Lou going around this junkyard and hitting brake drums to try to find the right note for his piece.

John invented the "prepared piano" by putting things into an ordinary piano to make the sounds come from other than what we think of as musical sources. Or using the sources differently, as Henry Cowell did, by strumming the wires inside of the piano or banging one's whole arm down on the keys. Later, John would slam down the lid to gain that sound.

Bonnie Bird once asked John, "What can I do to make music for children?" John said, "Why don't you have them play the room?"

SIMON: I met Merce in Paris when I was nineteen, in the early summer of 1949. I saw him perform a piece in a studio so small that it only had about four feet of space, and there were maybe thirty people sitting around the four feet. He was dancing with Tanaquil LeClercq and Betty Nichols. I was very excited, especially when I heard that Merce was staying in the same hotel as a friend of mine and was looking for a studio (the studio where he performed was not one he taught in). So I sat outside the hotel about four hours waiting for Merce to appear, and when he did I said breathlessly, "I hear you need a studio." That was the extent of my eloquence, unlike Earle's and Carolyn's when they met John. But Merce took the studio I told him about, and that's how I got to know him.

He returned to the States about the same time I did, and he started a class because he wanted to train people to dance the way he danced. I was the first student—in fact, the *only* student in the class for a couple of weeks, until Remy joined. After the first class Merce said, "OK, get into position." I did. And he said, "Now jump." I couldn't get off the floor. That was my beginning, quite different from Carolyn's.

In this first group that he was training himself, to Merce it was of the utmost importance that he use dancers who didn't have preconceived ideas about how movement was supposed to look. Why that was important became evident as we went on. Merce was developing movement that other choreographers were not, and he found it confining to use dancers who'd been trained by others and who had mannerisms and certain ways of going about dance.

About four months after the class began we gave a program at Cooper Union. Six of us did *Rag-Time Parade* (1950), which he'd originally made for untrained dancers. He called us his junior company, and we were not at all skillful. *Rag-Time* was outfitted from Second Avenue thrift shops, and it was quite wild and wonderful and funny. The other dancers in the class, whom we called the senior company, did *A Diversion* (1948). We got an encore and they didn't. So that was a wonderful introduction.

After the Brandeis festival, he stopped using dancers whom other people had trained, but by then we were good enough to become the senior company. He was beginning to make unique dances, although *Rag-Time* was quite unusual.

We underwent many shocks in the process of learning his choreography. *Springweather* was the most unusual score we had yet danced to. Merce was convinced that there was no way we could ever figure out from the score where we were to be or how to get together at different moments. After a while he asked, "How is it that you keep being together at these different times?" We said, "Well, we have musical cues." Except that we didn't, in the accepted sense. In our naîveté, we listened to whatever sound was presented and heard it as music and used it the way we would have traditionally. Hearing a squeak or a beep, we'd know that we were supposed to be in a certain part of the stage. Merce was quite surprised at our ingenuity.

Even then his way of dancing was very different from traditional modern dance, which was mostly Limón and Graham. Whether he was influenced by Zen then, I don't know. But what we learned was that we were doing just what we were doing and never anything else. It had nothing to do with drama or mental images or emotional responses. It had to do with our learning to be exactly where we were when we were there, doing what we were supposed to be doing. Merce insisted that we be very precise, that our movement be exactly the way it was supposed to look, that we fit into the frame of time the way we were supposed to; and to ensure that we always danced up to tempo, he made us move quickly and very lightly.

In secret, of course, we'd make up elaborate stories about what was actually going on. He'd laugh when we told him these scenarios, but they didn't bother him so long as they didn't intrude on his dynamics and timing.

CHARLIP: Once Merce was rehearsing a solo which absolutely freaked me out. I thought he was having a fit and said to John, "He's not going to do that in public, is he?" It was so amazing that it made possible my realization that I could do something as personal and intense, too. Particularly in his solos, what he danced was directly in touch with his feelings and had immediate emotional content. The group dances were quite different. He wouldn't tell us what they were about.

SIMON: He would deny that they were about anything, but we knew better.

A difference I've noticed between the early dances, particularly *Springweather and People,* and the dances now, is that when he was beginning to make chance dances there was an enormous amount of stillness. In *Springweather* we must have stood for fifteen minutes in one corner of the stage, four of us, doing nothing—actually, we were doing something: we were being still. But that seems to have vanished from Merce's dances today.

VAUGHAN: A little of the stillness is coming back, actually. It's one of those ingredients that goes away but returns.

The period when you were rehearsing both *Les Noces* and the *Symphonie pour un homme seul* (both 1952), utterly different pieces—was there a clear difference in the way Merce was making them?

CHARLIP: *Les Noces* we rehearsed to a recording. At the Brandeis performance, Leonard Bernstein conducted the orchestra. He got lost in the score and stopped but we kept dancing. The piece is most difficult to count. It goes: one-two-three-four-five-six-seven-eight, one-two-three-four, one-two-three-four-five, one-two, one-two, one-two-three-four-five.

SIMON: That's right.

CHARLIP: We'd memorized the whole thing, so we kept on dancing and shouted out cues to Leonard Bernstein when he got lost and stopped. He was aghast. But that was when Merce was choreographing to music.

We performed *Symphonie* to its tape, of course, but what was so completely different about that piece is that it was done with a stopwatch. Merce started the stopwatch at the beginning and stopped it at the end. We wouldn't rehearse with the music—or we would, it really didn't matter—but we'd always end the piece at exactly the same time, twenty-seven minutes and thirty-six seconds. It got to be astonishing.

BROWN: When I spoke of my *Indices* which he used for *Springweather and People*, I should've discussed the relationship of the choreography to the music. Before I wrote anything for him, Merce gave me his time structure, which I meditated upon and then ignored. I composed the piece in my own way, just making a relationship to his time, the time of his dancing. I remember the worry that the dancers, or Merce, or all of you had about using the music, getting to know the music too well, and keying off it too often. The score of *Springweather* if full of tremendously dense, chaotic things and also places where there's a long, long held note or two. The density of the music fluctuates widely. Merce did not know my music for the work when he choreographed the piece; and when I first experienced the music and dance together, I was astonished at how effective the lack of synchronization was, dramatically—if you let yourself be taken by the drama that wasn't put into it but was there anyway, intrinsically.

An extraordinary moment in it was Merce coming out of the wings in a leap at a point in the music when there was only one note being played on a violin. Merce flew on the one held note. A dancer other than Merce—a composer other than myself—would have supported that leap with a dramatic musical flourish. But I've always disliked what's termed Mickey Mousing the music, as in animated cartoons, where Mickey imitates the music, has a jiggly relationship with it. Merce's leap was stunning dramatically the way it joined that one violin note, much more astonishing than it would have been to anything else I could have written in order to support it.

Merce's use of the stopwatch as he choreographed influenced me a great deal. I had already done some work in what I called "time notation," which is nonmetric, nonfixed notation. Though it's highly specific, the musical performance can fluctuate somewhat. I wasn't sure whether this kind of notation would work for a small orchestra or a large orchestra.

Merce and his dancers were rehearsing a piece (not mine) one day in the Sheridan Square studio. He handed me a stopwatch and said, "Would you mind timing this? It's supposed to be fifteen minutes long." And with no music and no talking among themselves, the group and he danced the entire piece from the top. When they finished I stopped the watch—at fourteen minutes and fifty-five seconds, or thereabouts. Over a period of dancing for a quarter of an hour, without any musical cues or verbal support, they'd completed the work only about five seconds off. I realized they had used each other's moves throughout as cueing, and that supported my feeling about the possibilities of "time notation," now called proportional notation.

I want instrumentalists to listen to each other and know where they are through listening, rather than counting out the bars: one-two-three-four, two-two-three-four, three-two-three-four—bang! It's a kind of flexing, fluctuating situation, which is the nature of Merce's work. That amazing stopwatch experience confirmed to me that a group can stay together in a highly rational way without the ongoing support of metric music.

CHARLIP: The drama of that leap on one note reminds me of a solo Merce did in *Sixteen Dances*. He's wearing a big coat and he's a hunter and he shoots himself at the end of the piece. That's the plot. In the solo, every time Merce jumped into the air he grunted, and every time he crouched he made a high-pitched sound. Afterward, I tried to do that and it's nearly impossible. Because every time I jumped up I wanted to go up in my voice, and every time I crouched down I wanted to go down in my voice. The music phrase skipped along, and Merce would end it with "oomph!" He would be running around, the jump high into the air and grunt a low "oomph!" Then he'd sink to the floor and grunt a high "oomph!" It was very funny, but what made it even funnier was that it was all totally unexpected. You didn't quite believe what you were hearing or seeing.

VAUGHAN: Nowadays the company is used to the idea that not only do they not hear the music of the dance until the first performance, but that at other times they'll do the dance to completely different music. If they do a piece not in repertory but as part of an Event, it'll be to music it's never been danced to before and by a different composer, and the dancers won't hear it, either, until they're performing to it.

But when did the group first start actually rehearsing in silence? Was that with *Symphonie* or was it already Merce's practice, even with, say, *Banjo* (1953)?

SIMON: Many times we would learn parts of dances as part of our classes, because the middle part of Merce's class was always a dance sequence, and he'd try out portions of dances he was working on.

CHARLIP: Extra rehearsal time.

SIMON: That's right. So we rehearsed portions of dances that way, without music. And when we did the dances as such, the music didn't seem to matter.

Sometimes David Tudor would be there to play, and sometimes not. But we didn't really learn a piece to the music at all.

VAUGHAN: Of course you know the wonderful story about *Banjo,* that you rehearsed it sometimes with a pianist at Black Mountain who wasn't David Tudor. And everybody was wondering why they were dancing to this rather ordinary piece of jangly Gottschalk music, until Merce asked David Tudor if he would mind playing it once for the dancers, since he was going to play for the performance. David, in an extraordinary exhibition of virtuosity, really made the music sound like a dozen banjos, and the dancers understood why Merce wanted to use that music.

CHARLIP: What we were doing began to influence others. Up at Columbia, John did a piece of music for twelve radios, and I was one of the dial twisters. Then Jimmy Waring did *Dances Before the Wall* (1957). The wall was a gorgeous set by Julian Beck. Jimmy took his favorite pieces of music, cut them up to different lengths, and matched them with the different lengths of his dances. A dance got going, and right in the middle of it a new piece of music might start and go through to the middle of the next dance, when the music would switch to another piece, which could be everything from classical to popular music to sounds of dishes breaking. The dance, one of Jimmy's most beautiful, was the first by anyone but Merce to use the concept that you have the dancers follow your choreography but continually and arbitrarily change their music in the middle of the dancing. Of course Paul Taylor and others have choreographed a dance to one piece of music but performed it to another. Toby Armour made a dance she showed twice, once in silence and once with music. Some choreographers make different dances to the same music. So the concept of music and dance becomes wide open.

SIMON: From the dancer's point of view, the work we did on being extremely precise, doing the movements exactly the way we were taught, within the time frame imposed, at the speed that Merce insisted upon—perfecting all of this made it immaterial whether music or sound accompanied us. If we continually did Cunningham movement exactly the way we were supposed to, our bodies learned how much time a movement needed and automatically took up the right amount of time.

BROWN: That's why I called my notation "time notation." I believed a musician could have a kinesthetic memory as keen as a dancer's, which I'd seen confirmed by Cunningham's people working in that way.

VAUGHAN: The surrealists, whose work Merce would have seen in Paris and even earlier in New York, used chance. Did this influence him at all?

BROWN: One of the definitions of surrealism is that it's the simultaneous occurrence of mutually disparate objects, which is to say that anything can follow anything. That aspect of the surrealists' revolution influenced me—not to the extent of using chance, as Merce did, but the way it opened my whole world to events relating to each other just by being there.

CHARLIP: Surrealism to me is simply landscapes as portraiture, portraiture as still life, still life as landscape. It frees your seeing. The dadaists widened that freedom. Jean Arp dropped pieces of paper from above and glued them where they landed. Artists later covered the body with paint and pressed against canvas. In Japan, the Gutai Group, who predated the Black Mountain Happening, combined simultaneous events and juxtaposed space and activities. I was fascinated by a mud dance they did. We were aware of and influenced by all of these things.

BROWN: The Gutai were highly spontaneous; it was like action painting. People tearing through a series of brown paper frames. And that was a work of art. It was performed in front of you, and then it stood as a result.

VAUGHAN: Merce and John were also aware of what was occurring in American painting at this period; for instance, the way Jackson Pollock used space.

CHARLIP: Yes, just dripping something on the floor and that's what it is. Not conceiving anything beforehand. In one of my first conversations with John—I had just come out of Cooper Union—we talked about a concept new to me that I had learned: of how thrilling the surface of canvas and the matter of paint is, that it is the material one is working with that's of the utmost interest rather than what you're trying to say with it. For the first time I had realized that a canvas might be interesting whether it was covered with white paint or was left free, raw. And what is the surface? What does the surface mean in relation to when you put paint on it? These concepts were reflected in John's punching holes in a piece of paper to indicate notes for his music, or drawing a graph on ordinary blank paper and holding it up to the light, which would reveal imperfections in the paper. And those places were where John put his notes on the graph.

VAUGHAN: *Suite for Five in Space and Time* (1956) was done to music written that way; and Merce used the same process in making the choreography, to determine where in the stage space the dancers would be positioned. I believe there was a page for each of the dances.

CHARLIP: Yes. Take a page keyed to areas of the stage, hold it up to the light, and the imperfection you see within the sheet of paper places the dancers on the stage.

I was so excited by these concepts when I first heard about them. It was from John I first heard of the microcosm and the macrocosm, and what form is, and how you can "Play the room." Later, I would have students "Dance the room"—look at a window, for instance; consider a window as if it were a music score. "If that window was a dance," I'd have them say, "how many dancers would be in it, how long would it last, how many sections would it have, how would the costumes look, what would the space be like?"—and so on and on, deciding. You can dance anything: a chair, a table. At a design conference in Aspen, I had people dance their wallets. It was fun.

Those are the concepts that came out of that period, where the score itself is—

BROWN: A found object. To *find* the music rather than to *make* the music.

SIMON: Merce was most attentive to the way he used the material he had, which was the dancers. It was my impression during that early period in the fifties, that he gave us things to do that were based on who we were and how we moved individually. Furthermore, he made movements for us that were a bit beyond what we could do, so that we had to grow around them. Yet his dances were criticized as being abstract and dehumanized. I thought they were extraordinarily personal, because they had to do with who we dancers in the company were, how we moved, what our quality of movement was.

CHARLIP: *Galaxy* was a perfect example: Why he chose Viola for Water and Carolyn for Air.

VAUGHAN: This is still true of the company. The way Merce choreographs today has much to do with the dancers he has now, but some people still say his dances are dehumanized. Back in the *Dance Observer* days, Louis Horst reviewed the early concerts with more regularity and perception than most critics, and he had great respect for John as a musician; but didn't Louis and Merce part company at around the period we're discussing?

CHARLIP: Horst was still supportive, I thought. What he said privately I don't know, but he seemed to enjoy what he was seeing of Merce's.

VAUGHAN: But Louis himself didn't review many of the later concerts; others on the staff did. You remember the famous Louis Horst review of the avant-garde recital that Paul Taylor gave in 1957, when the *Observer*'s notice was merely a block of white space signed "L. H."

CHARLIP: That was for a dance where the women stood still forever; the billowing of their dresses in stage breezes was the only movement. So Horst drew a blank.*

VAUGHAN: But of course the Taylor piece was an extension of what Marianne was curious about, the stillness in Merce's dances.

CHARLIP: Merce said the two most difficult things to do onstage were to stand still and to walk.

SIMON: And we walked a lot. Merce developed this extraordinary technique, not for himself but for *us*, his dancers. He demonstrated and we learned the technique and did the choreography he gave us to do. The technique was

---

*Seven pieces were presented that evening. Generally, it is the work *Epic*, featuring Taylor standing still while a tape of the correct time was read, which is said to have inspired Horst's blank review.

derived from the way he danced, the way he wanted to create dances, but he never used it in his work for himself. He never moved like anybody else in the company when he danced with us, and you can see the difference in the early films. He looks like a gazelle or a lily blooming in the field or whatever, not like the man who had developed a great technique and was using it.

CHARLIP: Merce had an astonishing animal quality. You could never guess what he was going to do next. He could be on the floor one moment, up against the wall the next, but you didn't quite know how he got there or where he'd be next. There was a special kind of integrity in his movement. He was so possessed by dancing, and moved with such concentration, that you couldn't take your eyes off him. You might not have known what he was doing, but it was fascinating always.

SIMON: His own solos have been one continuous work from as far back as I can remember. The new one in *Quartet* is a continuation of every solo that he's ever done. That's amazing, isn't it?

BROWN: The solos that he did to Christian Wolff's music were always bizarre and wild. Actually, I used to feel that Merce had three choreographic styles. One was classic—not ballet, but classic and elegant in feeling. *Springweather* was one of those, it seemed to me. Then came the Wolff works. And then the Satie gamelike pieces.

VAUGHAN: That was the vaudeville element, which comes from Merce's early study of tap and ballroom dancing.

SIMON: "Bite your lips, pinch your cheeks, and you're on," Merce would say.

VAUGHAN: "Pure dance" and Cunningham are usually linked in the sense of the purity of his process and of movement done purely for itself. Does that imply that his movement is meaningless?

SIMON: The purity has to do with there not being any other meaning to the movement except the movement. The movement isn't symbolic, it wasn't designed to transmit a particular idea or feeling, only itself. That's basic to what he's been doing from the beginning. He trained us to dance that way.

VAUGHAN: With a kind of blankness, some would say. But weren't you concentrating on doing the movement and nothing else?

SIMON: What was going on in our minds was our own business, but what we projected was exactly what the movement was and nothing else.

VAUGHAN: When Merce is asked about the meaning of his movements, he says, "I simply don't want to impose on anyone." That's not to say he wants to exclude ideas or feelings as part of the observer's reaction to his choreography, simply that he doesn't want to dictate.

SIMON: He's been saying that from the start. But he understood that people watching would have thousands of different reactions and thoughts.

CHARLIP: That happens anyway. You might have an idea that you'd like to impose in a dance, but the dancer and the viewer may develop another idea. After eleven years of dancing with Merce, I went to see the company for the first time as audience. Steve Paxton had taken over my roles; and watching him, I said to myself, surprised, "Oh, *that's* what I did. Oh, *that's* what that's about! Oh, *that's* what we were doing?" It was really mind-boggling. I'd thought I was doing one thing, but I saw, when I actually saw it, that it was something else.

BROWN: That philosophy was certainly prevalent in the change in painting and sculpture and art attitudes, in which the object itself, like a Mondrian, doesn't represent anything except the colors and lines. The viewer is free to associate with such a painting in any way he wishes. That philosophy was strongly influential on both Merce and John. The "thing" in itself, as Gertrude Stein said; "It-ness," "It-ness" was a matter we felt very strongly about.

SIMON: When we asked Merce to tell us more about his dancemaking process, he might answer in conundrums. Once, though, he told us that he put different movements on a chart, such as "turn head" or "lift leg" or "raise arm" or whatever; and then, using chance, he would throw pennies onto the chart to indicate combinations of these moves. But if one movement was "squat on floor" and the other was "land from a leap," we had to get from one to the other, so he would devise a transition move. That's my understanding of how some of the choreography evolved.

CHARLIP: For some of the pieces he'd make a chart of, say, possibilities for the head: "look down," "look up," "look to the right," "look to the left," "turn back," or whatever; a chart of possibilities for the arms in second, fifth, parallel; and a chart of body placements: twisting, bending, stretching. Then Merce tossed coins at the charts. He might get a head looking up while the torso was turning while the arm was moving back. But he never had us work these moves out on ourselves. He made them on himself first, then he taught them to us. So every move we made at that time was always an accepted fact.

He'd work on his own all morning, then come to class and give us these insane combinations. He'd say, "Why can't you get it?" We'd ask him to show us again, but it would be slightly different.

Merce was able to do amazing moves, where you'd be heading in one direction with your body and suddenly your leg would be whipping you around in another direction. For the dancer, the challenge was always to do completely what he'd given you, down to the last syncopation, pinky, or whatever. That was really quite difficult and kept us so busy we didn't have time to think about anything else.

BROWN: Didn't Merce always have a tendency to include a tableau, where three or four dancers would hold their positions in relationship to one another? And there was always a whirligig near the end. Chasing tails.

VAUGHAN: In the fifteen-minute stopwatch sequence that so influenced

Earle, both of you were in that rehearsal. How did you manage to get your timing so refined? It couldn't have been a conventional sense of musicality, because you weren't dancing to any sort of music, but in silence. Had you developed a kinesthetic sensitivity to some sort of rhythm that would be an alternative to traditional musical rhythm?

CHARLIP: For me it felt like being a part of a family and cooking dinner, where you get all the food ready at the same time and everybody, knowing that dinner is on the table, collects in the kitchen. Because at that point we really were a family. I lived on 7th Street and Carolyn and Earle lived on Cornelia in the Village. I'd meet Carolyn for breakfast and we'd go to Antony Tudor's or Margaret Craske's ballet class. We'd have lunch and then go to Merce's class. We'd have a rehearsal, go to dinner, and then we'd perform or go to a movie or something like that. I mean, we were with each other constantly. We began to know each other's idiosyncrasies and pleasures. We developed Marianne's version of peripheral vision. She said that in teaching children, you must develop eyes in the back of your head so that you know which kid is about to throw the paint at you.

VAUGHAN: Wouldn't you agree that even though Merce doesn't work in a conventional way with music, his choreography is intrinsically musical? The best dancers of his choreography have always been musical dancers, and Carolyn, of course, is supremely musical. It's a question of one's sense of phrasing, which doesn't have anything to do with the kind of music being played.

CHARLIP: It was also the different musicalities that we got to know. Carolyn's sense of musicality was very different from mine. As in any company, all of us argued constantly about whether we started on one foot or the other, whether a phrase faces this way or that, and so forth. Dance was our life, so we worked on music and rhythm constantly.

VAUGHAN: When did the loudness of Cunningham's music become an issue?

BROWN: At Connecticut College, the American Dance Festival. Somebody was about to sue them. A problem was that the loudspeakers would be pointing toward the audience, but David and John were behind the speakers, so they were not conscious of what was happening to the audience. If you were in line with one of those tweeters and woofers, you could get your ears knocked off.

CHARLIP: Oh, they went out into the audience, too. They heard it.

BROWN: Then it was that loud even more consciously.

CHARLIP: They wanted the sound loud. The kinds of battles that went on about it . . . I can't tell you. I remember Carolyn being very upset about the loudness of the music.

BROWN: The use of contact mikes is basic to amplification, and the first time John experienced them was for *Quantitaten* by Bo Nilsson, the Swedish composer. It's the first piece of music I know of that calls for an amplified piano, and Merce choreographed it for himself and Carolyn, for Sweden. I was working then as a recording engineer for Capitol Records. David Tudor came in and we recorded his playing of *Quantitaten* with four or five contact mikes going to different loudspeakers. I put a mike on each loudspeaker, and we got the most incredible piano sound. It scared David right out of his wits. After that, John began using contact mikes frequently, and those led to the loud-speaker problem.

John and Merce both maintained an absolute integrity to the materials they used. In Merce's case the materials were the dancers—the way they moved, even just in walking, or the differences between the way they moved.

The same ethic prevailed with John in terms of his chance compositions. He always said he should have been a Methodist minister. He was absolutely disciplined—permitted himself no deviation—in his use of the chance process. It was not "anything goes." Of course in effect, the process is ambiguous. It's "anything goes" that the chance comes up with. In a word, only *that* can enter.

Cage is badly misunderstood by many people who take advantage of his work to veer off in directions he never did. Cage didn't do open-form pieces or improvisations. He uses chance as a means to remove his own memory and the memory of the musicians from the process, in order for them all to make an almost pure event. Chance is a very pure process, whether it uses squeaks or squawks or tin cans or whatever. It's highly disciplined and not random at all. There's a huge difference between the chance process and "random."

VAUGHAN: Which is why the Cunningham dances have very strong structural qualities. From working with him, what main influence of Merce's did each of you subsequently realize that you'd carried over into your own work?

BROWN: I didn't interact with him in the same way as the dancers, of course, but I spent a lot of time with and around Merce and his performers. I had played jazz, which is an intense kind of family-ship, and I was seeking confirmation of a lot of my deepest feelings about how people can perform together; can play, impeccably, music composed without rigid metrics. The performance art of Merce's dancers helped me to formulate my music.

SIMON: What comes to mind immediately is what happened once in a class. I was desperately trying to do something he had given us, and finally said in my most pathetically helpless way, "How can I do this?" Merce said, "Marianne, the only way to do it is to do it." His advice has remained as a brilliant light in the sky.

CHARLIP: For me it's Merce's courage to do the dance he wanted to do, in spite of everything. I was telling a friend who just did a concert—I was in a piece of hers, and the concert wasn't reviewed anywhere—I reminded her that the first fifteen picture books I published did not get reviewed. And I told her how Merce, if his early dances got reviewed at all, was demolished by critics. John Martin and most of the writers then thought Merce's work was the pits. But he continued despite it. That's very moving to me. It's given me the courage to go on.

Merce Cunningham as the Revivalist in Martha Graham's *Appalachian Spring*, 1944. Photo © 1955 Arnold Eagle.

Root of the Unfocus, 1944, double exposure. Photo © 1992 Barbara Morgan, courtesy the Willard and Barbara Morgan Archives.

Merce Cunningham and Pearl Lang, c. 1942. Photo © 1992 Barbara Morgan, courtesy the Willard and Barbara Morgan Archives.

Collage (Excerpts from *Symphonie Pour Un Homme Seul*), 1952, Part I: Solo. Photo © Arnold Eagle.

Collage, Part II. L to r: Remy Charlip, Timothy LaFarge, Marianne Preger (Simon), Anita Dencks (in background), Jo Anne Melsher, Carolyn Brown. Photo © Arnold Eagle.

Banjo, 1953. L to r: Carolyn Brown, Merce Cunningham, Anita Dencks, Timothy LaFarge, Remy Charlip, Marianne Preger (Simon).
Photo © Arnold Eagle.

Banjo. Merce Cunningham and Carolyn Brown.
Photo © Arnold Eagle.

Fragments, 1953. L to r: Merce Cunningham, Jo Anne Melsher, Marianne Preger (Simon), Carolyn Brown.
Photo © Arnold Eagle.

Suite for Five, 1956. L to r: Carolyn Brown, Merce Cunningham, Barbara Lloyd.
Photo by Marvin Silver, courtesy Cunningham Dance Foundation.

Nocturnes, 1956. L to r: Viola Farber, Merce Cunningham, Bruce King, Marianne Preger (Simon), Carolyn Brown, Remy Charlip. Photo © Arnold Eagle.

Nocturnes. L to r: Viola Farber, Bruce King, Remy Charlip, Carolyn Brown, Merce Cunningham. Photo by Louis Stevenson, courtesy Cunningham Dance Foundation.

David Vaughan

"THEN I THOUGHT ABOUT MARCEL . . ." MERCE CUNNINGHAM'S *WALKAROUND TIME* (1982)

The practice of commissioning decors and costumes for ballet from avant-garde painters and sculptors, initiated by Sergei Diaghilev in the second period (1917–1929) of his Ballets Russes, was continued by his emulators, Rolf de Maré (Ballets Suédois) and the Comte Étienne de Beaumont (Soirées de Paris), and, less boldly, by the émigré Russian companies of the thirties and forties. It has not happened often in American ballet in the second half of the twentieth century, largely because of George Balanchine's lack of interest—some might say lack of taste—in such matters. The modern dance has a better record, notably in Merce Cunningham's long series of collaborations with some of the most advanced American painters, which parallels his equally adventurous history of musical collaboration, particularly with John Cage, which is of forty years' duration.

From 1954 to 1964, Robert Rauschenberg was the Merce Cunningham Dance Company's resident designer. In 1967 Jasper Johns became the company's artistic advisor, in which capacity he not only designed scenery and costumes himself (for *Second Hand* [1970], *Landrover* [1972], *TV Rerun* [1972], *Un Jour ou deux* [1973] for the Paris Opéra Ballet, and, later, *Exchange* [1978]) but also commissioned them from other artists: Frank Stella (*Scramble* [1967]), Andy Warhol (*RainForest* [1968]), Robert Morris (*Canfield* [1969]), Bruce Nauman (*Tread* [1970]), and Neil Jenney (*Objects* [1970]). As is well known, one of

Cunningham's major innovations is the introduction of the principle of the independence of the elements of choreography, sound, and design, as opposed to that of integration, which characterized Diaghilev's productions. These elements are created separately and brought together only in the final stages, sometimes not until the first performance.

One of the few occasions in which Cunningham diverged from this principle was in *Walkaround Time* (1968), in which the collaboration, at one remove, was with Marcel Duchamp. In the late forties and early fifties, Cunningham and Cage were friendly with members of the New York School of painters (Willem and Elaine de Kooning designed the scenery for the production of Erik Satie's play *The Ruse of Medusa* at Black Mountain College in the summer of 1948, in which Cage and Cunningham were involved). It is often suggested that Cunningham's decentralization of the stage space, largely Zen-inspired, has much in common with the way painters like Jackson Pollock handled the area of the canvas. But there was an essential difference between what Cunningham and Cage were doing and the work of the Abstract Expressionists, whose subject, as Calvin Tomkins has said, was still "the heroically suffering artist."[1] This kind of content was of course precisely what Cunningham wished to eliminate from his choreography and Cage from his music (hence their involvement with chance processes). In this they were closer to Duchamp. Like him, they wished to erase the distinction between art and life. Just as Duchamp's "ready-mades" converted everyday objects into works of art by virtue of his having chosen them, so Cunningham used non-dance movement as an element in his choreography and Cage "admitted into the purview of music the sounds, and even noises, that are part of ordinary life."[2]

Although John Cage had met Duchamp as early as 1942, it was not until the mid-1960s that he and Cunningham became close friends of Duchamp and his wife Teeny, by which time Duchamp himself had long since "retired" from active involvement with art. It was largely through Cage's transmission of his ideas that Duchamp continued to be an influence on a younger generation of artists. A Duchamp collaboration with the Merce Cunningham Dance Company, however desirable, was unlikely. As Cunningham tells it, the genesis of *Walkaround Time* was casual, spontaneous:

> We were at dinner at Duchamp's apartment on 10th Street, John and Teeny were playing chess, and I was sitting there with Lois [Long] and Jasper [Johns], and Marcel was over there smoking a pipe, watching the chess game—he didn't have to watch, he knew what was going on without looking. And Jasper said to me, would you be interested in doing something with *The Large Glass?* And I said, oh yes—just automatically. So he said, then I'll ask Marcel. And he went over, and they talked and he came back and I said, what did he say? And Jasper said, well, he looked pained—he asked who would do all the work. And Jasper had said, I would, and Marcel said, oh, fine.
>
> That was the way that began. The only thing that Marcel asked was

that at some point it be assembled to look like the *Glass* as much as possible, and that's what happens at the end. Jasper figured out how to divide it, I'm sure he talked with Marcel—he had the idea of silk-screening [the images] on to some kind of transparent material. I think they had to do it twice— either the silk-screening wouldn't take, or it wouldn't stand up, or whatever. They wanted to do it with helium in it, like the [*RainForest*] pillows, but that wouldn't work. So it ended up with this idea of their being inflated: five of them standing and two hung.

Then I thought about Marcel. . . .[3]

Walkaround Time, then, differs from other Cunningham works in that all the elements are related to the central idea of a kind of *hommage à Duchamp*. The decor, as indicated, is an adaptation of Duchamp's magnum opus, whose full title is *The Bride Stripped Bare by Her Bachelors, Even*, supervised by Johns. The music is not by Cage but by David Behrman; its title, . . . *for nearly an hour. . .*, refers not only to the actual duration of the dance but to another Duchamp work related to the *Glass, To be looked at (from the other side of the glass) with one eye, close to, for nearly an hour* (1918). (Cunningham's own title for the dance comes not from a Duchamp work but from computer jargon: it refers to the time when the computer is running and the programmer can "walk around" until it is finished. At the end of the dance, when the seven inflatables have been assembled in an approximation of the original, the dancers do in fact walk around in a circle behind them, then sit.)

It is not surprising that Cunningham's choreography pays homage to various aspects of Duchamp's work in general rather than finding some kind of dance equivalent of the specific, erotic content of the *Glass* itself; such content is rarely to be found in his dances and in any case such a literal approach is alien to his method. Although he has said, "I put in lots of things about Duchamp and his work," he added, "I never tell anybody because this confuses people."[4]

The main thing, I think, is the tempo. Marcel always gave one the sense of a human being who is ever calm, a person with an extraordinary sense of calmness, as though days could go by, and minutes could go by. And I wanted to see if I could get that—the sense of time.[5]

Walkaround Time begins with the dancers disposed about the stage, surrounded by the decor. There is a long moment of stillness, and then they slowly begin to do various movements that anyone familiar with Cunningham technique will recognize as the opening warm-up exercises of his class (back stretches, knee bends). Cunningham customarily works out passages of choreography in his classes, and then develops them further in rehearsal, usually in the direction of greater complication, but here the exercises are transferred to the stage almost without alteration; hence, this is one form of choreographic "ready-made." Another may be found in the repetition in the second half of sequences of movement from the first half of the dance (Cunningham was

pleased when he heard that a small boy in the audience at the first performance had said, "Look, they're doing reruns").

Cunningham does not, as might have been expected, use everyday
movement as an element in the choreography of the dance proper, but in
between the two parts there is an intermission, when the house lights are
brought up and the dancers stroll onto the stage wearing bathrobes and do the
kind of thing they would ordinarily do during an intermission with the curtain
down—sit and chat, practice steps, lie down. Behrman's sound score gives
way to recordings of popular music (Argentine tangos, a Japanese soprano
singing *Tristesse*). All these, of course, are ready-mades in yet another sense.

The intermission also refers to the cinematic *Entr'acte* (by René Clair) from
the Dadaist ballet *Relâche*, presented by the Ballets Suédois in 1924, with music by
Satie and decor, costumes, and scenario by Francis Picabia, in which Duchamp
himself appeared. In the ballet, he appeared almost naked, as Adam in a *tableau
vivant* after Lucas Cranach; in the film, he is seen playing chess with Man Ray.[6]

Finally, the moment when one of the male dancers (originally Gus Solomons jr) is picked up and carried across the stage by the others, is interpreted
by Cunningham as follows: "You have an object—or a person if you like—and
then that object is transported and you see it, or him, in another circumstance—he's the same, but the situation has changed."[7]

Shortly after the end of the *entr'acte*, Cunningham enters, stands behind
one of the set pieces, and while running in place peels off one set of leotard
and tights and pulls on another. Both the striptease and the repetition of
movement while it is performed refer to Duchamp's *Nude Descending a Staircase*. Cunningham also tried to convey the sense of "stopping and moving at
the same time" that characterizes the *Nude* in Carolyn Brown's solo, where
stillness alternates with fast, large movement.[8]

Cunningham describes going into the studio and asking "one of the
dancers to do a back fall . . .; then I asked one of the men to fall over her, and
I asked another girl to fall over them."[9] It is possible to discern in the resulting
convoluted figure (which recurs several times, at different tempi, during the
piece) a reference to the machinelike images of *The Large Glass* itself. Again, at
various moments, particularly at the end, when the decor is assembled in an
approximation of the original (Duchamp's only stipulation), the dancers are
seen behind the set pieces, and we are reminded of an important aspect of the
Glass—that the images are not only to be looked at, but seen through.

Charles Atlas, director of the film version of *Walkaround Time* (1973),
suggests a further correlation with this aspect of the work:

> Cunningham has translated Duchamp's concern with transparency in
> terms of movements into a dance composition which explores the possibili-
> ties of lateral movements back and forth across a proscenium space. In
> addition to the "transparent" clarity of this way of shaping space (as
> against, for example, the use of a swirling space) this is movement that

retains its visual integrity as the dancers pass behind the see-through vinyl inflatables of the set. . . . The viewer is left to complete the dance with discoveries of Duchamp on many levels.[10]

Walkaround Time received its first performance at the Second Buffalo Festival of the Arts Today, at the State University of New York at Buffalo, on March 10, 1968 (it has been out of the repertory since 1972). Duchamp was present at the opening night. Jasper Johns has written: "At the end of the first performance, I told Duchamp that he should go on stage for a bow. He asked wasn't I going to. I said no. He said, as he went, 'I'm just as frightened as you are.' "[11] But as Cunningham remembers it, "Marcel came up the steps on to the stage and stood between me and Carolyn, and it was just as if he'd been doing it all his life."[12]

Notes

1. Calvin Tomkins, "The Antic Muse," *The New Yorker*, August 17, 1981.
2. Dale Harris, "Cunningham and Cage," *Keynote*, July 1982.
3. Conversation with the author.
4. Quoted in Ruth Foster, *Knowing in My Bones* (London: Adam and Charles Black, 1976).
5. Ibid.
6. René Clair, *A Nous la liberté* and *Entr'acte*, English translation and description of the action by Richard Jacques and Nicola Hayden (New York: Simon and Schuster, 1970); Henning Rischbieter, ed., *Art and the Stage in the Twentieth Century* (Greenwich, CT: New York Graphic Society, 1968).
7. Conversation with the author.
8. Conversation with the author.
9. Quoted in Foster, *Knowing in My Bones.*
10. Charles Atlas, note on "Walkaround Time," in *Film and Video Catalog* (New York: Cunningham Dance Foundation, 1982).
11. Jasper Johns, contribution to *Merce Cunningham*, ed. James Klosty (New York: Saturday Review Press/E.P. Dutton & Co, 1975).
12. Conversation with the author.

Marcia B. Siegel

COME IN, EARTH. ARE YOU THERE? (1970)

Somebody said it's okay now to hold your ears at a Merce Cunningham concert. I saw several people doing it during his spring (1969) season at Brooklyn Academy. In his good-natured way, Cunningham has always been in the forefront of the rape-the-audience crowd, and it is perhaps a measure of our acceptance of him that we no longer feel compelled to submit to all his brutalities. Certainly his choreography itself is no longer revolutionary. Without the music it would probably be either pure entertainment or pure boredom, depending on your degree of kinesthetic sophistication.

I don't know if the auditory documents of John Cage and his colleagues are becoming more violent, or if urban life has had a sensitizing effect on our hearing, but I find I have less tolerance for Cunningham's noise today than I had five years ago. Opening night at Brooklyn was performed in silence because of a dispute between the musicians' and the stagehands' unions as to who had jurisdiction over the indefinable activities in the pit. Several of Cunningham's most ardent admirers who were there remarked how lovely that concert was. And their impression of his new work, *Canfield*, was quite different from the one I got when the sound had been restored.

When you look at Merce Cunningham, you can either separate the various events that take place—the dancing, decor, lighting, accompaniment—or you can see them as a whole unit. Separating a Cunningham dance into its component parts is perfectly valid because the parts are created separately, often coming together only in performance. Not only do the dancers not dance to the music, they don't know in advance what the quality

71

and sequence of the sounds will be. In some dances, sections of the choreography are shifted around from performance to performance, so that there can be no set narrative or dramatic line. Cunningham's dancers don't attempt to relate to the decor in which they move, except in the most practical sense. When Andy Warhol's gently floating silver pillows get in their way in *Rain-Forest* they plow right through them. Or the visual imagery may change drastically from one performance to the next, as in *Scramble,* where Frank Stella's brightly colored rectangles of cloth stretched at different levels on aluminum frames are moved around so that whole sections of the dance might be invisible to some of the audience. In *Variations V* (1965), six projectors throw a cacophony of moving and still images onto the stage, but the dancers act as if nothing were happening. (Compare this with Robert Joffrey's popular but conventional mixed-media ballet *Astarte,* in which the music and the film/lighting sequence begin together and are precisely timed to coincide with and complement the dancing.)

Never to my knowledge has Merce Cunningham given an "interpretation" of any of his dances, nor do any of his associates. They will talk about the movement, what it is like, how it was made, what chance operations were used in putting it together, but they won't divulge the message or even the mood, as if it wasn't their business to be concerned with those things. Since I have no reason to believe that Cunningham and his people are either so naïve as to be unaware that they are always creating some kind of theater event, or so cagey as to pretend that they are not, I can only assume that they are deliberately maintaining their neutrality. There is in their attitude a certain fatalistic cheerfulness; they intend to do their job no matter what goes on around them. If every member of the audience has a different idea of what they're doing, or if the stage environment changes, still the integrity of their own task is constant. You can imagine them completing their appointed rounds in the dark, or if a dancer were injured or the theater were in flames.

Nevertheless, a Cunningham dance *is* a theatrical entity, especially in contrast to the work of some younger choreographers who have distilled his theories into more austere and concentrated forms. Judith Dunn uses nonsequential movement, Yvonne Rainer stresses the simultaneous, antiemotional quality of events, and Twyla Tharp turns chance operations into mathematical monotony. None of these choreographers uses other theater elements to the extent Cunningham does, and where their work seems cold and abstract, his takes on a dramatic life that he apparently neither dictates nor denies. The audience does have to find its own specific metaphors and relationships, but each piece usually has an overall sensibility that is apparent to everyone.

For me, Cunningham's dark pieces have suggested more specific "meanings" than his brighter works. The latter, which include *Field Dances* (1963), *Scramble* (1967), *Walkaround Time* (1968), and others, are expansive, flooded with light and color, pervaded with a general air of good fellowship and the joy of movement. In the dark pieces, the lighting and colors are somber, the movement is more restricted, the dancers seem more isolated from each other and at the same time more submissive to their environment. I feel in these works, especially *Winterbranch* (1964), *Place* (1966), *RainForest* (1968), and now *Canfield* (1969), that Cunningham is responding—perhaps unconsciously—to the ugly demands of civilization, rather than ignoring them.

There seems to be a progression from *Winterbranch,* where the dancers are crushed by merciless light and total darkness and a maniacally screeching sound track; to *Place,* where they rush frantically at the boundaries of some nameless enclosure and finally break out of it into some other unknown darkness; through *RainForest,* where they seem poised between their humanness and some nonhuman existence that could be either animalistic or artificial, and that they cannot attain in any case. Now, in *Canfield,* the dancers seem to have become resigned to a bland, computerized state in which both the joy and the rebellion have been diminished to faint emotions that can be easily countermanded by the more powerful hand of technology.

The dancers are in gray leotards against a white cyclorama and ungelled lights. The legs and borders masking the perimeter of the stage have been flown out; the space is enormous and the dancers look insignificant in it. A huge vertical boom travels constantly back and forth across the proscenium, with lights inside it, projecting onto the cyc. Sometimes the dancers are pinned in its glare, like escaping convicts in a searchlight; sometimes they drift in the gloom beyond its reach.

The movement seemed pale, the dynamics easy, without much thrust or conviction. There was rather more unison movement than in the average Cunningham dance, and an occasional theme of brushing past each other, making contact at the shoulder but without enough impact to upset each other's direction or momentum. Toward the end a huge bare leko bulb is projected on the cyc, then an indistinct man's face, then the lights in the boom begin to fade, looking somehow not like stage lights dimming but like the brown fatality of a power failure—and the curtain comes down on moving gray ciphers.

But it is the sound that dominates *Canfield,* a sound devised by Pauline Oliveros (*In Memoriam: Nikola Tesla, Cosmic Engineer*) that by its literalness and its overriding force insistently calls attention to itself in an unequal competition with what is going on on the stage.

Ever since Merce Cunningham began choreographing in 1942, his musical activities have been directed by John Cage. The two work amiably yet quite independently together. Each pursues his own inventions; the moment of collaboration is the moment of performance; and it is either a recurring accident or a figment of the critic's orderly mind that the two disparate parts seem so frequently to be in consonance with each other. Cunningham seems to have no egotistical notions about the dance being more important than the music, and on occasion the musical event was so shocking that it drowned out the dance until we became accustomed to it. At first we hated the catastrophic din of *Winterbranch*, but now it's hard to imagine that dance without it.

For the past couple of years, Cage and his colleagues David Tudor and Gordon Mumma have been experimenting ever more radically with sound, and *Canfield* once again pushes us beyond endurance. We may grow used to this too, but now we feel like the exasperated stranger who grumbled to me during intermission, "It's a secret pact to obliterate the dance."

What Cage and his cohorts are into now goes back, I think, to *Place,* when Gordon Mumma played around with distortion. That is, instead of distorting sound as Cage and many others before him had done via prepared piano, *musique concrète,* and other devices, the distortion *became* the sound. Radio feedback, hum, static, excessive amplification, and manipulation of other sounds generated by the equipment itself, not any sounds being fed *into* the equipment. Gradually the dial-twisting has become the primary concern; the original sounds, whether they are vocal, instrumental, or electronic, are important only as a medium for producing distortion, instead of the distortion being a means of modifying the original sound. In current performance of Cage's piano and orchestra score for *Antic Meet* (1958), there are now hardly any sounds left that even resemble a piano and orchestra.

In many ways this is a logical development. If you mike all the instruments and then ask the musicians to blow through the wrong end, put a trumpet mouthpiece on a bassoon, and bring along transistor radios and alarm clocks, as Cage did with *Antic Meet,* why not put the whole thing on tape and then reshape those distortions? Is there any difference between Cage climbing all over a theater, rubbing the mike against different wall surfaces, chewing aluminum foil with a mike in his mouth, to find sounds for *Story* (1963), and sending people all over the theater in *Canfield* with walkie-talkies to speak into the main sound system?

Well, there is some difference. More than ever the machine is in control. The chance activities that were produced by human beings doing unpredictable things have been submerged under the more powerful unpredictability of electronic equipment. The human input is simpler and less noticeable—all that's needed now is one long and two short blasts on a trumpet from the top of the balcony, or a voice-over test (testing one-two-three), or simply throwing the mike open. The tubes do the rest.

No matter how awful or boring or nerve-racking it was to listen to an amplified belch or the squeaks of a stool being dragged along the floor, there was a certain childlike charm in the idea of Cage doing it. That kind of sound could often arouse one's curiosity as to how it was being produced, what kind of transformations were being worked on common objects or activities to make them come out sounding the way they did. The effects of the intervening circuitry never quite obscured the fact that somewhere at the beginning of it all there was a complex and original mind searching for new ways to make sound, notate it, and get others to produce it.

In *Variations V* there was an elaborate system of antennae set up on the stage that were supposed to be activated by the dancers moving near them. Though I've seen the dance at least three times, I've never been able to detect any relationship between where and how the dancers moved and what sounds occurred. I was always interested to see how it would work out—something like an electrocardiogram maybe—the radios or whatever the antennae were hooked up to would, I supposed, get louder when the dancers approached them, suddenly louder if suddenly approached; but how would other dynamic and shape changes affect the sound? Two dancers instead of one? What would happen if somebody bumped into one and it whipped back and forth? I never found out. Whatever the antennae picked up was swallowed and digested into all the other sounds that constituted that score, or it was so misshapen at the controls that it couldn't be connected with its initiation when it came out.

There was a certain pleasant camaraderie between the dancers and the presiding technicians in the first version of *Variations V*, at Philharmonic Hall in the summer of 1965. The technicians, though somewhat patronizing, I felt, were always interested in what the subjects of their experiments would do next, sometimes consulting with them. On their platform behind the dancing space they presided but they also performed—they controlled the dance to some extent, but it was the *dance* they were showing off.

Now, in *Canfield*, with the arrogant competence of Rocket Control, they are running the show. Their cool, anonymous engineer's talk dominates the dance for much of the time. No matter how I tried or how uninterested I was in their matter-of-fact voices talking about unimportant things (John, where are you now? I'm under the stage. Give me a reading. One. One. Hmmmm, we didn't have that buzz in rehearsal), I couldn't focus on the dancing until about halfway through, when the jargon subsided into squeals and static—I couldn't get free of the busy multitude of disembodied taxicab drivers and policemen and disk jockeys who kept floating in and out on the walkie-talkie band. (Lotta guys on the line tonight.) Like all true radio nuts, even after they have obtained their tunings and levels, Cage and Tudor and Mumma keep fiddling. No pattern satisfies them. Nothing is good enough, or loud or unusual enough, to keep and use for something—it only serves to be surpassed by the infinite capabilities of their electronic superbrain.

It has been said that the visual sense is stronger than the aural, and in most instances at dance concerts I'm not specifically conscious of the music, even when I'm making an effort to relate the structure and phrasing of what I see to what I hear. The visual takes over. But not in *Canfield*. If you've ever been on the BMT when it grinds into those curves near City Hall station, or driven past Kennedy Airport when a jet was taking off over your head, you know that extreme noise can reduce or otherwise alter your perceptual powers. But even when it is not physically uncomfortable, the *Canfield* sound is literal, which can be even more distracting. What is it about words that makes us pay attention to them? There are ways of de-emphasizing a verbal dance accompaniment, as Cunningham does in *How to Pass, Kick, Fall and Run* (1965), where Cage and David Vaughan read low-key selections from Cage's writings, sometimes overlapping each other. Then we can choose to listen to one or the other, or to neither, letting their combined flow of words make an abstract background for the dance. But in *Canfield* the drama behind those banal dialogues is inescapable. How *could* I be interested in those efficient, faceless men with their dreary talk of inputs and readings? But I am, I'm fascinated, I strain to make out the words when the tuning drifts away. I hate myself and I hate the sound, because I'm missing the dance.

Well, maybe this *is* the dance.

A few days after the Brooklyn Academy season, *The New York Times* reported that an eminent biologist told Senator Edmund Muskie's committee investigating pollution that "in the process of creating new goods and services, technology is destroying the country's 'capital' of land, water, and other resources as well as injuring people." In fact, scarcely a day goes by that we are not offered pronouncements, pamphlets, threats, warnings, and predictions of disaster resulting from the masochistic and perhaps irreversible course of technological exploitation. Intentionally or not, Merce Cunningham is going beyond the tracts and the vague dread. He is showing us postmillennial man—wired for sound, dissolving into his colorless backdrop, ineffectually and without regrets, alive. The image is more vivid and more terrifying than all the dead fish in the Hudson and all the polemics in Congress. And our response is to cover our ears, as Merce Cunningham, wise as a stone, probably always knew we would.

*   *   *   *

Some time after this article was written, the astronauts landed on the moon. After watching their televised performance, Merce Cunningham's manager, Jean Rigg, told Merce Cunningham that the lighting effects on the moon were exactly what they had been trying for in *Canfield*. Merce Cunningham said, "Yes! And the sound too."

Stephen Smoliar

MERCE CUNNINGHAM IN BROOKLYN (1970)

I want to write about Merce Cunningham and the concerts given by his company at the Brooklyn Academy of Music during the month of January 1970. I suppose this means I want to write about dance, but it's not just a matter of writing about dance—even though in most cases, dance, music, and set are independent elements. It's a matter of writing about environments—however overburdened the literature of art criticism may be with that word already.

But that's all right. I've always regarded Merce Cunningham as being involved in more than just the art of making dances. He is an architect of the theater, building (in cooperation with musicians and artists) an entire world for his audiences—be it on a proscenium stage such as the one at the Brooklyn Academy or in a gymnasium or museum. I do not go to Cunningham's concerts simply for dance; I go for a total theatrical experience. This entails quite a universe, and many audiences are inclined to think it is more than they can handle. But one doesn't "handle" Cunningham's productions; one simply has to observe them. The rest is totally within the mind of the observer, who may direct his attention wherever he desires at any time and fashion his own personal experience. So in writing about Merce Cunningham's concerts, I am simply recording my own experiences—hence, the reason for this diary format.

The season began with *Canfield* (1969); and *Canfield* began with Pauline Oliveros's *In Memoriam: Nikola Tesla, Cosmic Engineer*, which started as the house lights were dimming. In an amplified conversation conducted from the orchestra pit and various other positions in the theater, the three musicians of the Cunningham Dance Company—John Cage, David Tudor, and Gordon Mumma—could be heard discussing their most recent sound experiences and giving a subjective acoustic evaluation of the Brooklyn Academy of Music. This subjectivity was only a prelude, however. It soon developed that this piece involved an *objective* analysis of the sound environment. Like scientists, the musicians worked independently in teams on a series of experiments—Cage and Mumma working together and Tudor working with an assistant, Jean Rigg.

Their activities consisted of making sounds, listening to them, and recording them—experimenting within the entire space of the Brooklyn Academy of Music, maintaining contact with one another by radio communications. In one experiment, for example, Mumma was sent up on stage (off in the wings) to play a bugle while turning in a circle. As he turned, the sound bounced off walls, sank into curtains, and was even affected by the dancers. One was reminded that such a procedure provides the necessary data by which bats navigate.

A music score of this nature defines an environment unto itself, regardless of any additional theatrical activity. It is an uncertain environment of unknown parameters which must be investigated and explored. In this particular case, it is also an independent component of the total experience of *Canfield*; I have been able to describe it without any mention of the dance. Similarly, the choreography may be described without any mention of the music.

The title refers to a game of solitaire; and Cunningham has choreographed a dance episode for each of the fifty-two cards of a standard deck. *Canfield* is one of the most difficult forms of solitaire, and very rarely do all cards come into play. I believe that the dance is determined by the cards which do come up during a given game. These are used to decide the order and length of a particular performance. By the nature of the game, two performances of it will almost never be the same.

I must confess that this was the first time I had seen *Canfield* and that I was so impressed with Pauline Oliveros's score that I had great difficulty paying attention to the dance. What struck me most of all about the choreography at this first viewing was its low entropy content—a security and commitment which contrasted with the exploratory uncertainty of the music. For example, the first card of this performance involved simply walking to a place through some path about the stage and then just standing there. After the stage became more occupied, a standing dancer would be set in motion as another dancer walked by, and would then proceed to another location and again come to rest—sort of like a thermodynamic system of Maxwell demons.

Admittedly, it is somewhat unconventional to view dance in terms of thermodynamics or information theory; however, in the case of Merce Cunningham, such as approach is not that far off base—particularly if one considers

Carolyn Brown's article in *Dance Perspectives 34* which interprets Cunningham's choreography as a physical system in space and time:

> I've always felt that almost no one has actually recognized what Merce has been doing all these years—his extraordinary use of space and his exacting concern with time. Although science and many of the other arts have been exploring the time-space concept, dance as a whole seems generally to have ignored it. Dances continue to be made as music visualizations or interpretations, or as translations of novels, plays, biblical, and historical events. And yet dance is far more basic than that. Dance is perhaps the only art form which is so primarily concerned with the time-space concept, not dualistically but integrally.

The decor by Robert Morris consisted of a vertical column containing white lights aimed at the back wall of the stage. The column was suspended from a little trolley which proceeded from side to side across the front of the stage. At first, its course seemed entirely predictable—first to one end and then back again. But then it became more indeterminate—stopping in the middle of its course to reverse direction. This was yet another independent component of the experience. The column served as a searchlight, although it did not "explore" the dancers or attempt to track them down. Its function was more like that of a lighthouse or a radar scan—systematically exposing portions of the stage and thus illuminating certain dancers and casting a variety of shadows on the wall.

Yet not only did the set interact with the dancers—by highlighting various activities—but also the sound of the trolley provided another source of exploration for the musicians. Furthermore, the semi-indeterminate behavior of the device fit right in between the musicians' cautious and studied sense of scientific method and the confident determinacy of every step taken by the dancers, providing the resulting system with a graded hierarchy of entropies.

In *Tread* (1970), the first new work of this season, the individual components were all oriented about a concept of interaction rather than one of contrast. Choreographically, each dancer was either in an "active" or "passive" state. If passive, the dancer could be moved about by the active performers. At the same time, an active dancer could receive energy from another active dancer; and the two would perform the same activity. In a sense, the work was a kinetic jigsaw puzzle in which the pieces themselves first defined the space and then determined how they would fit together. Bruce Nauman's set reflected the active-passive aspect of the dance with ten office fans, five of which oscillated (active) and five of which were fixed (passive). The music was also composed for the immediacy of interaction in a live performing environment. In Christian Wolff's *For 1, 2, or 3 people,* the performers communicate with each other through the process of realizing the score on their instruments. Again, the score is an elaborate system in itself; and unfortunately, this particular performance situation was not a live one. Rather, David Tudor used tape recordings from a realization he had already prepared on Richard Lippold's Schlicker baroque organ—a two-person realization accomplished by overdubbing.

From a purely subjective point of view, *Tread* was very enjoyable—even fun. One could safely call it refreshing, with all those fans blowing on the audience; but the beautiful thing about it all was the comfortable, relaxed attitude of the dancers throughout the piece. Some of the interactions involved strange and awkward contortions, but you never felt afraid to laugh at something that looked silly. The dancers themselves were quite prone to cracking smiles and the general atmosphere was one of—if you will pardon the expression—an antic meet.

Tread was followed by another cheerful piece—*How to Pass, Kick, Fall and Run* (1965). Here the movements were strictly physical—intentionally devoid of any of the tedious overtones too often associated with modern dance. The accompaniment consisted of an ensemble of stories by John Cage, read by Cage and David Vaughan, sometimes reading different stories simultaneously.

This type of accompaniment brought out a problem also present in *Canfield*—the dominating effect of the human voice. The Cage stories and the amplified discussion among the musicians had a tremendous command of the attention—enough to distract it from the stage. Perhaps the problem has to do with a subconscious desire for meaning which can be satisfied—at least superficially—by language.

I already mentioned my difficulties in trying to keep track of the choreography of *Canfield*. *How to* is a much more relaxed affair, and I never really feel I *have* to pay attention to anything. Things just seem to take care of themselves. It is impossible to mistake the generally bouncy atmosphere of the dance no matter how assiduously one follows the stories. *How to Pass, Kick, Fall and Run* can be taken strictly for fun—whether it comes from the stories, the dance, or a combination of the two.

* * * *

Scramble (1967) is one of the hardest dances for me to discuss intelligently. It may be because the work is what Gus Solomons jr. called "a real *dance* dance," and one can only grab a handle on it in terms of dance—that is, a fluent articulation of movement. If one is a dancer, particularly if one is well-trained in Cunningham's technique, this is not particularly difficult. Otherwise, *Scramble* is a work which demands several viewings. The bulk of Calvin Tomkins's *New Yorker* essay on Cunningham is about the making of *Scramble;* and I would like to quote two excerpts which describe the piece straight out:

> *Scramble* was certainly not indeterminate, nor did chance play much of a role in its creation. Cunningham kept experimenting with the order of its various parts. By the middle of June, he had blocked out three main sections of the dance. There would be four sections in all, and his idea was

that each one would be complete in itself. The longest section was the one that began with the whole company running four times across the stage. The fourth time across, Sandra Neels and Gus Solomons (whose part is now danced by Jeff Slayton) fell to the floor and remained there while the others went off; then, rising slowly, they began a sinuous, erotic duet, which led into Sandra's solo. This section also included the Carolyn Brown solo with the swimming movement and a Brown-Cunningham duet, which began with her taking extended positions while he scrambled (literally) under her outstretched arm or leg. The duet then erupted into a very active series of rapid leaps and pirouettes, criss-crossing the stage and ending when she made a startling head-first leap into the wings, where she was caught by Gus Solomons and Albert Reid (now Chase Robinson) . . . *Scramble* would begin with the section that the dancers had learned most recently, in which they came in slowly, one by one, from the wings, each with a different sort of sinuous movement, until they formed a tight group at the center of the stage. Cunningham then sprang into the quirky, complex phrase that had given Barbara Lloyd trouble earlier, and, one by one, they followed him until all of them were dancing the phrase in unison. This was followed by a new Cunningham solo, which the dancers now saw for the first time. The solo progressed through odd crouchings and twistings of the body to a passage in which Cunningham seemed to be making karate motions with his arms (he had seen an exhibition of karate and judo at Town Hall in the spring, and it fascinated him), and then he began a loose, loping, circling movement about the stage. As he was finishing the circling movement one day, he suddenly shouted—an angry roar that sounded more animal than human. The dancers thought for a moment that he had hurt himself. When he continued to dance, unperturbed, they realized that it must be part of the solo.

A few remarks by Cunningham on *Scramble* are also relevant to the performance: "The order of things can be changed, the timing. We can stop and start at any point. I've kept it that way on purpose. . . . It's taking its own shape and life, from now on my job is to avoid interfering with it . . . we can move the sets . . . oh, yes, it's going to work . . . have a good time."

Scramble is built about the ambiguities of its title—the physical action of scrambling about, the military jargon of scrambling a code, scrambling eggs. And the fact that the ordering of the dance was not fixed is yet another realization of the concept—this particular performance was a scrambling of the version described by Tomkins.

Between phonograph records and movies, we have been accustomed to believing that consistency of title implies consistency of contents. This is the first step on the road to the death of the live performing arts. The important thing about *Scramble* is that while two performances may not look exactly alike, they both look like *Scramble*. The question then, as far as this particular performance is concerned, is how did *Scramble* feel? Cunningham writes that the timing may be changed, and the timing of this performance was one which lent a very deliberate flavor to every movement. It wasn't that things were actually happening more slowly, but there was that feeling about it. In fact, the feeling was so subtle that it may not have even been intentional or—quite possibly—it was a consequence of the music.

Toshi Ichiyanagi's *Activities for Orchestra*, which accompanies the dance, involves an "orchestra" of whatever instruments are available. Under transformation by electronic equipment, the sounds of these instruments are manipulated and blended into a continuum of electronic sound. Performances of *Activities* have yielded long, steady streams of sound which support the ear as the crest of the wave supports a surfboard. Such was not the case at this performance. The sounds were more fragmented, less explicit; but every sound event left a deep impression on the ear and quite often provoked a broad spectrum of reactions from the electronic equipment. The musical sensitivity of every immediate event—for me—carried itself onto the stage. Every physical event drew itself out to fill its position in space and time. And while there was no electronic equipment to provide visual repercussions, the dance seemed to take care of that aspect with its own sense of momentum and propagation of energy.

*   *   *   *

Crises (1960) is a fantastic phenomenon—or maybe "fantastic" should be spelled with the "ph." It was, at the same time real and unreal—like the accompanying player piano rolls by Conlon Nancarrow which start out sounding like an ordinary piano and then get involved to the point of human impossibility. The transition into unreality is undefined; it's so nebulous that it never was there. It was the *reality* that was illusion, because you were never listening to a real piano.

Everything about *Crises* firmly holds the attention, but with the feeling that if you stare too hard it will fly into a thousand pieces. There is the whole element of human contact, which advances itself as a gesture of support and then turns on itself into a nightmarish hindrance. There is the trembling uncertainty of movement—particularly in Viola Farber's part—which keeps you on the edge of your seat as if she were on a tightrope. All this lends *Crises* an air of suspense and excitement which can rarely be found in the dance.

*   *   *   *

Canfield again, and a distinctly different game. Having read the comments in Cunningham's book [*Changes: Notes on Choreography*] about *Story* (1963), I was uncertain whether *Canfield* would change at every performance or whether, because of the complexity of such a structure, it would be necessary to fix an ordering for performance purposes. Apparently, the components are sound enough to admit of arbitrary changes in order and content. Why such a great concern about a piece not being the same at each performance? Primarily because the mass media seem dead set on conditioning the public to expect all performances of any given work to be strictly identical. When he delivered the

Charles Eliot Norton lectures at Harvard, Roger Sessions told of once having physically demolished several of his phonograph records. The performances on these recordings had become so rooted in his consciousness that he had lost touch with the actual music. It's like trying to appreciate a Calder mobile by looking at a single photograph of it. Reordering—or even changing—the contents of *Canfield* presents the same work from a different point of view at each performance. It is perfectly possible to have two performances of *Canfield* which are even *totally* different. A mobile never looks the same twice unless you restrict yourself to photographs—in which case it is no longer "mobile." Nonetheless, there are factors—which mathematicians call "invariants"—by which one knows that one is looking at the same mobile, regardless of the changes; and similarly, there are "invariants" which characterize *Canfield*. Some of these were obvious. The dancers wore the same outfits as at the Monday night performance. The decor was the same—the vertical column of lights traveling from right to left, changing direction indeterminately. The music was the same; even some of the sound experiments from Monday night were repeated.

However, these are all superficial similarities. The most important fact is that the individual units which make up the contents of the dance are always determined from the same deck of cards. Two games of Canfield are never the same; if they were, the game wouldn't be worth playing. The beauty of the game is that it entails an immediate encounter with chance which involves skill in the presence of an indeterminate sequence of events. Canfield is distinguished from other games of solitaire by its rules; and these rules are sufficient to enable an observer to identify the game. Similarly, the dance has its own set of rules in terms of the movement episodes associated with the cards; and purely on this basis, one may identify the work as *Canfield*.

This makes *Canfield* rather hard to "psych out" unless one is very familiar with its total contents. Imagine trying to observe the solitaire game if you had never before seen a deck of playing cards! Every experience would be a new one. You could spend hours just looking at the Queen of Spades, as you might look at a print in a museum. And if you watched many, many games, and if you really paid attention to what was happening, the contents of the entire deck and the rules of the game would gradually reveal themselves to you. This is the way it goes for the dance. There is far too much of it for one to be able to comprehend the entirety after only one or two viewings. However, this does not prevent one from relishing individual moments. Even the experience of a single shadow wavering as the light column travels by is worth savoring. A dance of this nature can be seen again and again and enjoyed as a new experience each time. And one need not exert oneself to understand the "invariants"; they will come of their own in due course.

The situation is a similar one for almost any new dance event, regardless of how indeterminate the structure may be. Last night was the first time I had ever seen *Crises*—although I had read much about it—and consequently, I saw many things in the second viewing which I had missed the first time around. For example, at first glance one notices that Viola Farber's costume is yellow while all the others are red. However, this is not so simple, because the red costumes range over a continuum of hues—from the dark, bold red of Cunningham's costume to Carolyn Brown's pale pink. In this context, the color of Miss Farber's costume takes on another interpretation. Not only is it a different color; but within this continuum, it is a color which is "falling off the brink" of the fading sequence of reds. This wording is particularly appropriate in terms of the qualities of her movement. The various quiverings of her body—particularly when they occur simultaneously with a long, steady extension—convey the impression of one on the edge of insanity. (As a matter of fact, there has been a fair amount of research in the matter of how body movements reflect a person's mental condition.) *Crises* is a downright terrifying experience. Not just because Miss Farber seems to be "falling off the brink," but because everyone else gives off that same hint. When Susana Hayman-Chaffey assists her in her jumps, Miss Farber appears helplessly dependent on everyone else. But when the other girls (there are four in the cast) start trembling the same way she does, or when they project those long, intense stares with ghostly empty eyes, it's as if the whole world was mad and she was the only one with even the faintest comprehension of sanity.

The third time around, *Tread* looked like it was being performed the third time around. The sparkle was missing, the house was very empty, and the audience seemed quite stolid. One sympathizes with the dampened spirits on stage. Tomorrow night they won't perform *Tread* and that's good. The piece needs a rest.

*   *   *   *

Walkaround Time (1968) serves as a fine introduction to Merce Cunningham and—for that matter—to the modern dance experience. The initial sequences of body stretches executed by the company are drawn straight from Cunningham's technique classes, and many of the combinations that follow could also have easily evolved from those classes. This is not to imply that the piece is elementary or simplistic. Quite the contrary—it's "what it's all about." It takes a series of movement structures which are so familiar to many dance students that they execute them without thinking, and places them in the context of dance—thus forcing one to think about them again. These exercises and combinations now become atoms of energy in the vast molecular structure which *Walkaround Time* envelops.

The title apparently comes from the computer jargon at the University of Illinois. It refers to that period of time during which the computer is running a program. In most circles this is referred to as "run time"; but of course that is from the computer's point of view. As far as the programmers are concerned, "walkaround time" is an appropriate expression.

The dance itself actually has such a period of walkaround time—that is, a period of waiting for something to happen before one can proceed. Halfway through the piece, the house lights come up; and although the curtain never descends, it is quite obvious that this is a period of intermission. At this particular performance most of the dancers just lay around in leg warmers. Mel Wong was doing exercises, and Meg Harper and Valda Setterfield were teaching some new steps to Douglas Dunn. The important thing about this episode is that it was totally informal—unstructured and spontaneous.

However, this provided a way of looking at the structured sections on either side of this intermission. The work was a carefully assembled montage of those activities which may be encountered during walkaround time—exercises, combinations for practice (in one series of leaps, Carolyn Brown looked away from the audience at Jeff Slayton, as if they were still practicing the alignment), and even idle recreation. Near the end of the dance, there was a period of work, as the dancers moved Jasper John's large plastic cubes based on the components of Marcel Duchamp's *The Large Glass* to the back of the stage. (The more ambitious computer programmers work on other problems during walkaround time.) Once this wall had been constructed, the dancers walked around behind it, and then sat down as the curtain descended.

The following background information was provided for *Second Hand*, the second new work of this season:

> In 1944 Merce Cunningham made *Idyllic Song*, using an arrangement for two pianos by John Cage of the first movement of Erik Satie's *Socrate*, a work for orchestra and voices having three movements: The Banquet; On the Banks of the Illysus; Death of Socrates. In the summer of 1969 Cunningham approached the work again with the plan to complete it. The two-piano arrangement by Cage was finished in October 1969 in collaboration with Arthur Maddox. Permission for the use of this arrangement was not granted by the copyright holder. The use of Satie's own arrangement for voices and piano solo was also not permitted. Cage, using *I Ching* chance operations with respect to seven modes and twelve transpositions of each, and applying these in a programmed way to his model, made a new composition preserving the rhythm and expressivity of the original.

Second Hand (1970) was totally unlike anything yet presented in the season. The only thing I can relate it to would be *Suite for Five* (1956), but it was even calmer and more placid than that. The first part remained an extensive solo by Cunningham, the second, a duet with Carolyn Brown. Only the final section involved the entire company. John Cage's music—a piano solo called *Cheap Imitation*—was soft, slow, and almost entirely monophonic. It was a true homage to Satie with all the purity of his simplicity, although the *I Ching* chance operations yielded melodic lines quite reminiscent of certain computer-composed melodies I have heard.

The dance itself does appear to be second-hand in a most remarkable way.

There are patterns, techniques, and gestures which go right back to Graham and Limón; and the opening solo—being *Idyllic Song*—may be regarded as second-hand Cunningham. Yet the piece as a whole does not reflect any of these earlier styles. *Second Hand* seems to do for dance what *Walkaround Time* does for more general activities. The movements are montaged without any reference to some concrete scenario. The movement is in this respect pure and the dance is quite classical.

There are more things to say about *Second Hand*. There are, for example, the costumes designed by Jasper Johns—tights and leotards which start in one color and fade into another. However, I have to see them several more times before I use up all my words. It is quite a substantial piece, and I suspect I shall have to work rather hard at it for the next few performances.

* * * *

Tonight's program began with *RainForest* (1968), the most "romantic" work of the season. We have a tendency to anthropomorphize everything we see and can infer a wide gamut of human emotions within the most natural movements of animals. *RainForest* allows such imaginative tendencies to run wild, and the effect is one of a supernatural jungle. The movements are all quite animal-like in their nature, but with a broad range of overtones. There is a simmering sensuality as Meg Harper winds about Cunningham's body in a serpentine fashion. The emergence of Chase Robinson upon this duet rings of a cold sense of competition, while Jeff Slayton strikes a more commanding note of disinterestedness. Finally, there is the energetic solo of Carolyn Brown, so reminiscent of a bird in flight, and the slower grace of Sandra Neels's solo which seems to reflect a larger, more earth-bound bird, such as a flamingo.

David Tudor's score is also fine food for the imagination. The sounds are obtained from wooden and metal objects which resonate with acoustic vibrations, but they are easily transformed "in the mind's ear" into a weird repertoire of bird calls and animal murmurs. Again, the effect is that of some supernatural limbo—neither total fantasy nor strict reality.

Andy Warhol's helium-filled silver pillows—which simply float about the stage subject to the existing air currents—best serve to define the imaginary aspect of this rain forest. Clearly, they are not a depiction of reality; but they hover over the scene as solemnly as the moving branches of a thick forest of trees.

I would like to discuss the elastic bands used in *Crises*. They are used very sparingly—only about once per episode and only in very brief movement sections. In fact, they seem more of a technical necessity than a key aspect of the piece. There is a great emphasis on physical contact. Viola Farber is subjected to movement in several situations—she is pushed across the floor by Cunningham at the beginning and assisted in jumping by Susana Hayman-Chaffey near the end. But many of the incidents of support turn back on themselves, like a crutch which suddenly develops a will of its own. Cunningham lifts an arm to support Miss Farber, but then it doesn't let go. Its grasp hangs on like a leech to become a frightening impediment. The elastic bands are particularly useful for such tenacious contact. Even if the two bodies try to separate, the elastic pulls them back together. They are caught in a spider-web of their own making, and each becomes a hindrance to himself as well as to others. The elastic makes the statement explicitly, but it is there implicitly throughout the entire dance.

Second Hand second time and there really isn't too much one can say. It is very "white"—encompassing all the colors of the spectrum and highlighting none of them. It leaves one peaceful—purged of chaos. It does not really invite a reaction. It simply occupies a time and space which it offers to share with the audience. As Cage would say, nothing is accomplished. But nothing has to be accomplished. It is all there.

* * * *

New thoughts on *Canfield*. As opposed to the more conventional form of solitaire in which one builds four piles of cards from ace to king, the "starting" card for Canfield is determined by chance and the piles are built cyclically—ace following king. My hypothesis is that the ordering of the dance is determined by the cards which are promoted to these piles. I further conjecture a connection between the numbered cards and the number of dancers in each section— particularly since the piece calls for ten dancers. I haven't yet been able to figure out an interpretation of the suits.

How does this affect the structure of the dance? If the game is won, it means that all fifty-two cards are performed. However, this is a very rare occurrence. In any event, the number of dancers used in each section will be approximately the same from section to section. If the first promoted card is an eight, the next will be either an eight of a different suit or a nine of the same suit, and so forth.

This provides a general coherence to the structure—allowing for perturbations when one pile grows faster than the others. But in general, it provides a microscopic control over the density of the piece. Like the laws of thermodynamics, it cannot govern the conditions at any particular moment, but it gives a good description of the overall effect.

I wish to emphasize the fact that this is a hypothesis; it is conjecture rather than proven fact. As a mathematician, I am quite accustomed to reading papers which advance new conjectures or further research alongside newly proven theorems. Since this is a personal diary, rather than a review, I feel I may allow myself the liberty of such conjectures because they reflect my impressions of the dance. More than any other work in the repertoire, *Canfield* keeps my mind churning away. Like a heckler in a game of solitaire, I am quick to make suggestions; but I really do not know the game well enough yet to play it myself.

I am not ashamed to admit that *Winterbranch* (1964) affects me more than any other Cunningham opus. I have always been thrilled by the macabre and bizarre; and while *Winterbranch* is explicitly neither of these, it certainly caters to that sort of imagination. The sporadic behavior of light in the midst of a general darkness and the sense of defeatism embodied in the action of falling both lend suggestions of a tremendous disaster to *Winterbranch*. The lighting makes it like a ride through a spooky funhouse. You are allowed only momentary glimpses as you are hurtled through a maze of terrors.

Is it worth mentioning the ill behavior of the audience? Was I naive enough to believe such things didn't happen in New York? Or is Brooklyn really that different from New York? Most of the dissidents were adequately put down by the accompaniment, La Monte Young's *2 Sounds (April 1960)*. It simply blasted the hell out of them and wouldn't let them complain. In fact, the tape ended early; and the entire audience heaved a collective sigh of relief in the final moments of silence. However, the enormous ovation at the end of *Winterbranch* best reflected the opinion of the heretofore "silent majority." After six years, *Winterbranch* still seems to pack the strongest punch.

*   *   *   *

With two days of rest, *Tread* returned—again cheerful and bouncy. There are so many precious moments in this piece! Sandra Neels's bursting energy as she climbs all over Jeff Slayton in their duet. The bemused look on Valda Setterfield's face as she is carried off on Chase Robinson's shoulder. And Meg Harper struggling to crawl through the fragment of space under Jeff Slayton's leg. *Tread* is not a string of gags. It is almost deadly for the dancers. Nonetheless, it is a highly amusing situation. It is curious that a piece like *Winterbranch*, whose movements are fundamentally simple, just seems to reek of disaster, while *Tread*, which is in reality a more dangerous work, can shine with a cheery disposition.

Like *RainForest*, *Place* (1966) leaves much to the imagination. However, while *RainForest* is essentially animal in effect, the implicit atmosphere of *Place* is more mechanical. Gordon Mumma's *Mesa*, which accompanies the dance, is as reminiscent of some surrealistic factory as *RainForest* is of the jungle. The sounds dig into the environment with the strength and determination of a buzz saw attacking a plank of wood.

Within this sonic context, the dance also takes on machine-like qualities. There are ensemble sections in which each dancer executes a periodic activity of different length, giving the overall appearance of some unworldly juggernaut constructed of human bodies. Furthermore, their faces are so expressionless that the effect is of a soulless, demonic machine—particularly when juxtaposed with Cunningham's contrastingly expressive solos. As in *Winterbranch*, where the feeling is also not explicit, there is a desperate sense of futility in *Place* which reaches a heartbreaking climax with Cunningham struggling within a plastic bag.

Once again, I was in a trance when *Second Hand* was all over. It is an unusual work for Cunningham in many respects. For instance, it was clearly choreographed to music; and this factor was so important that Cage was extremely careful to preserve the phrase structures of the intended accompaniment, *Socrate*, in his own *Cheap Imitation*. Also, the dance does not appear to be as seminal as other pieces. Rather than proceeding as a sequence of disjunct episodes, it appears to have a well-woven contrapuntal fabric which yields the sort of internal coherence one might expect from more classical works. Is not, then, *Second Hand* a reactionary phase within the context of Cunningham's innovations? I don't think so, because many of the ideas of these innovations are still being developed. Cunningham once wrote of one of his early solos: "The dance as performed seems to have an unmistakable dramatic intensity in its bones, so to speak. It seems to me that it is simply a question of allowing this quality to happen rather than of forcing it." Such is the case for *Second Hand*.

* * * *

Tonight *Walkaround Time* seemed to break down into three basic types of episodes. There were those sections which may be traced back to combinations from technique classes. There were the complex group constructions which have some of the same structural qualities as *Place*. Finally, there were the "walkaround" episodes which held the piece together.

In this respect, *Walkaround Time* was a dance about dancers. This was most evident during the intermission where the dancers were most free to be themselves. It was one of those exciting little "behind the scenes" glimpses of artists as they are "in real life." And the remarkable thing about *Walkaround Time* is that the Cunningham dancers were good about being natural when they were put on the spot in this manner.

Concerning the excerpts from technique classes—these were, of course, the building blocks of the entire dance. The work began, logically enough, with stillness; then it proceeded to the first set of exercises—a warmup, if you will. Finally, it progressed into the more complex constructions which we are inclined to call "real dance" (if there is such a thing). At the very end of the piece, the dancers went back to simply walking around and eventually sat down and came to rest.

The dance does go on "for nearly an hour" (the title of David Behrman's accompanying score), but a skillful articulation of the individual episodes does not make it seem overly long. The intermission is particularly valuable in this respect, and there is no real reason why the audience shouldn't be as free to "walk around" as are the dancers. After all, intermissions belong to everybody.

The music for *Scramble*—Toshi Ichiyanagi's *Activities for Orchestra*—had more of that sense of a continuum which I found lacking at the last performance; but the dance still seemed to have an isolated quality. That feeling of a pervading energy which drives the company—both individually and in groups—was missing. This may be due to a certain amount of fatigue on the part of the company. After all, every dancer has to perform every night. On the other hand, it may be due to fatigue on the part of the critic. It took tremendous exertion to devote my attention to *Scramble,* and then *Place* came along and walloped the hell out of me. All the sensations of a mechanistic nightmare were back again to haunt me.

This is one of the few pieces in which Cunningham really distinguishes himself from the rest of the company. He is a distinctly "different" figure who is either ignored by the rest of the company or treated with wild, abrupt movements. There are certain occasions when he tends to "blend" in with the rest, but they are very brief. He begins alone—surveying an empty landscape suspiciously and somewhat fearfully. He ends alone in a tormented struggle within a plastic bag which covers his entire body.

Unfortunately for the dancers, the biggest event in *How to Pass, Kick, Fall and Run* (1965) was John Cage's struggle to open his bottle of champagne. It took roughly half the duration of the piece, and the entire hall broke into a roar of applause when the cork finally popped out—soaring out over the orchestra pit.

Nevertheless, some very interesting things were happening on stage. Cunningham's part was being danced by Jeff Slayton and Carolyn Brown's by Susana Hayman-Chaffey. Slayton didn't have the intensity which is always inherent in Cunningham's appearance, but he was very capable. It's partly a matter of attitude. I don't think he can ever dance Cunningham's roles as if they were of his own making because they aren't. On the other hand, if he continues to perform the part for a while, it may take on a flavor distinctive to his own personality. Repeating the quotation by Cunningham: "It is simply a question of allowing this quality to happen rather than of forcing it." And that is very much a matter of time.

Carolyn Brown is notorious for enjoying herself on stage whenever she can, and *How to* certainly provides every occasion. On opening night, she pulled a beautiful manoeuvre with a long, sustained, flirtatious glance at David Vaughan between stories. Miss Hayman-Chaffey did not take such liberties with her part. She was obviously having a great deal of fun and emanated a very warm, good-humored nature; but it just wasn't Carolyn Brown's personality. Again, it is probably a matter of time. As she becomes more used to the part, she will begin to turn her own personality loose on it as Miss Brown has done over the last five years.

As far as the general atmosphere of the dance is concerned, John Cage tonight told one very appropriate story which deserves repeating:

> The Cunningham Company used to make transcontinental tours in a Volkswagen Microbus. Once, when we drove up to a gas station in Ohio and the dancers, as usual, all piled out to go to the toilets and exercise around the pumps, the station attendant asked me whether we were a group of comedians. I said, "No. We're from New York."

* * * *

Billed on the program as "Theatre Event," tonight's program consisted of *Canfield* in its entirety. As far as I was concerned, this was to be the ideal opportunity to test out the theories I had postulated in earlier notes. I can't say I was very successful. The performance of Pauline Oliveros's *In Memoriam: Nikola Tesla, Cosmic Engineer* certainly did not make it easy to watch this dance; and if you find my observations pretty skimpy for some eighty minutes' worth of theatre event, then you have only the musicians to blame. I have already mentioned that this piece has a tremendous command of the attention, between its use of conversation and the dramatic excitement of its explorations; and this large-scale version was so involved in filling the entire Brooklyn Academy of Music with sound that it was a significant distraction from the dance.

The problem is, unfortunately, that the piece worked so well over such a long period of time. It involved a series of sound experiments to determine resonating frequencies within the performing area. The added length of time provided opportunity for more experimentation and, consequently, for better results. Sure enough, I could feel my seat vibrating in the final moments of the work; and several people deserted their places to stand at a further distance from the loudspeakers.

All this did nothing to help *Canfield*. As is the case for most of Cunningham's choreography, the music served purely as landscape for the dance; but one must not let the landscape overwhelm the foreground. It would be like trying to do *As You Like It* in the Forest of Arden in the midst of a thick fog. I first found myself really watching *How to Pass, Kick, Fall and Run* when I saw excerpts of it in a gymnasium—without the distraction of Cage's stories. Now I find that during this piece I can divide my attention between Cunningham and Cage. I would like a similar crack at *Canfield*. I really think that if the piece were to be done in silence, it would be a revealing experience.

*   *   *   *

The last concert of the season presented those three works which made this season special—the two new works, *Tread* and *Second Hand*, and *Crises*, featuring guest artist Viola Farber. Now it is all over, and I have to go back to being a mathematician.

Crises was, for the last time, an experience of terror; but the terror was of a totally different nature from that of *Winterbranch* or *Place*. *Crises* is a much more personal experience. One can empathize with the character portrayed by Viola Farber far more easily than with any of the figures in either *Winterbranch* or *Place*.

I was relaxed during the final performance of *Second Hand*, determined to enjoy it; and I'm afraid that, technically, it was not as good as earlier performances. Cunningham got off to an unsteady start, and he seemed uncertain of himself for the remainder of the piece. I think that now that the season is over, the dancers deserve a well-needed rest; and I can start picking on these fine points when they are in better shape . . . if I have to.

Richard Kostelanetz

CUNNINGHAM'S SELF-BOOK (1969)

Among the more valuable traditions established in the late sixties was the practice of consequential vanguard artists creating imaginatively designed books primarily about their own work and esthetic position—not only Allan Kaprow and Claes Oldenberg, but Andy Warhol's *Index* (1967), Iain Baxter's *A Portfolio of Piles* (1968), Dick Higgins' *foew&ombwhnw* (1969), and John Cage's *Notations* (1969), among others. (The last book, by accepting within its own frame everything offered by selected other composers, is perhaps aesthetically more self-appropriate than Cage's two collections of essays, despite the patent compromise, in *Notations,* of such an unenhancing convention as presenting the contributions in alphabetical order.) Merce Cunningham's *Changes: Notes on Choreography* (1969) resembles its predecessors in the crucial aspect of being as much *like* as about Cunningham's dance.

The inside front cover has overlapping lines of crossing type on top of a photograph, a form reminiscent of the beams of light passing over dancers in *Winterbranch* (1964); a page in the middle has a column of type running down the center, superimposed over both a photograph and the program of *Variations V* (1965), very much like the disconnected simultaneity of the piece itself; and the structure of the entire book is as concentrated in discrete detail (the page) but as plotless and non-climactic in overall form as Cunningham's choreography. While materials relevant to a particular piece are generally grouped together, the fragments are not presented in chronological order, the author avoiding one compromise of convenience; and need one say that this is not the sort of self-book that either George Balanchine or Martha Graham would publish.

Just as Cunningham's *Walkaround Time* (1968) freely mixes movement, sound, stillness, and lights and decor, so *Changes* mixes with similar freedom shrewdly chosen photographs, reproductions of performance programs and handwritten notes, rough sketches and diagrams, neatly typed remarks that were apparently transcribed recently (on the same multiple-font machine that Cage favors); letters written to friends, scribbled replies to a questionnaire, aesthetic declarations, etc., etc. ("Dancing has a continuity of its own that need not be dependent on either the rise or fall of sound, or the pitch and cry of words. Its force of feeling lies in the physical image, fleeting or static.") Contained within this unpaginated potpourri are also some edifying descriptions of how chance procedures can be adapted to the gamut of choreographic variables.

In general, the pieces strike this nondancer (but sometime football player) as thoughtfully and thoroughly planned, even in their allowances for various degrees and kinds of indeterminacy (as in professional football—one hears, Cunningham's favorite spectator sport). Only an artist as unpretentious, unevasive, and succinct in his prose as Cunningham would admit, on one hand, that a 1944 dance, *Root of an Unfocus*, "was concerned with fear," or that in a more recent aleatory work "I find No. 9 and No. 10 were not used, did not come up as possibilities; and upon examining them carefully, I am relieved they did not." (The obvious point lost in the shuffling discussion is that while chance methods have the virtue of producing results beyond the conventions of premeditated choreography, not everything aleatory would be equally successful.)

"Dancing is movement in time and space," he announces early in *Changes*, and a book, by analogy, is filled pages between the frame of covers. Populating this canvas is the achievement of the writer and designer Frances Starr, who brilliantly adapted Cunningham's compositonal syntax to the bookish medium (that, need one add, more desperately requires stylistic resuscitation than, say, the ballet). It is true that texts printed upside-down provide a bit of a nuisance, while in the middle of the book is reproduced a program whose year-date is perversely blocked out or omitted despite Cunningham's handwritten inscription, "I date my beginnings from this concert." Nonetheless, scattered between the covers is much genuine information and explanation unavailable elsewhere.

This book-composition is also a highly contemporary way for an artist-still-in-progress to forge a permanent but incomplete record of his own career. However, since this volume eschews an explanatory preface or recapitulatory afterword, the reader is left the task of interpreting significances from the evidence presented. He who does not comprehend Cunningham's choreographic imagination is not likely to understand this book, for *Changes* demands the sort of perceptual procedures honed on Cunningham's dance, not to speak of Cage's music and perhaps William Burroughs's fictions, too.

For these reasons, though almost every Cunningham work is displayed, the book simply cannot serve as an effective introduction for those millions who have heard (or read) but not seen—perhaps nothing performs this initiating role as successfully as Calvin Tomkins's chapters in the paperback edition of *The Bride and the Bachelors* (1968)—and *Changes* has considerably less academic information than the Cunningham issue of *Dance Perspectives 34* (Summer 1968), while the intrinsically justifiable lack of page numbers (and thus of an index) in *Changes* makes information-retrieval a bit arduous.

This book was first announced as a collection of the essays on dance matters that Cunningham has published over the years; and as someone who has gone to considerable effort to ferret several of them out of obscure and defunct journals, I was anticipating a more convenient form of storage. However, as much as those essays are too valuable to lie forgotten, here is a different book entirely, less a guide to individual Cunningham ideas or dances than a key to his characteristic imagination; and, as an artist's bookish essay on his own endeavors, *Changes* is a masterpiece of its particular kind.

P.S. On second thought, perhaps Cunningham's willingness to use the convention of bound, evenly cut, equi-sized pages parallels his current commitment to a permanent company; for both are archaic conventions that, in our times, are likely to induce historically conservative, if not esthetically constrained procedures. This observation inspires conjecture over what kind of book-about-himself a post-Cunningham dancer might want to produce—say, Yvonne Rainer, Meredith Monk, or Kenneth King?

Jack Anderson

DANCES ABOUT EVERYTHING AND DANCES ABOUT SOME THINGS (1976)

M erce Cunningham has often been a problem. His nonliteral choreography has been a problem. His treatment of music and decor has been a
problem. His utilization of chance has been a problem.

The latest problem Cunningham has posed for dancergoers is that of the
Theater Event. Events, as Cunningham uses the term, consist of sections of
previously choreographed dances (and, occasionally, of new dances still in
rehearsal) performed not as a suite of detachable items, as they would be in a
divertissement, but rearranged so that they form a self-sufficient entity. These
Events—lasting about an hour and a half, without intermission—employ
musical scores and costumes different from those associated with the discrete
pieces from which the movements derive; and, given the extent of the Cunningham repertoire and the almost infinite number of ways sections from it
may be rearranged, it is likely that no two Events will ever by exactly the same.
As for their intended effect, Cunningham claims that Events "allow for, not so
much an evening of dances, as the experience of dance."

James Klosty's book *Merce Cunningham* indicates that Cunningham has
grown increasingly fond of Events. Certainly, in recent years, his company has
presented almost nothing but Events in the New York area. The first Event
ever took place in 1964 in Vienna; the first I encountered was #25 at Brooklyn
College in December 1971. A recent Event I attended at the Cunningham
studio—in December 1975, only four years later than my first—was #151.

These figures and dates in themselves attest to Cunningham's interest in Events.

One's first Event, if bewildering, may also be fun. It's a lark—"something different." But as Event follows Event, bewilderment may turn to dismay as it dawns upon one that Events, far from being regarded as mere novelties, have been legitimized as major endeavors by the Cunningham company. Moreover, they raise fearful questions, not only about the nature of Cunningham's art, but about art in general. The kinds of questions they invite are those implicit in the shocked exclamation of a friend a few years ago after attending some Cunningham Events: "He's dismantling his repertoire!"

As is often true of developments in the performing arts, Cunningham's current predilections may involve practicality as well as pure esthetics. By mixing older works together, Cunningham may keep much of his repertoire active. Simultaneously, he can try out new composers and designers. The flexibility of the Event format makes it possible to adapt his choreography to each fresh performing situation he encounters: Events fit easily into studios, gyms, museums, and lofts, as well as into conventional theaters. Yet, ultimately, these are Cunningham's concerns, not those of the audience. Audiences always want a "good show." If a certain performance procedure cannot produce one, then it should be scrapped, no matter how otherwise practical it is. Thus, we are led from practical to esthetic difficulties. And, to some dancegoers, they seem enormous.

Still, Events should not have prompted quite the amount of shocked surprise that they did, since they can be interpreted as logical outgrowths of basic Cunningham theories. Cunningham has always been fascinated by fluid performing situations, by live theater as something inherently unfixed. In dance of any kind, even when choreography is scrupulously set, no two performances will ever be exactly the same because of the cast's differing physical and mental conditions at each of those performances. To go to the theater is always chancy. Cunningham has long capitalized upon theater's uncertainties. For instance, he has created dances consisting of several parts which can be performed in any number of possible orders. Similarly, the music and decor for his pieces occupy the same space and time as the dance but usually do not imitate or logically relate to anything in the choreography—a practice which makes Cunningham simultaneously a Diaghilevian and a non-Diaghilevian choreographer: Diaghilevian because he commissions composers and painters, non-Diaghilevian because he makes no effort to have all parts of a production lock tightly together like pieces of a jigsaw puzzle. Once the parts of a single piece are regarded as potentially interchangeable, one is only a short step of the imagination away from thinking that all parts of all one's pieces are similarly interchangeable, and when that step is taken the Event is born. But some audiences may wonder whether that step ought to be taken. Has Cunningham this time really gone too far?

Unquestionably, the Events intimidate. To begin with, there is often nothing—or very little—that one can say about them. We are such verbal creatures that not being able to come up with a well-organized verbal assessment of our perceptions can be frustrating. No wonder a few critics are particularly annoyed by Events, for critics are by necessity the most verbal dancegoers of all. But what is there to say about an Event?

Well, one could try to describe it. Most Events are open in form, but some exhibit simple structural characteristics which may be noted. Thus, one recent Event was, whether by forethought or happenstance, constructed according to a pattern which Louis Horst, after gnashing his teeth, might have classified as extended ABAB or rondo form: a group section was followed by a solo which was followed by another group, and so on. One could continue trying to say something about an Event by recording in exact detail each action as it occurred. If one possessed the necessary skills, one could even notate it.

But what really would be accomplished by that? For there might still exist an inexplicable gap between the actions themselves and one's responses of delight, horror, or befuddlement. At least, Cunningham's individual dance works, though abstract, do seem to be "about" something, because each establishes an atmosphere or emphasizes some quality of movement so that, say, *Summerspace* (1958) looks genuinely distinct from *Winterbranch* (1964). The Events, however, remain impregnable. There they are: great hunks of theater, seemingly unapproachable.

There is, though, at least one way of regarding Events which can make them less forbidding, a point of view emanating from the philosophy which produced them in the first place. Cunningham, John Cage, and other artists in their circle regard art as an imitation of nature—but not in any literal sense, for that might result in nothing more than a superfluous replication of objects. Rather, they wish to imitate nature in its manner of operation. For them, the universe is Heraclitean, forever open to metamorphoses. Events, then, are attempts to reproduce in miniature the workings of the universe. In Events things happen and are transformed into other things happening, images are born and disintegrate and reshape themselves into other images. Everything has its own form, yet form is always subject to modification. Frequently, even when the choreography is vigorous, Events somehow possess an overall feeling of imperturbability or even serenity. They resemble such phenomena as the running of rivers, the formation of crystals, the orbits of planets, or the flow of traffic through the streets: they partake of some process which can be related to the basic processes of earthly existence. The "experience of dance" which Cunningham says he desires Events to provide is thus very much like the experience of life itself.

Even the length of Events is significant. Ninety minutes, uninterrupted, is a sizable chunk of choreographic time. It is long enough to seem an eternity. It is also long enough to prevent one from thinking in terms of beginning, middle, and end, as those terms apply to Aristotelian tragedy or French boulevard farce. Like the universe, Events have some sort of beginning and, as scientists say the universe will, in due course they come to an end. Otherwise, they are all middle—which is how we usually perceive life: life is something we are in the midst of. And just as choreographic incidents melt away and are succeeded by others, so individual lives die while life itself continues. Cunningham has managed to capture the processes of the universe in artworks which are models of that universe and at the same time objects subject to that universe's principles of change. He has created an art which is abstract, yet absolutely realistic.

Viewing Events this way allows one problem Eventgoers often fret about to be put in its proper perspective: namely, must one be able to recognize the original dances from which the movements in Events derive? Certain passages are easy to identify if one knows the Cunningham repertoire: a trio in which one dancer carries a stick comes from *Signals* (1970), as does a set of finger games; a swaying solo is out of *Second Hand* (1970); when Cunningham inches about on little cat feet that's the solo called *Solo* (1975), when his hands flutter like crazy that's *Loops* (1971), and when the dancers start falling and dragging each other about, that just has to be *Winterbranch* (1964). Being able to trace these episodes to their sources can be instructive, for one starts to realize how movements which have a certain character in one context may assume a totally different character in a new context, the most striking example being the movements which look so horrific in *Winterbranch* and which can also seem tame or gamelike in some of the Events.

Sometimes, however, I am unable to identify the sources of the movements I watch, even though the program note tells me that they come from pieces I have seen before. But perhaps that is nothing to worry about. Perhaps too great a fuss is made about the sources of the Events, whereas one's real attention should be focused not upon where the movement comes from but upon how it looks right now. It might be useful to compare Events with streets: if one knows the neighborhood, one can enjoy noticing that there goes Mr. Smith or Mrs. Jones, or that the corner store has a new window display. But if one is a stranger to the neighborhood, one may still find its buildings and people interesting to watch. Similarly, knowing the sources of an Event can come in handy, but not knowing them need not blunt one's enjoyment.

Nevertheless, the relationship of whole pieces to Events does prompt another worry, one less metaphysical in nature. The movements which comprise Events have to come from somewhere, and they usually come from previous Cunningham dances. Cunningham's preoccupation with Events can make one fear that any new dances he choreographs may not be terribly interesting as entities in themselves; they may only be repositories of steps he can later incorporate into Events. Such fears are probably groundless. In

Princeton last January, the Cunningham company offered its first repertory performances in the New York area in a long time. The programs contained two local premieres and a world premiere. Each piece was distinct in mood, each had its own recognizable personality. Judging from the Princeton performances, it does not seem as though Events are leading Cunningham to choreograph inferior dances.

Comparisons with city streets or natural forces suggest that Events might be called, in a sense, dances about everything, while most conventional dances, like most artworks of any kind, concern some specific thing: some idea, story, or emotion, as in narrative dance; or some particular way of arranging steps in space and time, as in abstract ballet. Artworks, as we usually conceive them, allow us not only to focus our attention upon something, they also, through their very finitude, provide opportunities for breaks of attention—breaks provided, for example, by the pauses which usually separate dances in the theater. The fluidity of Events prevents them from having this quality of focus which is ordinarily so important to art and which is one reason I hope Cunningham will never totally abandon programs of clearly separate dance works.

By their very sprawl, though, Events are reminders of the importance of paying attention and staying mentally awake. Just as we cannot truly savor the objects we pass while walking down the street unless we really pay attention to them, so we cannot enjoy Events unless we carefully observe everything which happens in them. No wonder they can be exhausting to watch. Curiously, one may need to pay more attention to Events than to individual pieces. The reverse would initially seem to be true: theoretically, because Events are so long one should be able to let them wash across one's consciousness, whereas the brevity of pieces should require intense concentration. In actuality, it is the Events, not the pieces, which usually require the greater concentration. The pieces may soon declare what sorts of things they are about, while the Events, simply because they are potentially about everything, must be scrutinized for new revelations at every moment.

In his separate pieces, Cunningham has tried to get us to look at things as they are. Now, through his Events, he wants us to look at everything at every instant. The task he has set us is far from easy. And rebelling against him on occasion are both our love of sloth and our love of art. For there are occasions when we do not want or need to look at everything but at one particular thing only. These are the occasions when we desire whole individual works, not Events. Yet having sharpened our eyes by looking at Events, we may, in turn, be better able to see the individual works. Similarly, by paying attention to Events, we realize that they, like all things around us, consist of one particular thing after another. Everything is but the sum total of some things.

By maintaining both pieces and Events in his repertoire, then, Cunningham has established a dialogue between everything and something. He not only provides us with different kinds of things to see, he reminds us that the same things may be seen in different ways. The pieces isolate and frame, the Events are all-inclusive. If we want to, if we need to, we can even put up our own frames of attention around the action in Events. Cunningham probably won't object: he gives us the freedom to make up our minds.

Carolyn Brown, Douglas Dunn, Viola Farber, Steve Paxton, Marianne Preger Simon, Valda Setterfield, Gus Solomons jr, David Vaughan

CUNNINGHAM AND HIS DANCERS (1987)

DAVID VAUGHAN: When Merce Cunningham was in his prime as a dancer, how did he work with his dancers in terms of communicating the choreographic material that made the early pieces? And as the advancing years have brought on physical limitations, how have his working methods changed—or have they? How has his choreography changed—or has it? Marianne Preger Simon was in the original company from 1953 to 1959. What can you tell us?

MARIANNE SIMON: My memory is that he gave us pieces to do for the middle of the class when there was dancing to be done, and they were usually portions of dances that he was demonstrating. That was how we learned some of them. Others he would demonstrate for us individually and teach us step by step.

VIOLA FARBER: When I first joined the Cunningham company—

VAUGHAN: Viola was in it from 1953 to 1965 and returned briefly as a guest artist in 1970.

FARBER:—Merce was working on two dances, and I don't think I knew that they had names. I never knew which dance we were learning parts of. When the point came that he said, "Let's do *Septet* (1953)," I thought, "Which steps are those?" I don't know if anyone else had that experience or if I was particularly stupid, but I do remember that. I'd no idea which dance we were working on, because we learned steps.

101

VAUGHAN: But at that time, of course, he was working on quite a large repertory, wasn't he, for the first performances of what became the Cunningham company?

FARBER: Yes. He was working on two dances.

VAUGHAN: Oh, just two? Do you remember what the other one was? I should point out that Marianne, Viola, and Carolyn Brown were the original female cast of *Septet,* being revived for the first time since 1964 by the company.

FARBER: We were working in the 8th Street studio—I can't remember what the other piece was.

VAUGHAN: Carolyn, do you? Carolyn gets the prize for longevity, having been in the company from 1952 to 1972.

CAROLYN BROWN: He started *Septet* before we went to Black Mountain [College]. I think we were probably doing the chance piece, the four-part chance piece?

VAUGHAN: Yes, *Suite by Chance* (1953). I think one of the things that's going to surprise people when they see *Septet* is the fact that it is a dance that is done to the music. You didn't learn *Septet* to the music, did you? Because *Suite by Chance* was obviously not learned to music.

FARBER: No, I would have remembered the music part very definitely.

VAUGHAN: So the music was added afterwards, as it is now?

FARBER: Well, Merce must have known what he was doing to what [music]. But we didn't rehearse to the music, because the music was performed live. I don't think we had a tape to it. If John [Cage] and David Tudor came to play—or just David, who could play four hands with two hands—if they weren't there, I don't think we rehearsed it to music.

BROWN: No, not in the beginning. He was experimenting just with movement. But at Black Mountain we rehearsed with David playing both piano parts or with a record of the Satie music whenever David was unable to rehearse with us.

VAUGHAN: Working on material in class, then, seems to be something that happened then and is still done, I think.

GUS SOLOMONS: Probably. I remember learning phrases—dance phrases—in class, but I really have very little recollection of how we learned solo parts and other things. I guess Merce demonstrated them and then right away *extracted* from us individually what he wanted to see. In other words, he would give us an indication of the movement—"This is a hip circle here"—and then he would watch us do it and say how it was wrong and how he wanted it to be done. For me, the process was almost invisible.

VAUGHAN: Yes, it is probably hard to say afterwards how it happened. Gus, of course, was in the company from 1965 to 1968. Before we leave this question of class material, though, is it true that the material was more *squarely* presented in class? Did he then fix it, play around with it?

FARBER: It wasn't so squarely presented in class, as I recall.

SIMON: I agree.

VAUGHAN: I meant *rhythmically* square.

FARBER: That's what *I* mean as well.

VALDA SETTERFIELD: About the solo material: My memory of it particularly with my *Walkaround Time* (1968) solo and also *Changing Steps* (1975), is that Merce didn't show me *anything*. In fact, for my *Walkaround Time* solo, he sat in a chair the whole time and said, "Can you do this? Can you try that? And maybe a little of this, and the other?" It was quite marvelous because I never saw it on anybody else's body—which, no matter how objective you can be, colors your sensibility about it.

VAUGHAN: Valda first danced with the company in 1961 as a sort of apprentice—well, no, you were in the original cast of *Aeon* in 1961—and then was a member from 1965 to 1975. Did Merce work the way she has described with anybody else on the *Changing Steps* solos?

DOUGLAS DUNN: Yes, he hardly showed me anything, either, about the *Changing Steps* solo, and he made me do one thing over and over and over again which I couldn't possibly ever understand. I don't understand to this day what he was asking me to do, but I finally did something that I guess he found okay to leave with me. It's interesting that now someone else does this part. I saw it once and it was . . . I think he had the same take. I guess he got it off the videotape. But I want to tell my own feeling about learning material from Merce. When I joined the company—

VAUGHAN: Doug was in it from 1969 to 1973.

DUNN:—Merce was making two pieces, *Second Hand* and *Tread* (both 1970). I could tell the difference between them because one obviously drove him up the wall, and he was having a good time with the other. The one that drove him up the wall was *Second Hand:* he was trying to make this dance to counts which were coming out of Erik Satie's *Socrate*. Again, he was not playing the music in rehearsal, but he had all the notes in his head, and he was trying to be very precise.

In *Tread*, though, he was being very fast and loose. And in that period, when I was first in the studio to learn these things, Merce was *showing* all material—he wasn't talking any of this material, he was showing it all. I remember standing there, and he was about to show me a phrase. I said to myself, "Now Douglas, watch which foot it is, watch what he does, just watch, watch." And then he would go across the floor, and he would be *here* and then he would be *there*, and I realized that I hadn't seen a single thing that I could take in as mechanics for doing it.

This was some of the most beautiful dancing that I had ever seen and I have no idea if he was making it up on the spot, or whether he had prepared it that morning, or a year ago, or whatever! I have *no* idea. Somehow he got across there in a way that was very exciting and very articulate, but not in a way that I could take in for what I wanted to do. I realized I had a real problem.

VAUGHAN: To say the least! *Changing Steps* was a piece that Merce made shortly after Carolyn left the company in 1972. She was the last surviving member of the original group and had been with the company a very long time, so it really meant a great change in the company when she left. Merce has said of *Changing Steps* that he wanted a piece in which each of the dancers in the company would have a solo, because he had always thought of them as soloists, and he wanted to show them as soloists. So that dance was made particularly on the individual qualities of the dancers concerned.

That leads me to another general question. Merce has an important characteristic that not all choreographers have. Perhaps you could say that choreographers are divided into two kinds—the kind that take material or qualities from the dancers they are working with, and those that come in with an idea that they impose on the dancers, no matter what. Well, Merce has always seen the individual qualities of dancers, and it may be interesting to ask how this fits in with his idea of a chance process, because he does work out the chance process *before* he comes into the studio. So how does that work? Can anybody give us an idea of how those two things relate?

STEVE PAXTON: Chance process can be applied to lots of different elements in making a dance. It seems to me that what he was usually working with was space and direction and abstracts like that, not qualities. I don't know how you would even *name* all the qualities in order to subject them to a chance procedure. So are those two ideas in conflict at all, really?

VAUGHAN: It's not just a question of quality though. It is a question of the actual movement, or the quality as it is *expressed* in the way the dancer moves.

PAXTON: Do you mean as *opposed* to the chance procedure or *linked* to the chance procedure?

VAUGHAN: Either one.

PAXTON: It seems to me that there were dances where he was focused on certain people—or *parts* of dances where he was focused on people—for their qualities. But that was unlinked to the chance procedures. For instance, if Merce was working with Viola's quality in an area of a dance and I was in that part, I was then supposed to deal with her quality somehow. Is that what you mean by him working with qualities of different dancers?

VAUGHAN: Yes, that could be.

SETTERFIELD: I think Merce is the only person who can answer this question.

FARBER: And he wouldn't answer.

SETTERFIELD: Yes, exactly. He simply wouldn't.

SOLOMONS: I think it is a combination of all the above.

PAXTON: The thing that surprised me the most about working in the company when I started—

VAUGHAN: In 1961; and Steve was a member until 1964.

PAXTON:—was that we didn't all sit around and throw coins. I had expected that we would all do that, and what we *did* was come and learn steps.

BROWN: Isn't it possible that the idea of accident (which was what [Robert] Rauschenberg used so much—accepting accident in his work) was what we dancers brought to the work? Chance now defined as accident? I mean, Merce didn't know all of us. He knew me all too well at the end, but he didn't really know us as he began to work with each of us. So when each new dancer would arrive in the company, that's where his focus would go, because that was new material and exciting for *him*. By that time, he already knew about the rest of us, so it was always the newest member of the company who stimulated his interest, and the rest of us would say, "Oh, gee, I wish I got that kind of attention." Steve, did that happen to you? Did you have that feeling?

PAXTON: Well, if you didn't know where Merce normally focused and you came into the company, you wouldn't notice, perhaps that he was focused on you. At a certain point he made *Winterbranch* (1964), which was partly made on me, but then I had hardly anything to do in it when it was performed. I think in the realms of working with chance, the possibilities are really quite broad. To think it is just the *I Ching* procedure or dice is really to oversimplify it. He had a lot of ways of tapping chaos or of working with indeterminacy; there were a lot of different levels, right down to the space of the stage.

One of the major things that affected the company was the size and shape of the stage that we performed on. If Merce was making something in a twenty-five-by-thirty-five-foot studio, and he went to a place where a semicircular stage was fourteen feet deep and twenty-eight feet wide, how did that affect the piece? How were the dancers able, for instance, to do *Aeon* at UCLA and to do it in the proper time with a minimum of rehearsal? It seems to me that chance has a part to play in that. It took real savvy and organizational capacity on the part of the whole company to do the dance there.

SETTERFIELD: *Practical* chance.

PAXTON: Yeah, yeah.

SETTERFIELD: You speak of chaos. Sometimes he produced a kind of *willed* chaos, and then as the dance was performed more and more frequently, he saw things that he found *too* chaotic perhaps, and he would draw in the parameters of possibility. It is my impression that if, for one reason or another, he didn't like what was there, he used his savvy, as Steve said, to make something conform more to what he wanted to have happen.

SOLOMONS: I remember that he threw away almost nothing. He didn't try things and then throw them away; everything he tried became part of the work. I sometimes wondered how he knew that something was going to work and where all the mistakes went. He didn't like to change things, either; he would try to make them evolve, because of his philosophy that everything was acceptable. He didn't want to reject anything. He would twist it into shape in some way, in some evolutionary way.

VAUGHAN: But this was *before* the dance was performed?

SOLOMONS: Sometimes before and sometimes after, depending on how it looked.

SETTERFIELD: I think, conversely, that sometimes in places where he desired chaos—perhaps we had gotten too comfortable with a passage—he would revert to timing it again, and usually we had slipped and made it slow. By taking it back to its original tempo, the chaos was restored, which made him happy. I think he did exactly what you say—he did both of those things.

BROWN: Perhaps Viola is also talking about two rare occurrences when he *did* use a lot of indeterminacy. One was in *Story* (1963) and the other was in *Field Dances* (1963). We had *so* much freedom in *Story* in terms of timing—or at least we thought we did—that perhaps he thought we were taking advantage of him in certain performances. I remember one situation in which we each had our own phrase to do—it was the "object" phrase—and one of our members stayed out there too long, and he didn't like it at all. He picked her up bodily and walked her off the stage. Because there were certain things that were extremely important to him—especially timing. Timing as part of the total structure of the piece. He has an extraordinary sense of timing and theatrical showmanship.

Another story about *Story*—Steve, can I tell about Cologne? You're *it* for this one. There're lots of stories to tell. In fact, I think Merce is writing a book based on his *Story* journal. We performed the dance all over the world in the 1964 tour. In each place, Robert Rauschenberg made a new set for it, and we rehearsed only the *elements* of the piece, the gamut of possibilities—our steps. And in Cologne—which was somehow a very dark time for Merce on that tour—we needed to be rehearsed, so he asked us to do our slow phrase, as slowly as we could. He went around the room, one by one, and it came time for Steve to do *his* slow phrase. Steve took Merce's instructions very literally, so that a half-hour later, Steve was *still* doing his slow phrase. The rest of us were out in the hallway, saying "Wow, how long is this going to go on?" But Merce had simply taken out his notebook and was looking at his notes, and Steve just kept doing his slow phrase. It was terrific! And Merce was still looking at his notes.

FARBER: Carolyn, that was Tokyo.

BROWN: Tokyo? I remember it in Cologne too.

FARBER: You did it *twice*, Steve?

PAXTON: I did it as slowly as I could. I remember it in Tokyo, too, but that was partly because I had been sick since Warsaw and was still ill in Tokyo. This was four or five months later on the tour—

FARBER: It was the sixth month.

PAXTON:—and at that point, I'm just glad he didn't say "Do it as fast as you can," because probably it still would have taken a half an hour.

DUNN: I was very struck when I was in the company by the intense rigor

of the work, the understanding Merce had of the material and the detail—
"rigor" is the word I like. At the same time, he was open on various levels at
different times and in different situations, to accidents and surprises.

The example that is most personal for me was when we were in a huge
gymnasium space somewhere in New England. It was a basketball court, only
bigger, and it had bleachers going up both sides—huge! Vast! It must have
held two thousand or three thousand people. And there were about twenty
people in the audience! We were doing a piece—I don't remember which
one—in which I have a run, a big semicircular run, and it was a vast space. We
were all struggling to cover this space and make the dance as big as we could
to fill the space. I took off to do this run, and right in the middle of it, I slipped
and fell, which was totally wrong—it couldn't have *been* more wrong! But
somehow, the way I fell, I was able to just roll and get right up and continue
running. I was terribly embarrassed. This was the third mistake I had made in
a piece in my career at that time, and I was humiliated: this was the worst thing
that could have happened to me.

I looked up and Merce was smiling, having seen it, and I realized he dug
it. He absolutely loved it. It didn't ruin the piece for him, it didn't cause him to
feel that it was out of control. It was beautiful. It fit right in.

SIMON: I don't remember anything ever being changed, or Merce saying
"That didn't look good" and then changing it to something else. I just
remember that whatever there was, we did it, as close to the speed and counts
as he gave it to us. But I don't remember him ever eliminating something
because he didn't think it worked.

FARBER: I *do* remember being taught things and attempting to do them,
and obviously Merce didn't like how I did them, so he said "Let's drop that."

SIMON: Well, that's because he asked you to do impossible things.

VAUGHAN: What about the repetition part of the rehearsal process? It must
really surprise people to see unison passages in a Cunningham work. The
unison is so close and everything always comes out together, and yet the
dancers don't have any music to hang on to. If you watch Merce rehearse, it
always seems to be a very quiet process. Merce sits there, and the stopwatch
is ticking away, and the dancers do the piece, and there is very little comment.
But somehow out of this comes an extraordinary unity. I think this has always
been the case, even if it is true that there is more unison now than there was.
Does anyone want to throw some light on this issue?

SETTERFIELD: The rhythms were always so incredibly strong. The audience
may not have heard anything, but the rhythms were pounding in our blood.

FARBER: I remember that sometimes rehearsals were very unnerving.
Merce would sit and look at his stopwatch, and the only thing he would say
when we had finished a dance was "You're a minute too slow." Sometimes we
had done other things that could be corrected, and when we were in good
shape, we corrected each other in the actual dancing—the shape of what we

were doing. But there were many times when it was just the time that was corrected.

PAXTON: In my era, one of the things he said relative to that was "If you want to get the time right, make every detail clearer," and that seemed to work. We would be able to shave fifteen seconds off a two-or-three-minute phrase that we had been slagging in a little just by sharpening up very small units inside the phrase—a tenth of a second here, a tenth of a second there—and finally getting it right.

As for the unison: I fell for this company in the first year I saw it because of *Rune* (1959), which had some amazing unison work in it, and it was done to music that didn't go with the steps. It was extraordinary in its power. At that point I was trying to understand the philosophy of Merce's work. It seemed to be based in Zen and it seemed to be dealing with chance—that's what was always put forth. And yet here was dancing in unison! Then I thought, "Wait a minute, indeterminacy has to manifest itself somehow. You can't see indeterminacy, except maybe in your mind. You can envision something which is ultimately chaotic, but in terms of actual manifestation in a human way, it has to be organized somehow. This is another manifestation of the possibilities."

There's a new theory about chaos. They say in fluidics that if you have a very clear pattern that becomes chaotic, a more recognizable pattern will emerge again underneath that chaos if you watch it long enough. There are organizing principles which we don't understand yet. The idea of chaos as it is regularly understood doesn't include the full range of its potential. It just sounds like a lot of blather happening—that's the way we use the word "chaos." But rigorously applied, it is actually a far more structured phenomenon.

BROWN: There is a big difference between the works that were choreographed by using chance procedures and the very few that were indeterminate in actual performance. The chance works were made precisely, with exact time, exact space, exact steps, and we were expected to do them precisely. There were very few indeterminate works. Although there are dances that have bits of indeterminacy in them, *Story* and *Field Dances* were really the only indeterminate works.

As to *Rune*, I think one of the reasons that we were able to do that unison material together was because in those days, at Connecticut College, we never worked with a mirror. We worked in a room in the music building that was more like a little library. There was no mirror, so we had to sense each other, we had to feel each other, we had to hear the beat in the floor, and we had to do the phrases over and over.

But, mind you, David said that rehearsals took place in silence. Not at all! When Merce was snapping fingers and clapping hands, it was noisy, and he was often talking too. It was only in the later rehearsals that it was quiet—

when he was *not* snapping fingers. So we had a real sense of that rhythm, and as Viola and Valda have said many times, the rhythm is *extraordinary*, and extraordinarily complex. It had to get into the whole body. We had to breathe together.

VAUGHAN: Do the dancers *count* very much in Merce's work? I think people have the idea that the dancers must all be counting like mad because the music doesn't help them, but would you tell us?

BROWN: In the beginning, when he gives you the phrase, he sometimes counts it, he sometimes does *not* count it—it's not always the same. Sometimes he says, "If I count for you, it will throw it off." He wants it . . . more subtle, more organic, and you just have to figure it out. Sometimes it changes on our bodies—something else happens because of the way we are built, and he accepts that. *That* is the area of accident—not chance, but accident, so important to Rauschenberg's work, is absorbed into Merce's work. *We're* the accidents.

FARBER: Earlier I was saying that things were sort of pulled back sometimes. I think that happened in the indeterminate pieces. For instance, there was a duet we did which was terrifying because we had sections to do but it was not decided beforehand *what* we did *when*. Rather, we gave each other cues for each section to do as the dance went along. It was perhaps *too* exciting. So Merce made it a little more set.

About unison: In *Rune*, the dance Carolyn talked about, which is an *extraordinarily magnificent* dance, there was a section where the whole company had to take a cue from someone (who shall be nameless!) who was behind us, and who danced very lively and lightly, so there was no pounding of feet. And we learned to do it. Somehow we learned to feel what was going on behind us. So I think we developed sensibilities that are quite nice to have. They were maddening, sometimes, to try to develop.

VAUGHAN: Viola, didn't Merce actually give you a dance image once?

FARBER: There's this idea of Merce being very abstract—there's *chance*, and it's *set*, and you *do* this movement, and it has nothing to do with anything but itself. Well, there was a dance called *Nocturnes* (1956) which was done to music of Satie, and in the last part of it there was an entrance. Once—not in rehearsal but in some kind of social situation—Merce talked about that entrance and said "I think of that being like branches waving in the wind."

VAUGHAN: Just recently he taught Rob Remley a solo that he had done in *Suite for Five* (1956) and told him that he had to be like an animal watching out of the undergrowth, which was such a concrete image. Rob was very surprised. But was it in fact as rare as that, that he would give you that kind of an image?

FARBER: As I remember, yes.

SETTERFIELD: I remember there being images, but they were always from nature, as the two of you cited. The only one he ever gave me was during the first time I performed with the Cunningham company—actually, I was doing a part of Viola's. Viola was injured. I had not been in America very long, nor had I worked with Merce very long. I was not informed if I was really going to do the part or if I should learn it, so I hovered around in the back, trying to figure out what to do. Carolyn said to Merce, "Why don't you help her?" He said (she told me later), "I want to see what she'll do with it."

So we went out on the road. We were in a terrible theater where the back curtain didn't come down to the stage floor, and you could see all the crossovers—bare feet going back and forth—and just before I went on, Merce said to me, "This, my dear, is an entrance worthy of Edith Evans. *Take* it." That was actually quite marvelous, because it was something that I absolutely understood, and he plugged into that.

DUNN: Merce often said something about "getting out of the way of the movement." To me there was never any question but that Merce was full of *all* these images and all this feeling about movement. But he did, I feel, restrain himself in general from making comments or suggesting images to the dancers about what he or she was doing, because he wanted most of all to have this directness, this simplicity. Deborah Jowitt used the image of the puppet, not to imply that the dancing is mechanical, but just that the plainness, the simplicity, the directness of movement as such, comes across without the dancer inflecting it greatly.

Merce once said that if the dancer has an idea about the work, something starts to happen, which is not necessarily so good for the dancer. A very interesting aspect of his work is that he gets so much from dancers by leaving them alone in a way that other choreographers do not, so I feel I get glimpses of the dancers themselves inhabiting, in a sense, Merce's world. Because the dancers are *themselves*, to a large extent, they are not becoming characters, and they are not making themselves up if they can help it. In a way you get *more* of the dancers, and that to me is what makes Merce's work go toward life and not completely off into his own fantasy world.

SIMON: I remember that in the very early pieces like *Minutiae* (1954) and *Springweather* (1955) we used to make up endless stories about what we were doing because it was so new for us. Sometimes we would tell him, and he would sort of smile enigmatically, you know. I remember feeling that it was very necessary to have something to hang on to, because it was so new.

BROWN: For the revival of *Septet* (1953), does the program list the sections' names?

VAUGHAN: No, he left those out.

BROWN: It's a very interesting ballet—something akin to Balanchine's *Apollo*, I think. And *Septet* has a very definite story. The section with three couples was called "In the Morgue;" it was about death. Another section is called "In the Music Hall"; another, "In the Tea House." Even when he was thinking about this dance, he had ideas about using candelabras for "In the

Morgue," and ideas of a set for "In the Tea House." But at the point it was beginning to happen, Cage's influence—to have no stories and no narrative—obliterated all that early history of the piece.

Remy Charlip wrote an article for *Dance* magazine [January 1954] about Merce's use of chance processes, and when Remy interviewed Merce he asked him a lot of questions about his earlier solos and the meanings of his solos. And Merce told him a lot of things about meaning, what the dances were about. But . . . it seems that Remy was told not to use that material. Now, *I* think *all* of his dances (and I'm not talking only about through my time there) are about something beyond just "the steps," and, as Douglas says, it's not important either that we knew it or that the audience knows it.

In the article I wrote for the [James] Klosty book [*Merce Cunningham*, 1975], I talked about *Second Hand* (1970), which was the story of Socrates. And it is there. The duet is not actually a duet of male and female; it should be a duet with two males. The story is there, but because the critics—because *everyone* believes what is written about Merce's work, they never looked further to think that, maybe, *Second Hand* was about something *else*—was actually *about* something. It was about Socrates's death, and it was very clear. It was very moving and very touching—the gestures that we all make toward Socrates at the end, dying in the back—it's all there. But everybody believed no, it's not about anything. Some people even said it's something about Graham technique, for God's sake!

Everyone! You shouldn't believe everything that is said to you. You really should not! If you read history books, there's not a whole lot of absolute truth there, either. You have to dig around to find out that there are other things going on in the work besides chance. That's the dogma. I know, but look deeper. There is a *lot* going on there.

FARBER: Douglas, elsewhere you've talked about Merce's "uninflected movement," but I don't quite know what you mean by that. Certainly when one saw Merce dance at the height of his powers, it was not dispassionate, uninflected movement. But there is a difference between putting something on *top* of the movement and letting the movement inform the entire person and, indeed, the entire space. Merce was not someone who was performing only technically exciting feats. Merce was totally *there*, and his character was totally in the movement. No one else danced like that, and in that sense, it *was* inflected. It was passionate; it was very personal.

SOLOMONS: When I was told to "do the movement fully," what that meant to me was to generate an emotion through the movement. But the emotion had nothing to do with some intellectual fantasy; it had to do with the physical feeling the movement gave me. It was never really a problem for me, because I always understood and worked that way myself. I still assume (probably more than I ought to) that people function that way normally.

I always knew inside my secret head that Merce had stories, and that they were very simple and almost silly sometimes. And that was the reason why he wasn't going to tell anybody what they were. Those "stories" helped him make a piece. When the audience saw it, they would put their own interpretation on it and see it in their own way—so why should he get in the way of that privilege which they would have? That seems the way people *should* function. It's a way of admitting the inevitable.

DUNN: I agree with Viola, with her use of the word "inflected." The way I used it was a poor choice of word on my part perhaps. But I agree with the way she describes Merce's dancing. I have a story about something that affected me greatly in this respect.

When Merce made a piece called *Objects* in 1970, there was a section in which about four of us had to sit down on the floor and mime playing jacks, and for the first and perhaps only time in my stint with the company, I was really offended and turned off. I thought, "What the hell is this guy doing? I came here to dance; and he has all this mythology about the steps, and I'm doing it, and that's great. And all of a sudden I'm asked to be a *mime*—something I wasn't comfortable with at all. I don't like that attitude about movement."

Well, we rehearsed this part for weeks and months. Carolyn and I did it—I don't remember who else. Then came the first performance, and I was really resisting. Suddenly, when the moment came to sit down in a circle, Merce *also* sat down. He had never done this in rehearsal, ever, and he had never *shown* us how to play jacks; he just *told* us to play jacks. And in the first performance, he sat down and we took turns. One of us would play and then we would mime (we didn't have any jacks) passing the jacks to the next person. Merce was last, and I had already humiliated myself by doing my turn in resentment. But when it was Merce's turn, he did it so *beautifully* that I was very angry with myself for not realizing that here was another potential.

The point of the story is that Merce has tremendous potential as an actor, a showman, another kind of stage presence. When he dances, he uses it all, but he puts it into the movement; he doesn't use it the way we conventionally think of as acting, or as a mime would. He pushes on it a little bit and it comes out a different way. It becomes ambiguous. "What's going on?" you say—you don't know that he's playing jacks all the time, so to speak. "The expression is in the rhythm," he used to say, which I think was slightly evasive, but it is an interesting comment.

VAUGHAN: He did a wonderful thing in an Event once at the Walker Arts Center in Minneapolis. He mimed making up—putting on stage makeup.

SETTERFIELD: Once in California apparently we had one more performance scheduled than we knew about and Merce did not have enough repertory, so we did an Event. He invited us all to contribute to it and do what we wanted. Everybody was a little shy. We had never worked with him in that way, and he was a little bewildered because we were shy. So he began to organize things, because he was impatient with the fact that everybody was standing there looking timid. But we came to and found things to do. Well, there was a point in it when Merce shaved. Do you remember that? Did he really shave or did he mime?

DUNN: He *really* shaved. He went right down center stage with his makeup stuff and upstaged—or downstaged—us.

SETTERFIELD: It was Merce shaving, but it was also that kind of attention to the brush and the action which was the same thing as when he was dancing. It gave one a real understanding of the fact that everything is important.

DUNN: Once backstage on a little staircase—four or five steps—he did an absolute soft shoe on it. He wasn't afraid to compete with Fred Astaire or Bill "Bojangles" Robinson. That was the only competition.

SETTERFIELD: For me, Merce was awfully good about sharing information. The only thing he needed was for you to ask; he didn't like to tell you things if he thought you weren't ready to understand them. But I asked, and I got the most extraordinary information, even if I had to say to him, "I can't figure out what is going on here, but it isn't feeling comfortable." We would thrash it out between us.

I remember a very straightforward incident when we were doing *Field Dances* (1963), which was originally made for four dancers. Then, when the company got bigger, we all learned those parts so everybody could be in it, including new people. We were doing it in Detroit for schoolchildren in the mornings, and there was a part where a man lay on the floor with his knees up and the woman lay across him, balanced on him, and the kids would call out "Hey, that's sexy stuff." I had a walk that had originally been Viola's, which had a lot of hip rotations in it, and the kids would call out all kinds of sexy things.

So I went to Merce and said, "I think this is really upsetting the balance of the piece. I wonder if I could leave it out." He said "Oh, no. Don't leave it out. If you do, you'll never get it back." And he talked to me about ways to incorporate it into the performance and not upset the balance of things: about maybe not shifting speed, about maybe pursuing the same direction that I was already working in, of paying attention to what else was happening and using somebody else's direction, or working with somebody else at that point. He gave me the most extraordinary understanding of stagecraft and improvisation and composition. He was fantastically generous and incredibly instructive, and I thank him for many, many occasions when he did that.

PAXTON: Getting back to Viola's remark about Merce at the height of his performing power—his extraordinary quality and attention. Last year I saw the company in Santa Fe, where they were suddenly dancing at seven thousand feet, having just come from sea level. They all had the flu and their plane was late—one of those typical disaster times for the company. The first evening of performance left me feeling . . . it's still a great company, but it isn't. . . . The second night was an Event, though, and I was moved to both laughter and tears for the last twenty minutes, because one of the earliest dances that I had learned, bits of *Suite for Five* (1956), was still being done in this Event. My own well-remembered movement, twenty years after leaving the company—still there, amazing! And suddenly being very grateful that I had left the company so I could once again *see* the company, because you *can't* when you're inside. Suddenly feeling that.

Later Merce did a solo, and maybe it's because I imagine that he is in pain when he dances now (I imagine—I have never discussed it with him) and I suppose that it's only years of stage adrenaline that allow him to address the idea of performance at all anymore. But when he started dancing, it was by far the best solo I have ever seen him do in terms of its communicative power. I think it almost might be because of the pain that I presume he is in . . . because he is able to take that in stride and still present this incredible physical manifestation, wherever it comes from. I was completely moved and I felt like Santa Fe had a kind of blessing, as occasionally happens in performance—when the manifestation is so completely clear and present that there is no denying anything, and you're there with it. The empathy with such a performer is such that the entire room is unified and everyone is there, no matter what their circumstances or their own background's pain.

Earlier, the "Caging" influence was mentioned. Once Cage said something about how composition is one thing and performance is another, and seeing a work or being in an audience is yet another. I think that once you step into that kind of appreciation of what's going on, what you as a dancer are trying to convey becomes different somehow, because you don't presume that you are conveying the message that you have *in* you, but rather that each person in the audience is unique; the meaning is always a matter of translation. Just because we are speaking in the same language doesn't mean that we all take in the same meaning. And Santa Fe was an occasion where something beyond reason or meaning in the dance was being conveyed. However, they only got about three bows there; there was no standing ovation at the end, so maybe nobody else was feeling that at all. I don't know, maybe Santa Fe just doesn't *do* that kind of thing—it's so *cool* there.

SETTERFIELD: Sometimes when you see something like that, you are not moved to make a great show of applause. It is a kind of quiet pleasure, for me anyway. So maybe that happened too.

PAXTON: I barely had time enough in those bows to pull myself together so that I wouldn't look a total fool. I would have been sitting there weeping, really. I literally needed the help of the people I was with to get up. We were in the back, so everybody would have seen this guy on the aisle weeping to himself for about ten minutes. I would have stood up and shouted a lot; I actually needed to release the emotion that he had provoked.

VAUGHAN: One often reads that Merce's work has become more or less of something—more balletic, that there is more unison in it, and so on. But it seems to me that, in fact, there is a great consistency. Looking at the company now, what changes do you notice compared to when you were in it?

SOLOMONS: Looking at films of early work, I was impressed with how little the movement has aged, and I wondered why. I haven't thought it through fully, but it is probably because it is so pure in its mechanics that it transcends any date, any time—any fashion—and I think that the purity is consistent. The speed has increased. The attention span—the size of the chunks—has decreased, consistent with our apprehension of the world since television.

PAXTON: The speed has *decreased?*

SOLOMONS: No, speed has *increased,* and the length of phrase has *decreased.* In other words, it comes in shorter shots, because we—the world—now perceive things in shorter chunks, and Merce is part of the world. And that affects what he *does* so well. But it also has to do with the showmanship that Carolyn talks about, because he is the kind of personality that is very aware of the audience and the effect on the audience. He doesn't cater to it, but he considers it in the way he presents what he does. I think that as he has gotten more proficient at understanding that, he has gotten more facile at serving that. I mean, at the beginning, part of his power was to disturb and offend the normal expectations of his audiences, in a way. And that was a way of getting the kind of attention that a performer wants. Over the years, his style has become more magical to people, and he has more power over his audience.

FARBER: I think his work has changed a great deal. As Gus says, the world has changed too, and Merce doesn't work in isolation from it. I left the company in 1965, and in 1970 I did a guest performance with Merce in a work that he had done earlier, *Crises* (1960). That was a five-year gap. I remember watching the rehearsal of the program—the part that I wasn't in, which was everything but one piece—and thinking that the piece from the good old (or bad old?) days must look very strange on that program because it was so different. I felt it would be a very odd program. Since I didn't see it as a program, I don't know if it was. But I very definitely had the impression that Merce had *moved on* to very different kinds of things.

PAXTON: Wasn't that always the case, though? The programs always seemed to me to contain radically different flavors.

FARBER: Really?

PAXTON: From the first programs I saw, there were dances to the music, there were dances to random sounds or prepared piano—whatever John and David [Tudor] had concocted.

SETTERFIELD: You mean *Antic Meet* and *Summerspace* taking place in the same summer, 1958? It was extraordinary.

PAXTON: Yes. . . . The *look* of the thing. Seeing part of *Suite for Five* on the 1986 company with whatever else he had included in this Event (I have no idea how far back or far forward in history he went), I was impressed with how the company kept the integrity of the movement—kept it relatively fresh. I find the company now able to dance longer and faster than we were able to do. He's training them, I think, in a slightly more. . . .

FARBER: They're technically more proficient generally speaking. I don't know if it is proper to say this, but I will. In *Septet* there was one part where we were to be in unison, but we never were. And I watched the rehearsal on Thursday. They *still* aren't.

BROWN: But there is a movie from Finland, and we *were*. On the button!

SOLOMONS: And that's what counts! It's *on* film.

BROWN: I think the work has changed a great deal. Merce has become now what I would call a master orchestrator. He has a larger company; he is interested in using larger ensembles. In the beginning, he was working with very specific individuals; there were only five or six of us—often five plus himself. He was starting out brand new; he was developing. Some of the early pieces were very, very spare. For instance, the early chance piece *Suite by Chance* (1953): it was the beginning, the *real* beginning, of him working totally with chance processes. It didn't have in it the gut busters you see the dancers doing today. But in the fourth movement, there were the beginnings of these things—but he was just developing that craft. Today he is like a composer writing for orchestra rather than for chamber ensemble. We were a chamber ensemble. Also, he *knew* us intimately. We travelled around together in a little bus. He knew how we ate, how we quarreled, how we slept. He knew everything about us, practically.

SETTERFIELD: We were more the same age then.

BROWN: We were very close, and John Cage was with us all the time. When I hear discussions now about the concepts and the philosophy of the work—that was simply a part of our diet then. We heard it constantly, we talked about it. Rauschenberg was in the bus with us; he talked about what he was doing.

Today it is *very* different. The dancers are much younger. They don't have the opportunity to live together as we really did. We were like brothers and sisters. I don't think it is the same at all now. Of course, a *lot* is the same, but I think Merce's interest now is in structure. He has always been a magnificent choreographer in terms of structure, and that's what we see now in these works. Structurally, they are mind-boggling, and the dancers are on another planet than the one we were on in the early 1950s.

PAXTON: We are *all* on another planet than we were on in the early 1950s. At that time, what Merce was doing was heretical from several different viewpoints, and, maybe most important, it was his heresy relative to the modern dancers of his day. At that point it looked as though modern dance was going to go on developing in the same way: that each of the major artists would develop a technique of his or her own that was different, and come up with a way of presenting that idea to the public—you know, rise and fall in Humphrey's work, or the idea of contraction and psychological symbolism of Graham's, and all of that sort of thing. Cunningham for some reason chose to employ a balletic mode. Carolyn, do you know why he did that?

BROWN: No, but when he was working with Graham in her company, he was only the second male that she had choreographed for. Erick Hawkins was the first, and he was a ballet-trained dancer. She said to Merce, "I can't train you fully in terms of speed and jumping," and she sent him off to study ballet. (That is where David Vaughan met him, at the Balanchine school.) I think Merce knew that the vocabulary needed to be extended into the legs and feet. So much of the Graham repertory in those years—not now, but in *those* years—was centered on the contraction and release and so much work on the floor (it is very difficult for many men to do all that work on the floor; their pelvises really aren't constructed to do that). So Graham is the one who sent him off to study ballet.

VAUGHAN: Yes, Nina Fonaroff, who was in the Graham company at that time and now teaches in London, told me that she thought that Graham had sent Merce to the School of American Ballet. Nina said, "She never told *us* to go. Of course, we *did*, but we wouldn't tell her that we did." But I think she sent him to [Lincoln] Kirstein.

PAXTON: But modern dance was the style for him, more or less, into which he would incorporate balletic arms and balletic legs—use them inventively, change the ballet, incorporating other things he had picked up, other ways he saw movement going, and later, doing it from his *own* work. Reinterpreting his own permutations, as it were, strikes me as being very odd and in some way as a great strategy, because his compositional means were to be so radical. I think if he had been working with *movement* as radical in those days as his compositional means were, it would have been completely undecipherable. There would simply have been no audience for it.

BROWN: There *wasn't* any.

PAXTON: There was a bit of audience. I was certainly one of them.

SOLOMONS: I never thought of Merce's movement as being balletic. That's a perversity of mine, I guess—a blind spot. I think Merce incorporates all the possibilities of human activity.

PAXTON: Bullshit!

SOLOMONS: Well, he does. That's his idea, isn't it? That all movement—all human movement, all possibilities—are his material. A straight arm and a straight leg, moving at right angles to the body, are among the possibilities, and because they happen to coincide with certain positions of ballet, they get called balletic. In addition, the dynamics and the clarity and the isolation with which he does things are also reminiscent of ballet, but I think they come from a different source. (I'm sure you disagree with me, but anyway, that's what I think.)

He uses the spine as another *limb*, with equal articulation in all the joints of that spine, and reduces the center from the whole torso to just the pelvis so that the spine becomes free as a limb. But when you look at that movement, at those dances, things are recognizable to you as *arabesque* or *attitude*. But I still think of that as a leg to the back bent, or a leg to the back straight. I may be unique in that perception, but I think it doesn't deserve to be called a balletic style. It's *movement*.

You know, when anybody does something that looks like a curved spine with sharp dynamic, it is called a Graham contraction, whether it is or not. It really should be said that ballet is "Mercean" in style, rather than the opposite.

SETTERFIELD: No, ballet has been going on longer. Give it its due. I think Merce's work is balletic. It is based on the formal structure of ballet, and that was what attracted me to it. When I came here from England, I was thrust into this maelstrom of modern dance which had no clear coherency for me. Then, suddenly, I was placed in a situation with Merce where there was a clear anatomical structure being used, and I understood it; it made sense. We also turned out front, side, and back, as you do in ballet class, doing a warmup which included all the things you did in ballet class, except we called them by an English name and not a French name. The thing that was marvelous was that we worked in parallel to sustain and maintain the alignment more clearly, which held as you turned out. One of the interesting things about Merce is that he is both radical and formal at the same time. I think he needs that. Obviously, he chose a very formal structure with which to begin.

BROWN: I disagree with Gus—that he needed to make pieces to shock. I don't think he ever did that. I don't think he set out to shock, and I don't think he set out to woo an audience. We all need to be loved, but I think his whole choreographic career indicates that he has simply plunged ahead whether anyone liked his work or not. Piece after piece that few people liked. There was a small devoted following, mostly of artists and musicians. But in general, people didn't go, or if they did, they didn't like what they saw. That was the situation for years. It didn't stop him. He never deliberately set out to make a crowd pleaser in his life.

SETTERFIELD: He has a force and a passion that drives him forward, and he was shocked when he shocked people. I think he was shocked once when he shocked *us*.

Carolyn, there was a time after you had left—we had been having class with Merce for years, three times a week at eleven in the morning. The warmup was very formal—structured, slow, thorough, terrific. Suddenly, we got to the center, and all hell broke loose. He began to make phrases that were *miles* long. He would show them once, twice. There were clear landmarks in them. Sometimes one stood still for a couple of beats, or there was a position, or one made a circle—there was something very obvious that one did at some point. He would show them, and he would say "Okay." We hardly knew what had happened, but we would sort of start. One would take something off this person, then another person would remember something, then I'd remember something, and somebody would feed back off me. I thought it was divine! I thought those sessions were the most amazing adventures I'd ever had in my life. I would wake up sometimes in the morning and think "Oh, God, I can't stand an adventure"—but I would get there, and pretty soon I was in *another* one and it was heaven.

However, the company went crazy. People said, "This is irresponsible. This is inappropriate. It could cause injury." Some people said (which I think was the truth), "I don't like being seen not knowing what the steps are." There was a meeting and it was all brought up. Merce got quieter and quieter and quieter as these protests were aired, and finally he said, "I'm trying to find out something for *me*; I've been teaching you for years. I always know what's going to happen. I've been trying to make loose and very dense phrases which I haven't fully worked out. I want to find out what you do with them. I want to find out in the class what is happening."

I said, "I'm having the greatest time I ever had." Everybody else still resisted, resisted, resisted. And he gave those experiments up, because there was not that kind of courage. But I think he was incredibly shocked by the safety-factor needs of the dancers at that time. He had no idea that he was violating something, that he was doing something we wouldn't be comfortable with—no idea at all. And I think that's what happened when he made work: he *made work.* He did not make work for an effect. He did what he had to do.

SIMON: Well, I remember all the way back to *Springweather:* it had a lot of stillness and silence. It was a very long piece for those days. I never saw it, so I can only speak about what it was like from the inside, but it seems to me that the pieces *now* don't have those lengthy, quiet, empty spaces that some of the earlier ones had. Maybe I haven't seen them all, but they seem more dense.

SOLOMONS: The world doesn't have patience for that kind of work anymore—for the stillness.

FARBER: And he has lots more dancers.

DUNN: Well, though, there's *Inlets* (1977); that's a piece that impresses me.

VAUGHAN: *Pictures*, from 1984, has a lot of stillness too.

SIMON: Something that always struck me was that Merce created this wonderful technique for us to learn that *he* never used because he just *danced.* We learned the technique to approximate what he did intuitively. I always found that fascinating, because, when you saw him dance a solo, it was really different from anything that we did as a group. The solo was this creature, just *being.* We, on the other hand, were *dancing.*

ROGER COPELAND: There has always been a distinctive form of concentration visible in the faces of Cunningham's dancers. There are no artificially plastered-on smiles, and there is a certain intense engagement in the business at hand. Is that distinctive concentration in part the result of having danced alongside sounds that you can't allow to distract you? It's not dancing *to* music and it's not dancing in silence. It's something, I think, that's tougher than either of those two possibilities.

DUNN: One of the things that I observed about Merce (which seemed perfectly natural, but contradicts somewhat the usual idea about the simultaneity of the music and the dance and the separation of the two at the same time) is that he clearly listens to the music. Whatever his counts or whatever the structure of his dance, he is listening. I could see, once I left the company, that he was dancing to the music—in a different way from dancing to the rhythm of the music, perhaps, but he was making it part of the landscape that he was dancing in. I didn't find the music distracting at all. If I found it distracting, I just tuned it out. And to the extent that I *could* listen, I *did*, and fed off it.

SOLOMONS: When I was dancing in the company, we were very busy with what we were doing—with all the elements of the movement we had to concentrate on including fingertips. Merce had a wonderful way of building concentration in the performer and keeping you from that word "inflecting"— that is, putting your *own* fantasy on top of the movement. There was so much to do that it took all your concentration to do it correctly, properly.

SIMON: I remember the first time we were given some of that very spare music to go with a certain piece. We had been dancing without hearing any music, and then we started to hear it. Within a very short time we had attached certain phrases in the dance with certain sounds that came from the music. I remember that Merce was very surprised when he heard that we had found *cues*.

SOLOMONS: We were never able to find cues, because the music was never the same from time to time. I remember one performance in Paris. We were in place and were coming down in the diagonal. The speaker was blasting from the corner. Now maybe this is in my imagination, but I remember that at one point the sound stopped. All of us were in a tight knot, moving down in a very difficult balancing situation. And when the sound stopped the whole company fell forward together. We had been literally pushing against the wall of sound. It was just remarkable, because I was not often aware of the sound. I never heard the continuity of the sound. It came in and out, so I was never aware of it, except in situations like that.

Another time, in Connecticut, we were dancing on Philip Johnson's lawn, and the speakers, God help us, were in back of us because there was no proscenium. It was just a platform. The volume was so loud that some of us got sick—physically sick—from the decibel level.

VAUGHAN: So did the neighbors.

JOHN MUELLER: There's much speculation about what Cunningham was thinking. Some of you've mentioned that you had no idea if Merce was inventing material on the spot or was picking some from two years earlier. Did anyone ever ask Merce, "Are you just making this up now, or did you have it planned?"

SOLOMONS: None of *us* did.

BROWN: *Valda* may have.

SIMON: I remember that, as we got to know that what we were often doing in class was learning a dance, we would *ask* occasionally, and he would tell us yes, he was working on a dance. I don't remember him ever being very detailed about it.

DUNN: One of the things I loved about going to Merce's class was that there was so little talking. Talking has a very different rhythm from dancing—from moving and getting warmed up and using your body through a given amount of time, as you know if you've danced or played sports. Some teachers and some choreographers are willing, or desirous even, of explaining as they go along, or stopping to chat, but Merce is not like that. He wants to build a class as a curve: you start slowly until you're ready, and as you're more able to do faster and bigger things, you do them. That is typical of a ballet class also, so it's not unique to him. In rehearsal, there was the same kind of intensity. You tried to get up there to your peak and do it, and if you stopped to talk that tended to go away. This was never discussed, but it was implicit in the situation. The communication was physical and direct. It doesn't assist you in your work to stop and talk about these things.

FARBER: All this discussion is retrospective, there are lots of speculations that one can indulge in now. But as Douglas says, we were busy *doing* the work, and it often seemed quite self-explanatory. We went on these endless bus tours where we were in close proximity. There was talk, as Carolyn has said, so we were not uninformed—we were not in the dark. We were doing the work and that was very occupying, and now we can think one way or another about it, but at the time it was very different.

DUNN: It's interesting to hear about the bus and conviviality. I was in the company in 1969. By that time, we didn't do a lot of bus traveling, and Merce did not talk casually with us.

CAROLYN: You were in a *big* bus.

DUNN: Yes, you could get away. But there wasn't this kind of banter among young artists that the earlier company members experienced. However, I had the same experience that Valda mentioned: that if I asked—and I did—I got extraordinary answers from Merce. One question . . . I was so embarrassed when I asked it. I'd been in the company two or three years, and was feeling horrible. I didn't exactly know why; I was just having a very hard time. So once at lunch, between class and the rehearsal, and without even knowing I was going to do it, I walked right up to Merce and said, "Gee, what do you do, Merce, when you're not enjoying dancing?" And as soon as I said it, I was completely shocked and wanted to run away: "Why am I asking this?"

He didn't bat an eye. It was as if he already knew I was going to ask him this horrific and insulting question. (This is my *choreographer*, you know!) And he said that when you commit yourself to something, you do it all the time, not just when you feel like doing it. You have a greater commitment to it than that. That in the times when you don't feel like doing it, you wait—wait until that feeling passes into some other feeling.

SOLOMONS: And while waiting, you keep doing it. That was the important thing, wasn't it?

DUNN: He didn't come out and say it, but that was definitely implied. It was extremely helpful; it was a very generous and helpful statement. While I was there, if you didn't ask you didn't get a lot. If the physical thing was enough, fine; you got that. But the other thing wasn't forthcoming unless you requested it, and it could be quite difficult. There was no way to process verbally—automatically—a lot of the feelings that go on in an intense work situation like that.

VAUGHAN: Did Merce feel that he was developing a technique for purposes other than training his company?

PAXTON: We learned a lot of the dances and a lot of the choreography in class, so the technique—the training method—and the choreography were intimately bound. Whatever he was doing was in a capsule. He could go from balletic work in the center and even movement across the floor into Cunningham choreography—which is supposed to be quite radical—without really having to shift technical gears. I think one of the reasons he did that is that he needed dancers who were there and available through all the rigors of being a dancer . . . which means whether you feel like it or not with the weirdest kind of schedule: lots of classes and rehearsals and performances, perhaps day after day—that kind of physical demand. He needed people who could do that. He knew that, with his training, we could fulfill those demands and dance his dances.

But then the dances, the movement, the development . . . Gus mentioned that the spine was used differently than in ballet, and there were many other differences as well. But I don't feel that all the movement possibilities are there in practice. Carolyn once said that Merce opened more doors for succeeding generations than he cared to walk through, and I think that's possible. But we've seen incredible new influences on movement in this country in the last twenty or thirty years, not only in the developments in modern dance and ballet, but also from the Orient and from Brazil—the Capoieran influence, for example. The movement world right now is broader than it has ever been before in terms of world exchange, so in light of that, Merce's work is quite conservative. (I mean the technical side of it.) Nonetheless, it is fully developed and beautifully made.

BROWN: We have to determine just what vintage of Cunningham technique we're talking about, because the technique itself has changed. It's constantly if subtly changing, depending upon his specific interests at the time. There are basic things that get done generally—the back gets warmed up, the legs get warmed up, and things like that. But, in the very beginning, in the early years when Marianne and Viola and Remy and I were in that tiny little studio on 8th Street, he was definitely exploring his technique—keeping things, tossing them out, finding out what worked and what didn't. The actual continuity of the class changed. There was a time when he did all the back exercises first, and then the legs, to see if *that* worked; then he alternated them. And that hasn't stopped.

When I go to the studio now, I feel that this isn't my home. I really don't identify with what's happening there now in terms of the technique. He is always developing the technique for the choreography. If he couldn't choreograph, or if he stopped having a company . . . since he's said he doesn't like to teach, I wonder if the technique classes would continue to evolve. When he was at the height of his powers, to take his class was so exhilarating it was almost unbearable, because he danced every step of it—he just danced it full out, every step of it. So that what one wanted to do, somehow, was to join that passion. He did not teach us the steps verbally; he never taught us how to do a thing by saying "If you did this and this, then you could do that." You learned by watching him. Some of us had to go elsewhere to find out how to do this awfully difficult stuff.

FARBER: One of his strengths, as a teacher at that time, actually, was that he didn't teach. That was what was beautiful about it! One could get absolutely lost, as Carolyn said, in trying to join him, in this extraordinary thing he was doing. It was just amazing.

BROWN: In the early years, even if we were in Connecticut, we took two classes a day with him, five days a week, and then we rehearsed with him for five or six or seven hours. The Cunningham dancers today go to ballet class; they only get him once or twice or three times a week for class, and of course they rehearse with him. That's different.

When Gus first joined the company (he wasn't an early member), he took the beginning class—I'll never forget it. He was in the company, but he said "I have to know what this is all about." He took the elementary class every day, he took the intermediate class, and he took the company class, because he wanted to know what the technique was about.

Today's company doesn't do that. The whole dance world is different. Martha Graham's people study ballet. Twyla's people—they don't even *have* a modern-dance class. Ballet's been around a lot longer, and I fear ballet's going to swallow it all up—it's going to bland it out.

Oh, I think probably Lincoln Kirstein is right. And since the ballet seems desperate for choreographers and since it's got the institutions and it's got money, and it's got theaters that modern dance doesn't have, it will absorb every new creative imagination it can latch on to.

VAUGHAN: I don't think we can open up that can of worms at this point.

David Vaughan

RETROSPECT AND PROSPECT (1979)

The inaugural performances of Merce Cunningham and Dance Company were given at Black Mountain College in 1953, twenty-five years ago. Cunningham is not, of course, given to celebrating such jubilees, but the programs of the two-week season of Merce Cunningham Dance Company at the City Center, September 26 to October 8, 1978, did provide a retrospective of his repertory over at least twenty years, going back as far as *Summerspace* (1958) and *Rune* (1959). The change in the company's title is small, but nonetheless significant, reflecting Cunningham's own desire to stress the company's present ensemble nature; for some years now the dancers have been listed alphabetically, including Cunningham himself, rather than hierarchically as they were at one time, with Cunningham's name at the top and the others in order of seniority below. He does not wish any one dancer to appear to be more important than another, though he himself inevitably remains more equal than the others.

This shift in emphasis is indicative of some important changes in the character not only of the company but of Cunningham's choreography itself—changes in the one naturally follow upon changes in the other. In many of his recent dances, Cunningham has been concerned with mass effects; he has used an increasing number of dancers, and made pieces in which longer passages of unison choreography occur, or in which individuals do not stand out even when everyone on stage is doing something different. One could trace this development at least as far back as such works as the third part of *Second Hand* (1970), *Landrover*, and *TV Rerun* (both 1972). It may be that *Un Jour*

124

ou deux, Cunningham's 1973 work for the ballet of the Paris Opéra, which used a large cast, intensified his interest in working this way. In any case, several of the pieces that came after *Un Jour ou deux* have been of this nature: *Sounddance* (1975), *Rebus* (1975), *Torse* (1976), the original *Exercise Piece* (1978), and *Exchange* (1978). The portions of the earlier *Scramble* (1967) and *Canfield* (1969) that have been retained in the material used in Events have mostly been those that can be performed by a large number of dancers.

At the Paris Opéra, Cunningham was more or less obliged to concentrate on mass effects because the dancers he worked with were necessarily novices in his technique and way of composing, even after several weeks of classes with him. This is manifestly not the case with his current company, but it is often stated that the dancers now available to Cunningham no longer include such strong personalities as Carolyn Brown, Viola Farber, Remy Charlip (in his original company) or Valda Setterfield, Susana Hayman-Chaffey, Meg Harper, Gus Solomons jr, Douglas Dunn, and others who have come and gone in the last ten or fifteen years—that the young dancers tend to seem "anonymous" on stage, are primarily involved with technique, and fail to project any character as individuals. To the contrary, I believe that the company Cunningham has now assembled is a nearly perfect instrument for his present concerns as a choreographer, the strongest group he has had for some time, and that this strength is not only in terms of technique but also of personality.

Foremost among those present concerns, according to Cunningham himself, are the possibilities and limitations of virtuoso movement, such matters of pure technique as swiftness of execution and the elimination of transitions between one movement or position and another. It may seem contradictory therefore to suggest that Cunningham does in fact want "character" from his individuals, in their way of moving primarily perhaps, but that is of course a function of individuality in personality itself. As Cunningham says, everyone in the world walks according to the same mechanism, but no two people walk alike, and that is what constitutes "expression." Like many great choreographers, Cunningham wants to get at that individuality, to draw it out, and draw on it, in the act of creating movement. In his present company of fourteen dancers in addition to himself, the largest ever, Cunningham has a group of people who work well together as an ensemble without losing their individuality. For evidence of the kind of individuality that interests him, one has only to look at the slightly different versions of the solo early in *Fractions* (1977) danced by Karole Armitage and Lisa Fox: Armitage performs the movement (flinging down her arms, swiftly turning legs in and out, coiling and uncoiling her torso) with the sharpness of a whiplash, while Fox does it with an extraordinary kind of looseness controlled from the center.

For every example that supports a generalization, it is possible to adduce another that refutes it. Cunningham's recent works include not only the dances named that stress ensemble movement, but also *Changing Steps* (1975), which gives each dancer a solo (and initially these solos were designed precisely to display the individual qualities of the dancers they were made for) as well as featuring them in duets, trios, quartets, and quintets; *Inlets* (1977) which like earlier dances such as *Summerspace, Rune,* and *RainForest* (1968) uses only six dancers; and *Fractions* (1978), which also uses a comparatively small cast (eight) and in its structure reminds one of earlier Cunningham works like *Suite for Five* (1956).

As a choreographer, Cunningham is amazingly and increasingly prolific; in the last year alone he has made three major works, *Inlets, Fractions,* and *Exchange,* the three small *Exercise Pieces* for use in Events or as part of the *et cetera* added in repertory performances to *Changing Steps* (which thus becomes a kind of mini-Event), plus several bits of solo material also for Events, some of which found their way into the new solo *Tango.* And though it is convenient for a critic and historian to group works together and trace lines of development, these recent dances are quite unlike each other in important ways. More and more, it seems almost impossible not to respond to Cunningham's work as drama, and this is as true of most of the ensemble dances as of those with small casts. This doesn't mean, of course, that he has suddenly changed his whole esthetic, abandoned his preoccupation with movement for its own sake, and started to tell stories, but that these pieces have a theatrical intensity that affects one as profoundly as any tragedy.

It is true that their nature as theatre pieces depends to some extent on the total effect of dance combined with music and decor, however independently Cunningham and his collaborators work, and that the dance material when divorced from these other elements, as we see it in Events, may not be easily identifiable as to its source in the repertory. But it is surely true of any choreography that it reaches its full theatrical potential only when combined with one or both of these elements. A lot of the drama in Cunningham's works derives from his own relation to the dancers in his company. The difference in age and agility between himself and the others, who are many years his juniors, is inevitably noticeable in performance. In one way or another, he is removed from them; he appears as a mysterious, controlling presence (as in *Rebus*), as an isolated, even tragic figure (as in *Inlets*), as a leader, or perhaps a tribal elder (as in *Exchange*); in *Squaregame* (1976), he is treated irreverently by the others, getting dragged around and tossed up in the air, but in the duet towards the end he is like some Pygmalion with his Galatea, tenderly guiding and steadying the woman's faltering steps; in *Travelogue* (1977), when he "plays dead," all the others stop in their tracks for a long moment.

Cunningham's relation to the dancers in fact often seems to be the "subject" of a piece. One could take *Sounddance* (1975) as a metaphor for the recent history of the company, or perhaps for the short, intense, often painful span of a dancer's career: the dancers come and go, entering from Mark Lancaster's tent-like structure, starting with Cunningham himself, who is also the last to be sucked back into it again at the end of some twenty minutes of fast and furious activity. That such interpretations of the dance imagery are bound to occur to one shows how nonsensical it is to talk of Cunningham's work as "abstract."

The drama of natural events has been a frequent subtext of his dances, going back at least as far as his first major group piece, *The Seasons*, made for Lincoln Kirstein's Ballet Society in 1947. (As a dancer, Cunningham is one of those, like Duncan, Nijinsky, Pavlova, or Sybil Shearer, who appears to be more a force of nature than simply human.) He returned to this theme in subsequent individual works: *Springweather and People* (1955) and *Summerspace* (1958); *Rune* (1959) was originally to be called *Autumn Rune*, and the tetralogy *manqué* was completed by *Winterbranch* (1964). I have said that the recent *Inlets* resembles *Summerspace, Rune,* and *RainForest* in that it has a cast of six; more to the point is its preoccupation with the cycle of time and tide. Its very title suggests the landscape of Puget Sound, and the climate and geography of the Northwest are strongly evoked both by Morris Graves's decor and John Cage's music. (Cunningham originally wanted Graves to design *The Seasons*, thirty years ago, and his first title for that piece was *Northwestern Rite*.) Choreographically, *Inlets* resembles *Summerspace* and *RainForest* in that the dancers move for much of the time as individuals—*RainForest* takes this structure to the extreme of not having any of the dancers return to the stage once they have gone off, except for Cunningham himself; in *Summerspace* and *Inlets* there are frequent entrances and exits for all the dancers.

It is no secret that former members of Cunningham's company and for that matter audience members with long memories find that dances revived from the past, like *Summerspace* and *Rune,* are almost unrecognizable in certain ways. The basic structure may be there, and the steps may be similar in outline to what they used to be, but not in such important matters as rhythm, weight, and phrasing, to say nothing of such intangibles as atmosphere. Such losses are perhaps inevitable with a choreographer like Cunningham, who uses the individual qualities of his dancers so much. Choreographers have notoriously short memories, and notes and even—nowadays—videotapes may not be infallible guides to reconstruction. Anyone who saw Cunningham, Carolyn Brown, Viola Farber, and Remy Charlip in their original roles in *Summerspace* and other dances is apt to find their images so indelible that they superimpose themselves on those of the people now dancing them. But for those who did not, there is no reason why, in *Summerspace*, for instance, Chris Komar, Louise Burns, Karole Armitage, and Robert Kovich should not make an equally strong impression of their own. Certainly the original cast of *Inlets*—Cunningham, Armitage, Ellen Cornfield, Lisa Fox, Komar, and Kovich—is fully capable of giving the work all the weight and atmosphere that Cunningham seems to have wanted for the piece, with its alternations of stillness and activity (he asked that the movement even at its most vigorous should have the quality of stillness).

There are those who go so far as to say that the revival of the earlier works is a futile exercise. I cannot agree: I think they are strong enough to stand up without their original interpreters and even in a form that does not reproduce the original with total accuracy. We gladly accept other dance masterpieces from the past on those terms, and we have to recognize a living choreographer's prerogative in changing a work as he sees fit. Balanchine's *Serenade*, for instance, is what he now says it is, which we know to be something very different from what it was originally. In Cunningham's case it would even be possible for him to go to the extreme of remaking a work according to its original chance process, with equally valid, albeit different, results. (In fact, one section of the video piece *Westbeth* [1974] was made according to the process used in the trio and quartet from *Suite for Five*.)

The chance process, assumed to be evidence of Cunningham's lack of reverence for traditional methods of composition, is not as totally arbitrary as might appear. As with any other compositional device, the quality of the result depends on the quality of the imagination at work. Cunningham has said that using chance methods frees him from the limitations of habit and of his own intuitions, but clearly talent is still involved, in the invention of the movement gamut on which the chance process is brought to bear, and in the sheer craftsmanship needed to make everything work. One gasps, for instance, at the way in which certain patterns in *Torse* resolve themselves, like the moment when people enter from the wings and feed into the circle of dancers that suddenly fills the whole stage, with everyone spinning around and at a certain moment reversing direction.

It is passages like this, presumably, that caused the San Francisco critic Robert Commanday to describe *Torse* as "barefoot Balanchine." The Seattle critic who thought that *Torse* was "a spoof of ballet" was clearly wide of the mark—as if Cunningham would waste his time making a fifty-five minute spoof—but was probably misled by the resemblances between Cunningham's technique and that of ballet. Cunningham technique is based on the pelvic turnout, fundamental to his movement even when executed in a parallel position. The Cunningham equivalents of ballet's eight directions of the body (*croisé devant, quatrième devant, effacé, écarté, à la seconde, épaulé, quatrième derrière, croisé derrière*) keep recurring in *Torse*, but the swift transitions between one and another, and the extreme degree of tilt in the torso (hence the title) which Cunningham demands are very different from what one usually finds in ballet nowadays (according to Frederick Ashton, though Bronislava Nijinska, in her classes, used to make the dancers move their upper bodies in ways not dissimilar from Cunningham's).

Torse is perhaps the purest Cunningham work of all, for his technique provides not only the vocabulary but the very subject matter of the piece. This is Cunningham at his most austere and his most classical. Yet *Torse* is quite uncompromising in its use of a complex chance process, based on the *I Ching*:

there are sixty-four phrases, as many as there are ideograms in the *I Ching*; the chance process ensures the repetition of these at various points, and thus imposes a kind of formal structure, though not one that follows the kind of "rules" of composition laid down by Louis Horst and Doris Humphrey.

It has become commonplace to speak of Cunningham's classicism; this does not mean that he has become any more orthodox with the passage of time, only that people are recognizing something that has always been true of his work, which has always been classic in its rigor, its clarity, and its economy. If *Septet* (1953) and *Nocturnes* (1956) could be revived, many people might be surprised by the almost conventional use of Erik Satie's music, but even *Suite for Five* would no doubt seem classic in its purity and simplicity. It is difficult to believe that only a few years ago, a piece like *Suite* was considered iconoclastic in its rejection of conventional methods of composition, with some reason since it used a chance process based on the imperfections in sheets of paper to determine both the spatial plan and such things as the length of a given phrase. *Suite* was one of the most radical works in its use of space; in the trio and quartet sections, Cunningham proposed and uncompromisingly followed the principle that each dancer was to be his or her own center.

I have suggested that the recent *Fractions* in some ways recalls *Suite*, and this fragmentation of space is one of them. In its original video form, *Fractions* involves the use of monitor screens that show action occurring in other parts of the studio simultaneously with that in the main space. *Fractions* thus brilliantly avoids that besetting problem of video dance, the spectator's acute awareness of the limitations of the dancing area. In the stage version, the use of the monitors is vestigially indicated in the moments when one or two dancers enter and take up positions at the side of the stage.

Cunningham's treatment of the stage—or any other performing space he uses—as a "field" in which no one area is more "important" than another is among his most significant innovations, together with his insistence on the independence of dance, music, and decor, and his rejection of literary and psychological pretexts for dancing. I am surprised, though, that few writers have commented on his extraordinary use of space in the sculptural sense, the way he changes the space around the dancers by the shapes their bodies make. The configurations of arms and legs and bodies at different heights and angles continually astonish us by their beauty and originality, especially in his duets—only Ashton and Balanchine among contemporary choreographers make duets as beautiful as Cunningham's. The duet between Armitage and Kovich in *Fractions*, the designs they make in space as their arms and bodies fold about each other, is only one example in a work full of such felicities, and in this respect is reminiscent of duets in earlier works like *Rune* and *Scramble*.

Exchange belongs in the category of what I think of as Cunningham's epic works, like *Aeon* (1961), *Canfield* (1969), *Un Jour ou deux*, works that seem to deal with the passing of time in terms of epochs. It's no coincidence that, in most of these pieces, he was able to use a larger number of dancers than ever before: his company was enlarged before *Aeon* and *Exchange,* and for *Un Jour ou deux* he was able to use twenty-six dancers from the Paris Opéra Ballet. The scale is large in every sense. *Aeon* had its playful side, especially in some of the inventions in Robert Rauschenberg's designs—for example, Carolyn Brown at one point wore a rope tied around her waist, with various objects hanging from it, a sneaker, a cowbell, a bit of cloth (analogous, of course, to certain elements in his decor for *Travelogue* sixteen years later). *Canfield,* as is well known, was composed according to a process derived from the card game of the same name. Choreographically, though, both *Aeon* and *Canfield* had a kind of majestic sweep and grandeur that made them seem macrocosmic in scale.

Exchange is that kind of work: watching it is like watching history unfold before your eyes. Some of this feeling comes from Cunningham's use of the two generations within his present company: the first section is danced by the more recent recruits, Meg Eginton, Susan Emery, Lise Friedman, Alan Good, Catherine Kerr (returning after a year and a half's absence), Joseph Lennon, and Robert Remley, led by Cunningham himself. Then in the second, these "junior" members are replaced by the seniors, Karole Armitage, Louise Burns, Ellen Cornfield, Lisa Fox, Chris Komar, Robert Kovich, and Jim Self. As befits their status as the most senior members, Komar and Kovich at times seem to assume the roles of deputies to Cunningham, the leader himself. Only in the final section do the two groups intermingle, with some switching of partners among the couples.

Exchange, like *Un Jour ou deux,* was designed by Jasper Johns, and shares with it the somber feeling that comes in part from the dark grays of his decors and costumes—relieved in *Exchange* by touches of color in the women's leotards and at the ankles of the men's tights, though even these are overlaid by gray. But in both works, the feeling comes equally from the choreography: there is a kind of sober inevitability as one movement follows another, each moment seems totally realized, so that the overall effect is monumental. The choreography of *Exchange* constantly reorganizes the space not only in terms of area but of volume, displacing whole blocks of air above the stage: it is this which gives the work a positively architectonic sense of weight and solidity. *Exchange* is a major work, worthy to be named in the same breath as Nijinska's *Les Noces,* Graham's *Primitive Mysteries,* Balanchine's *The Four Temperaments,* and Ashton's *Scènes de ballet.*

That Cunningham's latest work should be one of his greatest encourages one to believe that there need be no end in sight to his choreographic career. As a performer, it is clear that he is as much in his element as ever on the stage. His new solo, *Tango,* reminded us, as do his "Dialogue" performances with John Cage, that he is one of the great clowns of our time. In recent years, Cunningham has gradually been relinquishing some of his roles to younger dancers. Several years ago Douglas Dunn danced his part in *Winterbranch,* and

now Chris Komar dances *Summerspace*, Robert Kovich *Signals*, and the two of
them alternate in *Rune*. The breadth and freedom of their aerial movements
recall Cunningham's own in former years, even if his magnetism as a performer is inevitably lacking. It may be true that Cunningham himself can do
less and less, but he finds more and more ways to do it; one of the exciting
things about *Exchange* was that he seemed to have found several new movement possibilities for himself, notably an undulation through the torso, that he
will no doubt continue to explore. In any case, the power of his gesture and the
authority of his presence are such that he could easily command the stage even
if he just stood absolutely still.

Many people have spoken of the irony of the fact that Cunningham, the
iconoclast, the *enfant terrible* of yesteryear, out of whose concerts members of
the public—not to mention the critics of metropolitan dailies—used angrily to
stalk, has now become accepted as part of the dance establishment. As Nancy
Dalva remarked in *The Daily Texan*, "Cunningham has not gone establishment,
but the establishment has gone Cunningham." It's no exaggeration to say that,
in their tours of the United States in the late forties and early fifties, under-
taken in conditions of hardship that today's dancers, with their union-set per
diems, could not imagine, Cunningham and Cage and, later, the original
dance company played as important a role in developing audiences for contemporary dance as Anna Pavlova did for ballet. I sometimes wonder how
conscious Cunningham himself is of being a part of the mainstream of dance
history—a position many people would have denied him even a few years ago,
and possibility still do. That he is a part of it seems as incontrovertible as that
he has diverted its course in the second half of the twentieth century.

Changeling, 1957. Photo by Richard Rutledge, courtesy Cunningham Dance Foundation.

Antic Meet, 1958. L to r: Barbara Lloyd, Viola Farber, Shareen Blair, Merce Cunningham, Carolyn Brown. Photo by Fannie Helen Melcer, courtesy Cunningham Dance Foundation.

Summerspace, 1959. Viola Farber and
Carolyn Brown. Photo by Richard
Rutledge, courtesy Cunningham
Dance Foundation.

Summerspace, 1965 production.
Photo © Jack Mitchell.

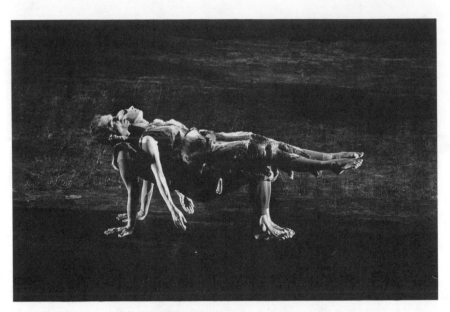

Nightwandering, 1958; 1965 production. Merce Cunningham and Carolyn Brown. Photo © Peter Moore.

Crises, 1960. Viola Farber and Merce Cunningham. Photo by John Wulp, courtesy Cunningham Dance Foundation.

Crises, 1965 production. L to r: Merce Cunningham, Carolyn Brown, Sandra Neels, Barbara Lloyd. Photo © Peter Moore.

Merce Cunningham and John Cage, 1963. Photo © Jack Mitchell.

Merce Cunningham, 1963. Photo © Jack Mitchell.

Variations V, 1965. L to r: Albert Reid, Gus Solomons jr, Sandra Neels, Photo © Peter Moore.

Variations V, 1967 production. Photo © Peter Moore.

The Cunningham Company musician/composers at work.
L to r: John Cage, David Tudor, Gordon Mumma. Photo ©
James Klosty, courtesy Cunningham Dance Foundation.

Merce Cunningham giving a lecture-demonstration at Hunter College, 21 April 1966. Photo ©
Peter Moore.

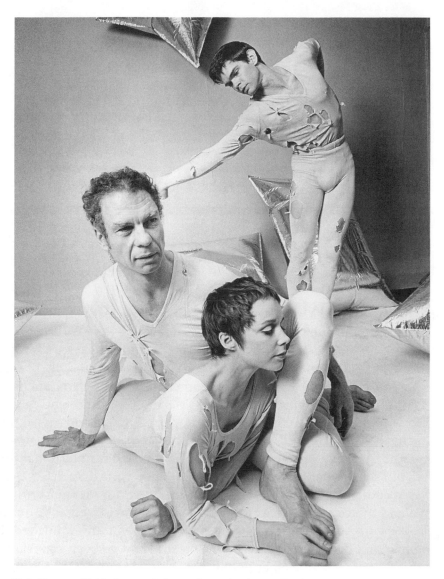

RainForest, 1968. L to r: Merce Cunningham, Barbara Lloyd,
Albert Reid. Photo © Jack Mitchell.

Arlene Croce

THE MERCISTS (1978)

Spring thaw in New York always brings us the modern dance. Would that it brought us another name for that species of theatrical performance which developed largely outside the spectacular opera-house ballet tradition. Modern dance is, like Romantic ballet, a historical phenomenon. Labels are prejudicial and confining, but we need some other way to refer to dancing that is more than one generation removed from Martha Graham, who is going on eighty-four years old. I have heard "post-modern," and its very weakness and temporariness recommend it. For the recycling age we live in, post-anything sounds right. Actually, in dance there's a fairly explicit tradition that for years has cried out to be called—after its preceptor—mercism. If Ruth St. Denis and Ted Shawn could become a noun (Denishawn), why not Merce Cunningham? We have had mercist companies for quite a while now. Even as Cunningham himself goes on dancing and choreographing, companies headed by his descendants and disciples pop up everywhere. They've been especially ubiquitous in the past few weeks, appearing at Dance Umbrella, at the American Theatre Laboratory (A.T.L.), and at Cunningham's studio in Westbeth. The climax of the series was a two-week stand by the Cunningham company itself at the Roundabout Theatre.

Mercism isn't the only kind of downtown dance activity, and its manifestations are diverse. But generally one identifies it by a commitment to dancing exclusive of music or decor. This commitment to the dancer moving in silence and creating his own space reflects one of Cunningham's paramount concerns—the one that he has held on to longest. Passing concerns of his (happenings, improvisation, non-dance experimentation) recur ghostily in the work of the permanent radical fringe that borders both dance and the spoken theatre. At the moment, we can see one of those periodic inflations of a Cunningham idea taking hold in this sector. Just as the younger generation in the sixties inflated Cunningham's proposition that any movement can become *part of* a dance into "Any movement can be a dance," there are those who are now expanding his insight about the ambiguity of movement into a fascination with ambiguity in all things. Often surface appearances aren't merely allowed to contradict each other, they're directed to. Applied ambiguity blankets many post-modern evenings. One is apt to find more decor than dancing; sound runs to verbal texts. Dance reviews, with their endless speculative remarks about roses that could be noses or whatever the mind supposes, are beginning to mirror the lifeless quandaries posed by these students of the mystique of ambiguity. When faced with one of their impenetrable puzzles, I think of John Cage's advice to Richard Kostelanetz: "Use your experience no matter where you are." It is good advice. Taking the responsibility for the effect of a piece— following what Cage called (in Kostelanetz's book about him) the "non-intentional" aspect—can sometimes be the only way to watch it. And there's always the possibility that what is not intended may be more effective, and even more productive of "meaning," than what is. In Mel Wong's *Harbor*, at A.T.L., the dancing became involved with a display of conceptual art. After about twenty minutes of total inscrutability, I knew I was going to have to get *Harbor* unjammed from an unworkable intention. Wong happens to be a skilled choreographer in the mercist vein, and I found I could enjoy the dancing even though I couldn't tell what it was meant to be about. *Harbor*, though, is far too long to experience just on this level. I couldn't play with pure dance and accidental ambience for the nearly two hours that Wong had chosen to press his intention. As he became more abstruse, with the dancers declaiming numbers or speaking fragmentary sentences or pouring colored water from various plastic containers, I had to become less so—less privately and more professionally interested in what I was seeing. It's not my favorite way of watching, but one can't make mystery out of ready-made *misterioso*. One can't and still hold on to one's respect for the dance craftsman that Wong so truly is.

At mercist lecture-demonstrations, audiences will sometimes ask how much they should know of the creative methods used in a dance in order to appreciate it. The question, not at all a dismissable one, means that they've detected the presence of a process that doesn't disappear into a result. It may also mean that the process looks as if it would be more interesting to watch or to know about than the actual dance it has produced. Process is often deliberately on view in mercist pieces; it's right up there in Viola Farber's works, inseparable from production. My difficulty with Farber is that the process is too obvious: the sectional construction, for instance, that tells me where one day's composing ends and the next day's begins. And one day is as good as another—the process isn't selective. Farber may be the purest mercist around, although I'm told she has no intention of imitating Cunningham's approach to composition. Her work is like Abstract Expressionist painting. You follow it (as you follow all dancing) for the *act* of creation, not for the sake of some disembodied product that creation leaves behind; but you also get the record of what creation involves—you get interruptions and distractions and second thoughts and wipeouts. If Farber were capable of virtuoso brushwork, a long, chuntering piece like *Dinosaur Parts,* seen at Dance Umbrella, might be wonderful. In a new work, *Turf,* she seems to have narrowed and concentrated her means. I watched it with absorption and wondered how much the use of Poulenc's organ concerto alongside the dancing had to do with the relatively flexible and tidy effect. (The David Tudor score used for *Dinosaur Parts* affected me like a dentist's drill.)

Cunningham has initiated more new ideas for theatrical performance than any other choreographer. It's no wonder he has so many followers. Because the material he has brought into being is so richly suggestive, any number can play. When a Cunningham-inspired idea fails, one is still glad it has been tried. Yet ideas by themselves don't make art; they do tend to disappear the moment they're realized. In Cunningham's own best work, as in all works of art, a negotiable idea becomes transparent expression; nothing is left of it but the talent that produced it in the first place. No one who has been influenced by him is working anywhere near Cunningham's level, and one sees—and hears—lots of ideas. Many choreographers, mercist and non-mercist, have tried to get spoken words to work as an accompaniment to dance. The mercist method is to have no direct correspondence between the words and the movement. However, not even Cunningham himself has managed to make them equal partners. Words always dominate; arranged in nonsensical patterns, they still steal the attention away from dance. (The relationship is like that of words to music. Most people identify a song's meaning through its lyric, not through its music. Irving Berlin's "Blue Skies," for example, is a "happy" song, even though its music is a dirge.) Margaret Jenkins, a San Francisco-based choreographer who taught for many years at Cunningham's New York school, collaborates frequently with a poet, Michael Palmer. A voice-over, speaking words in several of the Jenkins pieces that were done recently at Westbeth, forced me to consider meanings that didn't seem to belong to the dances. *About the Space in Between* had a text dealing with Ludwig Wittgenstein, but for me it was really "about" what the title declared it to be about. Jenkins has a keenly sculptural sense of negative space, which she often exploits choreographically both in her own dancing and in that of the group. A void may appear, speaking volumes, only to be retracted, altered, or recharged by a solid shape. Jenkins's dancers are firmly centered (centering to dancers and potters means the same thing), and though not especially wide in turnout, they have a powerful thrust from the inside of the thigh. The strong legs and strong, flexible feet are legacies from Cunningham, emphasized by

Jenkins. Such emphases give these dancers a uniform non-eclectic technique. The foremost mercist company on the West Coast, they appear to be specialists in a very special, insular sense. Not that they're provincial; at least one piece, the epigrammatic *Videosongs*, would have made the reputation of any New York company. But both in the excessively brainy pieces and in the straitened technique there's a little too much hothouse conditioning. More New York appearances would be good for them and us.

A very impressive sound accompaniment to a couple of Cunningham's Events in his Roundabout series was devised by John Cage from his *Mesostics re Merce Cunningham*. The *Mesostics* (a variation on acrostics) are made of words, but they impinge on the ear as pure sound consisting of discrete syllables. Cage published his puzzle poems a few years ago, using within each one many different Letraset typefaces and sizes. He then used the typefaces and sizes as musical notation, letting them dictate pitch, timbre, loudness, and duration. At the Events, the *Mesostic* songs didn't reverse the usual effect of verbal texts on dance, and this was because their performance by the Greek tenor Demetrio Stratos was overwhelming in its virtuosity. Stratos has a voice like no other I've heard; he can switch registers so that they seem to overlap, he can produce drones and ululations with uncanny bell-like overtones, and from a lesser artist than Merce Cunningham he would have stolen the show. I saw the second of two performances with Stratos. Cunningham performed more than he had the week before, when the sound was electronically produced by David Tudor. He was obviously responding to a challenge, and he drew from himself an extraordinary variety of movement, some of it unmistakably and unerringly timed to coincide with Stratos's singing. He is just now in excellent diabolical form, and the occasion brought out his weirdest strokes of wit and drama. He twice held a difficult pose on a bench a very long time while the company danced. He did a slow, foppish solo, full of sly, curlicuing wrists and implied flashes of lace handkerchief. After an appalling minute of complete silence on an empty stage, he entered wearing white coveralls and lay face down, without moving, for another minute. Perhaps his best dance moment was a kind of fractured conga in those same coveralls. Cunningham, now in his late fifties, avoids extremes of movement; he holds to his middle range and makes it seem like a full diapason. All his effects are concentrated, delicate, precise, yet never small. As for the company, the constant addition of new members keeps it looking on the green side, although much individual progress is being made. At the two Events I saw, the choreography was drawn in full or in part from *Torse* (1976), *Winterbranch* (1964), *Changing Steps* (1975), *Canfield* (1969), the wonderful and seldom performed trio called *Cross Currents* (1964), and *Westbeth* (1974), a made-for-TV work. Cunningham's personal repertory consisted of an apparently endless supply of solos that he keeps in his sleeve.

No one who saw Gus Solomons jr, performing with the Cunningham company in the sixties can forget the impact of his tall body and fantastically long legs—as long and thin above the knee as they are below. Solomons could easily have been a male Judith Jamison; instead, he has become a serious choreographer. The company he brought to the Dance Umbrella was the second one of his I've seen; it's young and sunny. Solomons still looks all line, with relatively little muscle—a man who has grown stilts. He did a solo called *Signals* while his music director, Mio Morales, attempted a bit of Demetrio Stratos. *PsychoMotor-Works,* an ongoing company project, had a lot of classical ballet in it, in the form of syllabus positions. Two excerpts were performed; both ended with lively sets of allegro in which Solomons tried for speedy, dexterous footwork—the only one of Cunningham's adherents, as far as I know, to do so. But outside ballet, no one except Cunningham has the secret of allegro. *Bone Jam* was about life experience. It bounced along in episodes broken by blackouts. The dancers, wearing half-masks, appeared in everything from underwear to overcoats, and the movement, which included a good many jokes, ranged from ragdoll limpness to long, clear sweeps and hard, directional changes on a big scale. It was one of what might be called Solomons's junk dances, but there weren't so many bottle caps this time. A good, entertaining piece.

Speaking of life experience, the remarkable thing about the mercists is their esthetic unity. Their backgrounds are widely dissimilar (Mel Wong is of Chinese descent; Gus Solomons jr, is black), and their dancing has been a melting pot. Mercism is really about dancing as experience; it has a built-in dryness and objectivity, and from both dancer and spectator it demands a certain taste for the leaner virtues, for moral disinterestedness. Many people, especially Europeans, find that anti-theatrical. Privileged deprivation may be an exclusively American trait—WASP American, at that. *Théâtre du Silence*, a French company with a modern repertory, opened its New York season (at the Beacon) with a highly unreticent version of Cunningham's greatest lyrical piece, *Summerspace.* The Rauschenberg stippled backcloth was bathed in an orange glow, the sparse piano score, by Morton Feldman, was overamplified, and the dancing was heavy and coarse. It's a company of lusty athletes; one gets the impression that, for the French, avant-garde dance is a form of *le sport* or *le sexe.* Whether they know it or not, the French are temperamentally non-mercist (*non, merci*).

I heard people say that, before they knew better, they took the *Théâtre du Silence* to be a deaf-and-dumb theater. That made me think of Remy Charlip and how much I wish I'd seen his work for the National Theatre of the Deaf and the dances that were derived from it. Charlip was once a member of the Cunningham company, creating roles in *Summerspace* (1958), *Rune* (1959), and *Antic Meet* (1958), among other pieces. He's a noted designer, an illustrator, and author of children's books, as well as a dancer and choreographer, and his gift for visualization and animation stops, apparently, at nothing. There never has been anything like his collaborations, a decade ago, with Al Carmines, the most amazing of which actually wrung a dance oratorio from *The Sayings of Mao Tse-tung*. These days, he is working in theater mostly as a soloist, but in any one of his appearances all his talents manage to be on view. At his Dance Umbrella concert, he began by having his silhouette traced head to toe on brown paper with the arms showing different positions. Then he painted the silhouette blue and flew it as an ensign for the rest of the program. Everything about Charlip suggests consistency, smoothness, and wholeness. His cookie-cutter silhouette, his drawings, and his dances all resemble each other. His art is mime-based, but he is able to draw more abstract inferences from mime than many choreographers can from dance. In *Glow Worm*, he moved about the stage telling stories of his boyhood aloud and using the sign language of the deaf as a counterpoint to both movement and speech. The words, the mime language, and the mime movement supported each other gracefully, but the clear separation between them suggested melancholy dissociation. It's an effect Charlip gets by means of pure mimicry in *Meditation*. As Massenet's insulting, silky music plays on, he slowly contorts his face in a series of agonized or inane expressions divorced from emotional contexts. Charlip works on a very small scale with exquisite balance and discretion. He is someone who might look at home in Japanese ceremonial dress. A light-weight, yes, but also a master.

Merce Cunningham

A COLLABORATIVE PROCESS BETWEEN MUSIC AND DANCE (1982)

What follows concerns a selection of the works that John Cage and I have collaborated on over the past four decades. It is in no sense a complete survey; there are numerous others not included. But these are some of that history that reflect to me a change or enlargement of the underlying principle (with the sole exception of Second Hand [1970]) that music and dance could be separate entities independent and interdependent, sharing a common time. There is a continuing flexibility in the relation of the two arts. We are involved in a process of work and activity, not in a series of finished objects.

Whatever tremors it may have provided for the various dancers who have shared these experiences with me, I think they would agree that it is also exhilarating and adventurous. It keeps one on one's toes, and jumps the mind as well as the body.

The first program that Cage and I shared was presented in New York City in 1944. The evening consisted of six solos by myself and three pieces of music by Cage who had also composed the music for the dances.

At the time, he was working in a way he called rhythmic structure, and all of the dances with the exception of *Totem Ancestor* (1942) were choreographed involving this use of time. What was involved was a "macro-microcosmic rhythmic structure" in which the large parts were related to the small parts in divisions of time. This was a way of working between the music and the dance that allowed them to be separate, coming together only at the structural points. For example, in *Root of an Unfocus* (1944), the original phrase was structured 8–10–6 beats. The dance was in three parts, the first section being 8 × 8, the second 10 × 10, the third 6 × 6. The tempo for each section varied as did the time lengths (one and one-half minutes; two and one-half minutes; one minute). This use of a time structure allowed us to work separately, Cage not having to be with the dance except at structural points, and I was free to make the phrases and movements within the phrases vary their speeds and accents without reference to a musical beat, again only using the structural points as identification between us. Each of the five dances made this way had a different time structure and length which came out of my initial working with the movement for the particular dance.

DANCE	TRIPLE-PACED ROOT OF AN UNFOCUS TOSSED AS IT IS UNTROUBLED
MUSIC	THE PERILOUS NIGHT: SIX SOLOS SONGS: SHE IS ASLEEP THE WONDERFUL WIDOW OF 18 SPRINGS AMORES: PRELUDE; TRIO; WALTZ; SOLO
DANCE	THE UNAVAILABLE MEMORY OF TOTEM ANCESTOR SPONTANEOUS EARTH

Studio Theatre, 108 W. 16th Street, April 5th, 1944

I had written *Four Walls* (1944), a dance-play lasting an hour that was to be presented in the Perry-Mansfield Summer Theatre. Cage wrote a piano score for it. I had asked if he could make the score fairly simple, not being certain of the pianist's capabilities in such a situation. We devised a rhythmic structure that included time-lengths for the script and the dancing, and then he composed the work for the white keys only. The rhythmic structure left me free to work with the dancers and actors in such a way as not to pin the words or all the movements to specific notes, although the structural connections were observed. Cage was not present at the summer school, and at one point in the rehearsals, Arch Lauterer, who was co-directing and had designed the set and lighting, pointed out one part he thought too long. "You must cut the music there." I agreed that the section dragged, but did not feel that to cut the music was a solution, and would not have chosen to do so anyway. Searching about for another answer, I changed the dance movements and rephrased the timing of the scene; in other words, used the allotted structural time differently. The next rehearsal Lauterer said, "You see, it is much better with the music shortened."

FOUR WALLS
a dance play

under the joint directorship of
Merce Cunningham and Arch Lauterer

Choreography: Merce Cunningham
Design: Arch Lauterer

Perry-Mansfield Theatre, Steamboat Springs, Colorado,
August 22nd, 1944

In the spring of 1948, Cage and I were touring, giving joint programs of music and dance. One of these was presented on a small stage in the Richmond Women's Club, the "oldest in the country," we were told. The oldest member had been informed ahead of the program about the prepared piano, so that when the sounds were heard she would not be too disturbed. At one point in the program, there was a piece that Cage had arranged for piano and flute. She confided loudly to her companion, "Well, I understand how that other music came out of the piano, but if this one did, then our piano's broken."

Later on that same tour, at a college in Virginia, we were asked to give a lecture-demonstration. We chose not to do the conventional talking and demonstrating, but rather to make a short dance and piece of music in front of the largely student public. Explaining first about the rhythmic structure and what this particular one would be, we proceeded to work separately, he at the side of the stage with a piano, and I in the stage space itself.

As I remember, the structure was 8 × 8, divided 2–2–1–3. At the completion of any section, any 8, we would try it together, the dance and the music, the public applauding as each point was made. I had explained we did not expect to finish the work, that it was more of an act of process. But we did, to my amazement.

The *Sixteen Dances for Soloist and Company of Three* (1951) was special for me in my work. It was a long piece intended to fill an evening. It was also the first time the use of chance operations entered into the compositional technique.

The choreography was concerned with expressive behavior, in this case the nine permanent emotions of Indian classical esthetics, four light and four dark with tranquillity the ninth and pervading one. The structure for the piece was to have each of the dances involved with a specific emotion followed by an interlude. Although the order was to alternate light and dark, it didn't seem to matter whether Sorrow or Fear came first, so I tossed a coin. And also in the interlude after Fear, number 14, I used charts of separate movements for material for each of the four dancers, and let chance operations decide the continuity.

The work had an overall rhythmic structure to which Cage wrote the score, generally after the dances were finished. He composed it for both piano and small orchestra, distinguished by a number of unusual percussion sounds. Although each dance was a separate entity, we were beginning to use "poetic license" in disregarding connecting points within the dances.

16 DANCES FOR SOLOIST AND COMPANY OF THREE

Solo:	Anger
Trio:	Interlude
Solo:	Humor
Duet:	Interlude
Solo:	Sorrow
Quartet:	Interlude
Solo:	Heroic
Quartet:	Interlude
Solo:	Odious
Duet:	Interlude
Solo:	Wondrous
Trio:	Interlude
Solo:	Fear
Quartet:	Interlude
Duet:	Erotic
Quartet:	Tranquillity

Hunter College Playhouse, January 21, 1951

At the Black Mountain Summer School in 1952, Cage organized a theater event, the first of its kind. David Tudor played the piano, M. C. Richards and Charles Olson read poetry, Robert Rauschenberg's white paintings were on the ceiling. Rauschenberg himself played records, and Cage talked. I danced. The piece was forty-five minutes long, and, as I remember, each of us had two segments of time within the forty-five to perform our activity. The audience was seated in the middle of the playing area, facing each other, the chairs arranged on diagonals, and the spectators unable to see directly everything that was happening. There was a dog which chased me around the space as I danced. Nothing was intended to be other than it was, a complexity of events that the spectators could deal with as each chose.

THEATER PIECE

Speaker:	John Cage
Music:	David Tudor
Dance:	Merce Cunningham
Poetry:	Charles Olson
	M. C. Richards
Paintings:	Robert Rauschenberg

Black Mountain College, North Carolina, Summer, 1952

Cage had written the pieces *Music for Piano*, the sequence of sounds for which had been found by noting the imperfections in pieces of paper, and applying chance operations to this. I decided to do the same thing to ascertain the space points for a dance called *Suite for Five in Space and Time* (1956). The *Suite* eventually came to comprise seven dances. The spacial plan for each dance was the starting point. Using transparent paper as a grid, a bird's-eye view of the playing space, I marked and numbered the imperfections, a page for each dancer in each of the dances. In the "Duet," the "Trio," and the "Quintet," I superimposed the pages for each dancer to find if there were points where they came together and would allow for partnering or held poses, some form of liaison between them. The time was found by taking lined paper, each line representing five-second intervals. Imperfections were again noted on the paper and the time lengths of phrases obtained from chance numbering of the imperfections in relation to the number of seconds.

This was one of the first dances where meter was completely abandoned, and we, the dancers, had to rely on our own dance timing to guard the length of any phrase, and the timing of a complete dance.

Cage's *Music for Piano*, which was played with the dance, is variable in time. Although the dancers came to know the sequences of sounds, the sounds do not necessarily happen at the same points from performance to performance. And, as sometimes occurred, with the addition of pianists and pianos, the sound was augmented and the original piece had other layers with it.

The total length of a given dance, however, remained identical each time. Through many performances, the duration of the pieces varied little. After a period of, say, three months of not rehearsing, the dancers (assuming they were the same ones, of course) would come within five to ten seconds of a two-minute and forty-five-second dance.

SUITE FOR FIVE IN SPACE AND TIME

the music is from *Music for Piano*

Solo:	At Random
Trio:	Transition
Solo:	Stillness
Duet:	Extended Moment
Solo:	Repetition
Solo:	Excursion
Quintet:	Meetings
Solo:	For the Air

The events and sounds of this ballet revolve
around a quiet center, which, though silent and
unmoving, is the source from which they happen.

Piano: David Tudor
(First Performance)

The University of Notre Dame Concert and Lecture Series, May 18, 1956

My company and I were in residence at Connecticut College in 1958, and
there was to be a festival of programs the last week. We would appear on two
of them. So I made two dances, *Summerspace* with a commissioned score from
Morton Feldman, and the second, *Antic Meet,* using Cage's *Concert for Piano
and Orchestra.* This was one of the first times I gave him only the length of the
total dance (twenty-six minutes), but no time points in between. His score is
indeterminate in length, and also in the proportions within the piece, so even
though the dance was set, we could not count on the sounds as cues, as they
never fell in the same place twice. The dancers' unsupported timespan was
expanding.

ANTIC MEET

Merce Cunningham, Choreography
David Tudor, Pianist
John Cage, Conductor
(First Performance)

Connecticut College, New London, Connecticut, August 14, 1958

The *Events* were originally intended as a means of giving performances in
unorthodox surroundings. Since then they have sometimes been given in

conventional theaters. The first *Event* was presented in the *Museum des 20 Jahrhunderts* in Vienna during a world tour. The music was Cage's *Atlas Eclipticalis* and was played by six musicians who were seated apart from one another in the corners of the large hall in which the *Event* took place. Since the performing area was unconventional, just an open space in the museum, it did not seem to us that a conventional presentation of three or four dances was appropriate, and so we chose to present a single length of time, an hour and a half, in which the music and the dance could be heard and seen. I put together a series of sections out of the repertory. At times during the program there were several dances going on at once. There was no separation between the dances; we went directly from one to another. The audience was seated mainly in front of us, but also extended onto the two sides. The musicians played continuously for an hour and a half. Since we, the dancers, had no awareness of what the continuity of sound would be, we were free to involve ourselves in what we were doing.

We continue to present *Events* in orthodox and unorthodox situations, usually with four musicians. In recent years they have been Takehisa Kosugi and Martin Kalve as well as Cage and David Tudor. Each is a composer, and each makes a sound ambience separate from the others, using the *Event* time as he chooses. The dance material now consists not only of pieces from the repertory, done in whole or part, but also dances and actions made specifically for the *Events*.

MUSEUM EVENT   VIENNA 1964

Mittwoch 24. Juni 1964   19:30 Uhr
Gastspiel
Merce Cunningham & Dance Company, New York

Museum Event Nr. 1
(Erstauffuhrung)

Tänzer
Merce Cunningham

Carolyn Brown   Viola Farber
Shareen Blair   Deborah Hay   Barbara Lloyd   Sandra Neels
William Davis   Steve Paxton   Albert Reid
Schlagzeug:
John Cage
Friedrich Cerha
Peter Greenham
Judith Justice
Petr Kotik
David Tudor
Musik: John Cage (*Atlas Eclipticalis*, 1961/62)
Dekor, Kostüme, Beleuchtung: Robert Rauschenberg, Alex Hay

The French-American Festival had commissioned Cage to prepare a score and me to make choreography for it. For this work, *Variations V* (1965), Cage decided to find out if there might not be ways that the sound could be affected by movement, and he and David Tudor proceeded to discover that there were. Several, in fact, only two of which finally worked out for use in the piece, the rest being impractical due to cost, or requiring machines not usable in the theater, or simply too clumsy. The two ways that were used were not differentiated with respect to the dance, but were different for the musicians, the technicians, and the stage set-up. The first was a series of poles, twelve in all, like antennae, placed all over the stage—each to have a sound radius, sphere-shaped, of four feet. When a dancer came into this radius, sound could be triggered. Each of the twelve antennae had different sound possibilities. The metal rods were five feet high and roughly one inch in diameter. I had not known the exact dimensions of the poles nor their placement previous to the stage rehearsal the day before the performance, as the technique necessary to ready them had been in a constant state of experimentation, but I did know they would be upright and the number would be twelve. So I had prepared the choreography and the dancers—there were seven of us—for the possibility of instant changes of mind. But I did wonder about our feet stepping on the wires which would be running from the base of the poles across the floor and up to the electronic systems which controlled all this. Fortunately, it was a surmountable impediment.

The second sound source was a series of photoelectric cells which were to be positioned on the floor along the sides of the stage. The stage lights would be focused in such a way as to hit them, and when a dancer passed between the cell and the light, more sound possibilities were triggered. This did not work out precisely, as the stage lights were too distant to strike the sides of the stage strongly enough. After all, they were focused on us and we were prone to be in the middle of the area. So at the last minute the cells were put at the base of the twelve poles throughout the area and this was a viable solution. The general principle as far as I was concerned was like the doors automatically opening when you enter a supermarket. The dancers triggered some of the sound possibilities, but the kind of sound, how long it might last, the possible repetition or delaying of it, was controlled by the musicians and technicians who were at the numerous machines on a platform behind and above the dance space. They utilized tape machines, oscillators, and short-wave radios.

Film and television images were also used in this work. Stan VanDerBeek and Nam June Paik both showed visual elements on screens behind and to the side of the performing area. There were also various props: a plant, a pillow, a pad, a table, and two chairs, to which contact microphones were attached and which, when moved or touched by the dancers, added to the sound possibilities. At the end of the piece I rode a bicycle, the wheels wired for sound, through the space, around the poles and the photoelectric cells, and then exited.

New York Philharmonic

French-American Festival, July 23, 1965 at 8:30

John Cage: *Variations V*
(World Premiere)
Merce Cunningham, Carolyn Brown, Barbara Lloyd, Sandra Neels,
Albert Reid, Peter Saul, Gus Solomons jr
    Electronic Devices: Robert A. Moog
    Film: Stan VanDerBeek
    Distortion of Television Images: Nam June Paik
    Technical Consultant: Billy Klüver
    Musicians: John Cage, Malcolm Goldstein, Frederick Lieberman,
            James Tenney, David Tudor
    Lighting: Beverly Emmons

One of the earliest of my solos, called *Idyllic Song* (1944), was made to the first movement of the *Socrate* of Erik Satie. Cage had arranged the music for two pianos. Over the years, he had suggested I choreograph the other two movements, as he had planned to arrange them for piano also.

On one of our tours in the late sixties in the Middle West, David Tudor and Gordon Mumma, the musicians with us, explained to me that it was difficult for them to make different electronic set-ups for each of three separate dances for the performances and what could be done about it? Cage suggested I choreograph the *Socrate*. He had completed the two-piano arrangement. I worked on the dance, remembering the early solo for the first part, making a duet for Carolyn Brown and myself for the second, and a full company dance for the final movement. A month before the scheduled first performance, Cage telephoned from Davis, California (where he was in residence at the University of California) to say that the Satie publisher had refused permission for his two-piano arrangement, but not to worry as he was writing a new piece for one piano, keeping the structure and phraseology of Satie's music but otherwise using chance operations to change the continuity so there would be no copyright problem. When he told me this, I replied, "But you will have to rehearse with us and play the music so we can learn the new continuity." "Don't worry, I will," he answered, "I'm calling my version *Cheap Imitation*." "Well, if you're dong that, I'll call mine *Second Hand*." It was the last time I made a work following the phraseology of a musical score.

Second Hand	John Cage
	(Cheap Imitation)

(First Performance)

Part I	
Merce Cunningham	
Part II	
Merce Cunningham	Carolyn Brown
Part III	
Merce Cunningham	Carolyn Brown
Sandra Neels	Valda Setterfield
Meg Harper	Susana Hayman-Chaffey
Jeff Slayton	Chase Robinson
Mel Wong	Douglas Dunn

Decor: Jasper Johns
Piano: John Cage

Brooklyn Academy of Music, January 8, 1970, 8:30 P.M.

In the fall of 1973, I spent nine weeks in Paris working with dancers from the Opéra Ballet. The *Festival d'Automne* and the Paris International Dance Festival had jointly commissioned this work to be choreographed utilizing dancers from the Opéra on the Opéra stage. I asked Cage if he would compose the music, and Jasper Johns if he would design the decor. They agreed. It was to be an evening-length work without intermission and would involve the full Opéra facilities. The work was to be called *Un Jour ou deux*.

Cage had originally wanted to use the works of Satie in various juxtapositions, to make a circus of Satie's music, but Salabert, the publisher, refused permission. So he composed the work *Etcetera*, for orchestra, which involved twenty musicians and three conductors. Cage arrived in Paris a month before the first performance, and proceeded to have consultations with Marius Constant, the principal conductor, and the other two, Catherine Comet and Boris de Vinogradow. When the first musical rehearsal came, there was a problem. From what I understood, the musicians, upon learning that they were to make choices about which sounds they played, as indicated in Cage's score, asked for more money, pointing out also that it was chamber music. Rolf Liebermann, the then Director of the Opéra, spent a good part of the day with them, eventually solving the difficulty by giving them two marks (double pay) for each rehearsal and performance. Cage was worried about setting a precedent. Constant said, "Don't. It's the Opéra. It would have happened anyway."

Each day, I was in the top of the building working in the ballet studio with the dancers, many of whom were worried about dancing without musical support, and what would happen when the two came together? This fear increased as the piece grew longer, one or two of the soloists becoming quite upset at times. I thought it had to do mainly with an idea about their image, and assured them they were strong enough as dancers not to be thrown off by it.

At the first rehearsal of the music in the theater without the dancers, a sound like rain on a number of roofs came out of the pit. The large handful of spectators rushed forward to see what was producing it. Each musician had, as a supplement to his instrument, a French cardboard carton which he used as a drum at various moments during the piece.

Several days later, at the first full rehearsal of the work with the dancers on the stage and the musicians in the pit, I had to repeatedly calm several dancers as to their dancing with the music. Finally the rehearsal began. I was nervous enough trying to keep track of the dance and the timings within it and what was working and what wasn't, so any difficulties they might be having with the music were not immediately apparent to me. Afterward, upon my questioning, they said, "The music? No, we didn't have any trouble."

UN JOUR OU DEUX

Choreography by Merce Cunningham
Music by John Cage: *Etcetera*
Decor and Costumes by Jasper Johns
Assistant: Mark Lancaster
Conductors: Catherine Comet,
Marius Constant, Boris de Vinogradow

Théâtre National de l'Opéra, Mardi 6 Novembre 1973 à 20H30

Our *Event for Television*, presented on the National Educational Television's "Dance in America" series, was a collaboration among the dance company, John Cage, and David Tudor. This was an hour program which in this instance became fifty-eight minutes and forty-five seconds. Charles Atlas, with whom my video and film work has been done, and I spent four weeks working out the dances and excerpts of dances we planned to present. The excerpts that were from the repertory were remade and angled for the camera; in some cases they were shortened, as I feel one receives information quicker and more directly on television than on the stage.

Cage and Tudor decided to share the hour, Cage having the first section for which he played *Branches,* music for plant materials. He was interested in sounds from nature and had found that the spines of cacti, when touched and amplified, produced resonant sounds. At the point in the program, when the dance *RainForest* (1968) appeared, Tudor's music for it began, and this continued through the balance of the hour. Both musics were introduced into the program after the taping and editing had been completed—that is, several weeks after the actual shooting of the dances.

Working with dance in video requires a constant adjustment in terms of space, often on a small scale. A six-inch shift can seem large on the camera.

This also can cause a displacement in the timing requiring a change in rhythm, or the amplifying of a dance phrase, sometimes necessitating a cut or speed-up of the movement. In the conventional music-dance relationship, this could require a constant recomposing or rearranging of the sound. But since I work separately from the music and not on a note-by-note relationship, I was free to adjust the dance phrases and movements through the camera in a visual sense.

EVENT FOR TELEVISION

Minutiae
Solo
Westbeth
Septet
Antic Meet
Scramble
RainForest
Sounddance
Video Triangle
Music: John Cage (Branches)
David Tudor (RainForest)
Taped at Nashville, Tennessee, 8–11 November 1976
First public showing, WNET/"Dance in America," 5 January 1977

The most recent collaboration that Cage and I have been involved with was the International Dance Course for Professional Choreographers and Composers held in August 1981 at the University of Surrey in Guildford, England.

The workshop was a two-week period that involved eight choreographers selected by audition from professional companies (ballet and modern) on the Continent and in the United Kingdom, and eight practicing composers, with a nucleus of twenty-seven dancers and five musicians for the various choreographers and composers to use as working personnel in the projects.

With one exception, Cage and I decided to conduct the workshop by means of chance operations. The exception was the time length of each project. The decision here was to make the original project four minutes in length and to increase the daily project by a minute; thus, the final project would be fifteen minutes long.

Other than this, the rest of the decisions concerning the daily work were decided by chance operations: the number of dancers or musicians any choreographer or composer would work with each day, the actual dancers and musicians involved in a given piece, and the composer-choreographer relationship.

Each day after the morning class and lunch, I would suggest a project to the choreographers and dancers from ideas I had employed in dances in the past. These ranged from simple time and space problems to complexities involving multiple spaces and superimposition of movements and phrases.

Then each choreographer would be informed as to the number and names of the dancers he or she would be working with that day. The dances ranged from solos to octets. Following this, the choreographers had the balance of the afternoon, roughly three to four hours, to work with their dancers in the separate studios the university provided.

With the composers and musicians, Cage talked each morning about the ideas in his music. He gave a survey of it from the earliest pieces to the latest work, pointing out the musical ideas he had been working with in each instance and the philosophical concerns with which he had been involved. He did not present a particular project to the composers, preferring to leave them free to make their own choices.

Neither the choreographers nor the composers knew during the afternoon working period which music would be played with which dance.

Each evening for the twelve days of the workshop there was a program of the dances and the music that had been made during the day. And it was then, again using chance operations, that the decisions were made as to the choice of music to be played with any given dance. At times, there would be two choreographers' works being presented to a single composer's music. At other times, two separate pieces would be played along with one of the dances.

One came to the evening's program with a certain amount of anticipation and, although not all fare was gourmet, there were an astonishing number of times when the music and the dance seemed to have been made for each other.

The original plan of having a minute added to the length of the works each day was relinquished after the first week. A number of the choreographers felt it was difficult to deal with the increased length each day due to the short working period and their unfamiliarity with the dancers. They made their own decisions about the length, although several of them elected to continue the one-minute addition. And choreographers who, during the first week, had worried about doing a longer work each day, found a ten- or twelve- or fifteen-minute length not intolerable, but provocative and feasible.

The sharing of dancers, musicians, and ideas; the non-impinging atmosphere that resulted (as well as the extraordinary amount of music and dance that was made, rehearsed, and presented each day) was exhilarating, giving a feeling not of things finished, indexed, and catalogued, but of work that was being done, and could continue to be done and shared.

INTERNATIONAL DANCE COURSE FOR PROFESSIONAL

CHOREOGRAPHERS AND COMPOSERS

University of Surrey, Guildford, England

Sunday 16th August–Saturday 29th August 1981

David Vaughan

LOCALE:
THE COLLABORATION
OF MERCE CUNNINGHAM
AND CHARLES ATLAS (1981)

M erce Cunningham often speaks of the profound impression that the films of Fred Astaire made on him when he was growing up in Centralia, a small town in the state of Washington. Astaire was concerned with the dance for its own sake, and was always trying out new ideas, new rhythms, new steps—it is said that he used to screen his old movies frequently to make sure he would not repeat himself. Cunningham, throughout his forty years as a choreographer, has also pursued a restless search for new ways to move.

In recent years Cunningham has emulated Astaire in another way—when he went to Hollywood, Astaire decided that he had better learn the craft and technique of filmmaking if he wanted to keep control of the way his dances were shown on screen. Cunningham made a similar decision with respect to video when it became clear to him that this was a medium that would allow his work to be seen by a wider public. As early as 1961 he had choreographed a short work for Canadian television, and there were telecasts during the Cunningham Dance Company's 1964 world tour (including one of a live performance in Helsinki, from which *Story* [1963] is now distributed as a film by the Cunningham Dance Foundation). In 1968 Cunningham choreographed *Assemblage*, filmed on location in Ghirardelli Square, San Francisco, under the direction of Richard Moore, for KQED-TV. But in these cases Cunningham was not able to exercise full control over the way the dances were handled, and was not always satisfied with the results.

In May of 1974 he collaborated for the first time with Merrill Brockway, then director of the CBS program *Camera 3*, on a show called "A Video Event," in two parts—a television version of the kind of performances Cunningham's company had been giving in museums, gymnasiums, sports arenas, and other non-theatrical spaces for the past ten years. Cunningham and Brockway worked closely together on the adaptation of the material for this program, which included class work and rehearsal shots as well as excerpts from the repertory. (Later they were to renew this collaboration on a more ambitious scale for the "Event for Television" Cunningham devised for a program in the first WNET "Dance in America" series, made in the fall of 1976, which included one specially choreographed segment called *Video Triangle*.)

The next logical step was for Cunningham to begin making video pieces of his own. He had already begun to use videotape as a means of recording choreography, which he felt to be preferable to any of the existing notation systems because it provides a direct visual image of the movement itself rather than representing it by means of graphic symbols. Moreover, videotape's capacity for instant replay makes it a useful tool in the actual creation of choreography. The Cunningham Dance Company's technical director, Charles Atlas, is a filmmaker in his own right (who had already made a film of one of the dances in the repertory, *Walkaround Time* [1968]), and Cunningham began collaborating with him on a series of video and film pieces, most of them devised specifically for the medium. The first of these, *Westbeth*, was taped at the Merce Cunningham Studio in Westbeth, New York, in the fall of 1974. In the following year they made *Blue Studio: Five Segments* for the WNET/Lab, a solo piece using the chroma-key system. This was followed in 1976 by a video version of an existing piece, *Squaregame (Squaregame Video)*, also made at Westbeth.

Having familiarized themselves with the grammar of videodance, Cunningham and Atlas began to increase the scope of their experiments, using more elaborate technical means. *Fractions* (1977), an original work for video, played with the idea of the fragmenting of images among a number of screens—action taking place simultaneously in different areas of the studio was seen on the main screen and also on monitors set up within the range of the main camera. Like *Westbeth*, the choreography of this piece was later adapted for live performance, a reversal of the usual practice. *Westbeth* became part of the body of material from which Cunningham put together Events, and *Fractions* was recast as a discrete stage piece.

Even more complex was *Locale*, a filmdance shot in the Cunningham Studio in January–February 1979. In the previous pieces, Cunningham and Atlas had dealt principally with movement within the frame rather than movement of the frame—using, that is to say, a mostly stationary camera and with no fancy editing (Cunningham prefers to keep cuts to a minimum, at strictly logical points in the dance). Now they were ready to explore the possibilities of a moving camera, which can be treacherous when used to film dancing—one kind of movement can have the effect of cancelling out the other. Because they wanted the camera to move not only along with but around and amongst the dancers, and also at different speeds, its movements would have to be choreographed as precisely as those of the dancers. Three kinds of camera were used: Steadicam, Movieola crab dolly, and an Elemac dolly with a crane arm. Because of the expense of renting this kind of equipment and the limited rehearsal and shooting time available with the dancers, Cunningham and Atlas did as much advance planning as possible; the logistics were figured out as far as possible on paper beforehand, then Atlas had one weekend to practice with the equipment without the dancers. Then he rehearsed along with them, to set the path he would follow when using the Steadicam. When it came time for the actual shooting, certain adjustments had to be made—as Cunningham has said, there are certain things that the camera "just won't do"—but for the most part things went according to plan.

One of the most obvious differences between dance as seen on the stage and on television or film screen is that in the former the spectator is free to choose where to direct his attention, while on the screen the viewpoint is that of the camera, controlled by the director and, in Cunningham's pieces, the choreographer. The difference is in fact even more extreme in a Cunningham work because in his stage pieces he favors a "field" approach to the use of space, in which a number of different things may be occurring simultaneously so that the spectator is more or less obliged to make a choice of what to look at, whereas in more conventional forms, such as ballet, the focus is to a large extent inherent in the choreography, which reflects the hierarchic set-up of ballerina and partner supported by lesser soloists and backed up by the *corps de ballet*.

In the first section of *Locale* the camera moves at sometimes dizzying speeds (on a large screen this can be quite disorienting, so that some spectators have experienced something close to motion sickness), back and forth, up and down the length and breadth of the studio space, revealing different groups of dancers who appear in the camera's field of vision (instead of entering as they would have to on stage). Some of them—on camera anyway—are more prominently visible than others, according to whether they are in the foreground or background of the picture. Some people, watching *Locale*, have even complained of being robbed of their autonomy; the critic Marcia B. Siegel, for instance, wrote in the *Soho News* (April 2, 1980) that "I'm . . . impelled to give up my own center and submit to an external motion that I can neither predict nor control." As Arlene Croce pointed out (in the *New Yorker*, February 25, 1980), it is with Cunningham's own "eye and mind" that we see the choreography of *Locale*—"communication as direct and transparent as any we have had on film since the hand of Picasso drawing in *Le Mystère Picasso.*"

Perhaps to simplify things for the spectator by not forcing him to register too many different kinds of movement information at once, Cunningham choreographed his first section mostly in terms of stop-motion poses. The second section begins with a sequence of short passages separated by cuts, during which the movement becomes more fluid. (In the first section whatever cuts are necessary are made as unobtrusively as possible, usually at moments when the camera passes a blank wall.) The timing of the editing here is often virtuosic, as when Joseph Lennon leaps off some steps, crashes to the floor, and immediately Lise Friedman is lifted by Alan Good—the surprise of this sequence of movements works perfectly on camera in a way that it never can, quite, on stage. In a later section, the camera moves again, at one point executing a complete 360-degree revolution around the studio space, finding dancers in corners or catching their reflections in the mirror, that is as technically dazzling as the opening shot of Max Ophüls's *Madame de . . .*

The making of *Locale* was recorded in a brief documentary by Atlas called *Roamin' I* (which can be read as Roman One or Roamin' Eye), consisting of some material specially shot during the filming as well as outtakes from *Locale* itself. This is a hilarious and instructive glimpse behind the scenes, or behind the camera, showing the dancers scuttling around to make their re-entrance on another side, climbing over cables, jumping out of the way of the dolly or crane. An elaborate system of pulleys was devised to pull the cables out of shot as the camera pursued its restless path, and one sees this in operation, with the accompaniment of shouted cues to the technicians in charge. (The soundtrack of *Locale*, which consists of electronic music and some ambient sound recorded during the filming, was added later.)

The latest Cunningham-Atlas collaboration, *Channels/Inserts* (1981), has already been seen on stage, during the Cunningham company's recent City Center season. The film is, at this writing, still being edited. This time the collaborators used the entire premises of the Westbeth Studio, not just the main studio itself. The stage version is certainly among Cunningham's most impressive recent works; word is that the film version will look very different, which is certainly true of *Fractions* and *Locale*, but one may be sure that it will yield plenty of surprises.

Cunningham's work as a choreographer has been based on an innovative approach to the nature of time and space in the theatre. For instance, he rejected the notion, proposed in Doris Humphrey's book *The Art of Making Dances*, that certain areas of the stage are "weaker" or "stronger" than others, and the time element of his dances is not governed by conventional notions of "build-up" and climax. It is not surprising, therefore, that he has shown an instinctive grasp of the nature of these elements as they are perceived in video, realizing, for instance, that time can be treated elliptically because the spectator absorbs information much faster than in the theatre, and that space appears to widen out from the small aperture of the screen, giving an illusion of greater depth than in fact exists. Cunningham's video pieces are composed with such characteristics in mind. (Other choreographers have "reconceived" their works for television, but Martha Graham, for instance, in reworking her *Clytemnestra*, retained sequences whose repetitiousness seems excessive in terms of television "time," while George Balanchine has usually preserved the symmetrical spatial configurations inherent in the balletic hierarchy.) Cunningham is the first to agree that dance on the screen can never have the immediacy of a live performance, but his video and film dances prove that work in those media can have a vitality of its own—just as Astaire's did.

Merce Cunningham

DIARY OF A CUNNINGHAM DANCE (1981)

During the six-week work period of the film/dance that Charles Atlas and I have made, I kept a diary of the work in progress, *Channels/Inserts*.

It was understood from the beginning that this work would also be performed on stage during our two-week season at City Center, and that the stage adaptation would be made after the camera version had been completed. For the stage you have to choreograph entrances and exits, whereas with film you need only shift the camera to eliminate a dancer.

The piece, the fifth Mr. Atlas and I have filmed in my studio at Westbeth, was to be twenty-eight minutes long after editing. He and I planned all the cuts in advance, and all filming was done with those in mind. Three cameras were available: a still camera—that is, one in a fixed position; a "dolly," a camera mounted on a small wheeled platform to be moved during filming; and the third, a Steadicam. This last was a camera suspended in front of Charles Atlas, who wore a brace to support it and was able to move about freely while using it.

The work is comprised of sixteen sections varying in length from ten seconds to three minutes. Each section has a different number of dancers, although six seem to predominate.

Herewith my jottings:

Dec. 23—First day of rehearsal with the dancers. Labyrinths of notes and drawings I've made working by myself during the past months to turn into steps and placements. After three hours with five dancers, we had a little more than a minute of the complete work—two couples and a girl dancing in an eight-foot diameter of space (disco in an elevator).

I will work with the dancers during the week, Tuesday through Friday, using a small viewfinder as a helper, and the filming will be done on the weekends when the dance studios are freer from their ordinary allotment of classes. The various sequences are to be shot mainly in our large dance studio, with several being made in the small studio and in the corridor running between them.

Dec. 27—Camera work is basically uncooperative with dancing—limbs getting out of the camera frame. The dance is to be shot in both film and video, the film for eventual broadcast possibilities and the video for instant playback, essential for seeing what it is you've done.

Dec. 28—I tried out some fragments for the long two-minute corridor sequence. It has all the dancers in couples appearing in and out of doorways. Where do they go when the camera gives them only walls and inches?

Jan. 3—First time with all the dancers and the whole crew. There are twenty-two of them with Charlie Atlas, the two cameramen and assistants. And fifteen of us. Big production. Rehearsing for filming. At first glance through the cameras, nothing works. All the angles are wrong: try again. Then all the cameras and monitors go blank; so while remedial practices are applied to the instruments by the crew, I work on a section for the men—a still camera sequence with the dancers leaping into and out of camera range.

Jan. 4—Long technical day. Constant attention is what it's about. No arm let go, no pose thrown away. Charlie's continued concern for each single shot is admirable if exhausting. But dance on camera seems to require this or it stumbles. Also we are planning the cuts from one camera to another, and this requires a stop or a clarification of the dance action to make the cut possible. A cut in film takes the place of eye-shift in theater.

Jan. 5—Sat with Charlie looking at the video playbacks of Sections 1 through 4, watching for technical errors and ways to enliven the angles. Dancing on film doesn't seem to have presence.

Jan. 6—I started on another section, this one with three couples again. Looking through the camera at what I'd made previously, muttering to myself, "That phrase has to be re-angled; now Karole's too far out; if Cathy and Robert move over and the rhythm is quickened there, the three couples are O.K.; why's this look so flat?; oh, that works!; but wait a moment! stop! stop!" Go back and begin again, almost frame by frame, and after a half-hour of that, where's the dance life?

Jan. 9—After years of watching dancers in the flesh, it is still difficult for me to turn my back while they are dancing and see them only in the monitor.

Jan. 10—The first film shooting day. The dolly is moved onto the dance floor, the camera positioned, the decks and monitors stretched out on the edge of the space. One of the cameramen stoops over the dolly, hands on the handle ready to push it along the floor. This bent-over position is his for the next three weeks. He manages it with humor.

Jan. 11—The studio is completely changed. The company room's a costume and make-up headquarters; the women's dressing room has become a small café complete with coffee urn and bench covered with croissants, fruit, and cheese, and various members of the crew and company munching. Charlie's room is full of film equipment, and the main studio has become this black walled and floored vault. No light from outside allowed to enter.

After two days of shooting, we have about seven minutes filmed.

Jan. 15—I asked the dancers to go through what we had of the piece, some twenty minutes, to give them the chance to do something fully and give myself the opportunity to see it. Great deal of activity.

Jan. 16—The sound engineer tapes "room sound," the ambient noise, with each take. This will be added during the editing, as will the music being composed by David Tudor. Since my choreography is not set to music and not governed by musical phraseology, I am free to change it as need be in terms of camera angles and cuts.

Jan. 19—We had about twenty minutes' rehearsal on the thirty-second sequence in Section 3 where the Steadicam is used. Charlie, rushing about in the midst of the gyrating dancers, with that brace on and the camera suspended in front of him, looks like some large leaning animal trying to avoid collision with a bunch of humans each going in a different direction.

Jan. 22—Grand entertainment in a way, this dance/film experience. Shocks the sense of time, and makes one aware of minute differences—like lengths of arms. How'd they get so long? Dancers have an automatic way of putting arms out to balance and counterbalance what the rest of the body may be doing. But often on the camera they have to do the opposite to keep them in view—moving toward the edge of the space and dropping an arm instead of raising it to the side.

Jan. 23—The studio has a black cavernous look now with the curtain drawn totally around, the stage framed in black flats, the floor covered with black marly. It takes an hour after the morning class to ready all the curtains, flats, lights, and cameras before the dancers appear. Then there's about two-and-a-half hours to try as much as we can, with the dancers and the equipment, before it all must be removed, the window shades lifted, the piano pulled out of the corner, the floor cleared, and casts exchanged—crew and company leaving as students troop in with dance bags and aspirations. The teacher appears, the pianist begins, and there is again the formality of a dance class.

Jan. 24—"What's that on the floor? Is that oil?"

"The dolly's leaking."

"Dancers, sit down and relax!"

Jan. 25—Getting dance on camera is a process that demands constant attention in multiple directions, during the brief period of a shot—say ten seconds to three minutes—and immediately afterward looking at the video playback to note omissions (loss of a hand, a lift cut, an angle that covers one of the couples), and the undesired additions (top of the curtain, an inadvertent foot from the sidelines, a flare in the lights). The dancers have maintained a remarkable calm under the weeks' strain. After the fifth take of a sequence which has gone well for them, ill for the camera, they do it again with good spirits.

Jan. 27—I saw a sampling of the footage from the Steadicam episode in the corridor. Like a ride on a horizontal roller coaster. Some of the shots in the tape look O.K., giving us some confidence in the eventual product.

Jan. 29—One of the odd things about working in this medium is the time differential. The performers have finished the show, but the public can't see it until several months elapse. Charlie's editing intervenes.

Feb. 1—Final shooting hours. We started at noon and ended at 8 P.M. The last shot was of a duet in the small studio, with the Empire State Building out the window as a backdrop. The dancers exit, and Charlie sets up a special camera which uses a time-elapse mechanism, and which, operating through the night, catches the Empire State lights going off at midnight and the change as dawn arrives. He plans to run it under the credits.

"All right, everybody, one more time."

"What take's this?"

"Seven."

"O.K., ready; roll tape, Jenny."

"Dancers in position; silence; roll sound."

"Speed."

"Slate it, Bob."

"Roll camera."

"A one insert 3, take 7, sound 195."

"Dancers, ready."

"Go!"

Don Daniels

CUNNINGHAM, IN TIME (1985)

To see the American Ballet Theatre production of Merce Cunningham's 1980 *Duets* is to see Cunningham acquired by the ballet boutique. At ABT, Cunningham's repertory staple becomes a prestige item. At best, it's a remedial exercise for deprived ABT dancers. (Where else in the rep—so goes the apology—can ABT's budding soloists encounter equivalent challenges?) The Met audience reacts with the mildness it brings to all the seasonal imports on display. Although *Summerspace* (1958) may not have settled in at New York City Ballet back in the sixties, today *Duets* does so with ease across the plaza. And, at ABT, it's not merely a matter of stylistic subtleties lost in the transfer. Rather like the recent ABT production of Balanchine's *Symphonie Concertante*, everything is there but the dancing.

Take, for example, the perception of the metrical weight of Cunningham's dance style. By "weight" I am not referring to a physical weight used by performers in the production of Cunningham dance on stage. (Cunningham's dancers are asked to use their *ballon* with more variety, and more regularity, than the ballet-trained ABT dancers.) I mean something like the viewer's awareness that the dance has an insistent metrical order. Dance metrics govern Cunningham's work, aid in its production, sometimes even become the preponderant expressive element out of several (attack, dynamics, *plastique*, etc.). I know trained dancers (with no background in Cunningham classroom training) who say that they can "count" a Cunningham dance while watching it being performed. I'm not sure that this is literally true, but I think I know what they mean. With no immediate or detailed competition from conventional musical accompaniment, Cunningham rhythms are exposed and "held" in a way that dance audiences may sometimes find assertive. The very charm of this exposure—its blatancy and frankness—allows the audience a sensitivity to dance rhythm that can startle. It seems so at times to me—for example, in Cunningham's large-scale ensemble works like *Torse* (1976) and *Rebus* (1975). When Cunningham himself or his best soloists perform his best material, they add many rhythmic values, lighten the texture, complicate it. On the other hand, when the group performs in concert, basic principles are nakedly revealed, and the Cunningham metric can seem flatly rhetorical.

In this respect the Cunningham approach to dance rhythm may derive from John Cage. Cunningham and Cage met in 1938, one year before Cage's composition *First Construction (in Metal)*, a score organized according to durational proportions—the relationship of temporal lengths in musical materials. In a lecture delivered in 1948, Cage summed up this durational approach to structure: "There can be no right making of music that does not structure itself from the very roots of sound and silence—lengths of time."[1] As late as the *String Quartet in Four Parts* (1950), Cage continued to use a "rhythmic structure": "Sounds, including noises, it seemed to me, had four characteristics (pitch, loudness, timbre, and duration), while silence had only one (duration). I therefore devised a rhythmic structure based on the duration, not of notes, but of spaces of time. The whole has as many parts as each unit has small parts, and these, large and small, are in the same proportion. Used for the first time in *Construction*, this principle appears in nearly all my work (symmetrically or asymmetrically) until 1952."[2]

The 1980s dance public recently saw the young choreographer Douglas Wright present his dance *No Man Standing* to Cage's *Six Melodies for Violin and Piano* (1950), and the audience at the Bessie Schönberg Theater was able to recall the prealeatoric, pre-magnetic-tape Cage.[3] In the *Melodies*, Cage's durational rhythm allows a stepwise construction in the music—each intervallic shift held upon by the rhythmic controls—so that the listener is made aware of the monophony (these really are melodies) and of the shifting sense of time frames through which the components are viewed. As the music slowly accumulates in its unveiling, a series of overlapping "dissolves" in the listener's perception of the musical form continually frames the components in new ways. Each temporal unit is thus filled regularly and variously through the structural imbrication. The music has a drama both in the immediate, moment-by-moment response to such local configurations and in the listener's growing sense that more discoveries are to come—the present lack of knowledge about overall shape forces a suspension of conventional musical appetites in light of the accession to come. So dense, in fact, is the immediate sound-sense (the pressure of inspection allowed by monophony and by the restriction of violin and piano to twenty-three tones) that the listener's need for release from the musical logic leads to the mind's imposition of the structural frames as though by mental reflex: such involuntary perception of local and accumulated shape offers a promise of freedom from immediate pressure toward the system's anticipated self-disposal.

It was during the early 1940s that Cage and Cunningham began their collaboration. (Their first piece—*Credo in Us*—was presented in 1942). In 1944, Cunningham devised a dance, *Tossed as it is Untroubled,* whose choreography is said to have followed Cage's proportionally arranged musical structure. (In other collaborative works, Cage followed Cunningham's lead.) Cage's compositional technique (like Arnold Schoenberg's) freed his music from any structural dependence on a harmonic system, and it may have represented a general attempt by Cage to strengthen the rhythmic component in advanced music making at that time. The sound of such music has a "primitivistic" feel about it similar to qualities in the music of Erik Satie and George Antheil. The very title of *First Construction (in Metal)* suggests constructivist forebears—that is, a style simultaneously primitive (in the steady, quantitative outlay of information) and sophisticated (in the manner by which constituent units are manipulated to "free" the sound or to contrast macro- and micro-layers of rhythmic information).

As late as 1955, in his essay "Experimental Music," Cage continued to see the basis of musical rhythm as a matter of duration: "Rhythm is duration of any length coexisting in any states of succession and synchronicity."[4] I have never encountered a published discussion of Cunningham that has suggested that Cage's approach to musical rhythm may have been influential in any specific, technical sense on the formation of the choreographer's dance rhythm. (Possibly this is because the whole subject of the relationship between musical and dance rhythm is relatively unexplored. The two are not necessarily the same.) Neither am I privy to Cunningham's specific compositional techniques. (Cunningham has stated in interviews that music and dance share only one element—time— and that all other correspondences between the two arts are "intellectual" constructs.) But I suspect that the durational emphasis in Cage's composition of music may have its equivalent in Cunningham's dancemaking.

Indeed, there may have been a period influence on both Cage and Cunningham. The swing music of the thirties brought about a new appreciation of Bach's musical rhythm. Virgil Thomson has characterized swing rhythm as "quantitative."[5] Borrowing the term from prosody, Thomson has contrasted music that is accentual in its organization (including much popular dance music) with music that is organized according to "a unit of length." For Thomson, both big-band swing and a "Brandenburg" concerto are examples of quantitative rhythm, metrical units made up of lengths or durations of musical sound. Accentual music thus becomes "beat" music. Quantitative music de-emphasizes beat; it floats, it shimmers, it burnishes; it stickily and sweetly "jams." According to Thomson, much of the freedom of improvisational jazz is made possible by an unexpressed, steady, underlying quantitative rhythm. The durational values are hinted at in the musical decoration—anticipated, traced, or brushed in, allowed to hover through the percussive strokes of drum, cymbals, or double bass—providing impetus and ground rather than offering that immediate, multilayered play of pulse and pattern to be found in music based on an accentual rhythm. I suggest that John Cage's attempt to structure his rhythms according to a durational principle may have been his contribution to this area of musical discourse during the thirties and forties.

Listeners can recognize the decoration of a Bach concerto or the drive of a jam session. Cage's durational music features a similar free flotation and steady state; it is a music of powerlessness in power, of passivity achieved out of organized activity, of contrasting movement and stasis. In the 1950 *Melodies*, the aural weight builds up a chastened version of baroque or swing momentum. Each unit is under such immediate compositional pressure, such availability for the closest inspection, one would think that all impetus would die, fragment, evaporate. (And in some late 1940s musics, Cage investigated just such effects.) Which is to say that the durational element is substantive in Cage's work, and that this value may have its general relation to what Thomson has described as a "quantitative" rhythm.

The reason that I find the evidence of a mutual interest on the part of Cage and Cunningham in this aspect of rhythm to be of use when watching the choreographer's works is that otherwise I know of no other way to explain the particular experience of Cunningham rhythm—its weight, its inclusiveness, its environment. Any dancer brought up through traditional classroom training in ballet, tap, flamenco, etc., knows that there is something special and enveloping about the Cunningham metric. Whether the educated member of the audience finds that metric liberating or claustrophobic is a matter of taste, education, or prejudice. But I think that something like the quality I am describing is identifiable in Cunningham's dance.

Such a view would explain certain enduring and characteristic features of his style. For example, simply to say that Cunningham's dances have an extraordinary command of large-scale rhythmic strategies is to say very little. Those big proportions are obviously not arrived at after the fact; they are not in any simple sense an inheritance from Martha Graham's commodious idea of theatrical time; they are not applied from "outside"; and they are not in any simple sense macro-versions of smaller dance units. It is as though Cunningham had found a method to de-emphasize any conventional "accentual" dance components in his work (except for purposes of satire or allusion). By working for durational qualities, Cunningham may have derived a method for avoiding all the clichés of conventional dance, all the encrusted "accentual" patterns that have grown up around dance forms—folk, theatrical, balletic. Freshness in dance material is thus forced by Cunningham through a singular approach to compositional method. Perhaps this also explains why some audiences and dancers—trained by dance styles formed out of a residue of accentual dance rhythms—experience an initial difficulty adjusting to the Cunningham metric.

It would also explain why a production like American Ballet Theatre's *Duets* proves inadequate. If Cunningham's dance rhythm possesses a strong durational element, then certain seductive charms of his dance classicism would be vulnerable to misinterpretation by ballet executants. For example, I suspect that, for Cunningham, *plastique* is merely one more means of "filling" the dance duration; *plastique* does not have the substantive powers of rhythmic extension that it has in ballet. At best it would work—like Bach's harmony and counterpoint—to hold attention *through* the metrical unit. It is guide rather than destination. (Actually, the choreography of Petipa, Bournonville, and Balanchine at times also exploits that kind of plastic guidance.) Cunningham works regularly to control *plastique,* to de-emphasize inherited ideas about sculptural values in dance, and to use his version of such values to concentrate and expose the underlying rhythmic idea. He allows his best performers to generate additional layers of rhythmic information over his material, to thicken the mixture, whereas in classical ballet the choreographer readily accommodates such layerings, builds them in. Those of us in the ballet crowd can—these days, must—take our pleasures where we find them. But the fan of both ballet and Cunningham makes allowances for the stylistic differences involved. Only an ABT can afford to level them. Cunningham asks his followers to watch all dance objectively. In that sense, the ABT production hadn't a Cagean chance. Not only does the version say little about Cunningham; it does little for the training of the ABT dancers—except postpone balletic choices of real stylistic consequence.

Seen in this way, Cunningham's percussive dance patterns—his variations upon his dance themes—would be the choreographer's free "improvisation" over the rhythmic ground, as in Bach and swing. (The improvisation is a compositional achievement rather than a performance choice.) Cunningham would thus purchase the freedom for brilliant "baroque" variations from the discipline of the durational control. As in those forms of modern music where harmony and counterpoint no longer dictate matters of rhythmic structure, Cunningham's *plastique* and local accent are deliberately subjugated to the controls of his dance rhythm.

This may be why my dancer friends claim they can "count" Cunningham. The durational lengths are something like an unexpressed, expanded ostinato beneath the dance phrases; they may even help beginning Cunningham dancers learn to orient themselves in a form of dance so independent of conventional musical "counts." (The question would be, what are Cunningham's dancers counting? Accentual patterns? Time lengths?) Indeed, the educated response in any viewing audience would be to locate a pulse beneath such dancing, especially when its phrasal elements are irregular and unpredictable. In *Rebus* (1975) or *Torse* (1976), Cunningham stretches the boundaries of a dance dynamics and sustained allegro invention: the experiment locates the viewer's sense of durational rhythm around the borders of its possible sustainment, and the dance rhythm—forced and highlighted—acquires a quality of an amplified "beat" such as is found in certain forms of music that are obviously accentual in their organization. Perhaps this is one reason why so many of Cunningham's postmodern followers have used varieties of "pulse" music (both yesterday's swing and today's "pulse" exploit a motoric rhythm). In interpreting the master, in updating him for the eighties, the postmoderns often parody Cunningham's durational rhythms, turning them into inflated accentual ones, as rock music in the fifties simplified and exaggerated the accentual components of popular jazz dance rhythms in pursuit of the big beat. Today's postmoderns glance at Cunningham's rhythms, hear-tell of a metrical process, and then mass-produce in their own work the squarest possible dance phrasing under the banner of a theoretical triumph.

The best recent Cunningham dances (*Landrover* [1972], *Sounddance* [1975], *Solo* [1975], *Fractions* [1977], *Quartet* [1982], *Phrases* [1984]) would resemble Bach or swing on one level: they so advertise their freedom from the underlying metrical ground that we are tantalized into trying to locate any "beat" at such heady distance. Once Cunningham had enunciated his approach to dance rhythm, any other dance project that evidenced a compositional reliance on the inheritance of accentual rhythmic ideas—a tradition of impulses and formal guides that had always sustained and educated choreographers in conventional dance styles—would be seen by Cunningham and his followers as marked by facility, by a lack of proper and rigorous investigation of dance basics. Accentual rhythm in a dance equaled conventionality. Durational rhythm became the post-fifties avant-garde given (as it was for Nijinsky in *L'Après-midi d'un faune*).

A conventional choreographer—by that I mean one who assumes that the unconventional component of dance is self-evident—lives rather easily with the accentual residue of the past. He observes it, absorbs it, reconstitutes it. And a traditionalist like George Balanchine sometimes joins a durational metric to his primarily accentual one: an example would be the play with tempi and deaccelerando devices in his choreography to Hindemith's *Kammermusik No. 2*. Again, the interplay of accentual dance rhythm and durational musical accompaniment in Balanchine's *Concerto Barocco* is one source of that ballet's continuing challenge to performers. (Among other things, Balanchine used the big-band link with Bach to highlight that area of female adagio technique that is quasi-durational in its rhythm.) An unconventional choreographer like Merce Cunningham, on the other hand, suspects the residues of accentual dance rhythm to the extent of devising a method of self-protection against them. There is a sense in which Cunningham's defensiveness toward the matter of traditional dance may represent a last gasp of nineteenth-century vitalism, with its emphasis upon the purification of the spirit via radical disciplinary means. If so, Cunningham may not have purged his work of a "vitalistic" element as completely as Marcel Duchamp's antivitalist esthetic requires.

Many of the "radicalisms" used to characterize Cunningham's dance are subservient to this use of durational rhythmic values. The fractured, evenly exposed, "elemental" dance components signal their integrity—their service to a temporal control. An aesthetic of assemblage (facets organized within a field) works ironically to throw attention onto the original "free" selection of materials. (Such freedom is restated in the absence of traditional stage focus or hierarchical stage patterns.) The neutral (because geometrically simplified) *plastique* of the dancers serves to carry primary rhythmic information and to frame the rhythmic content. The *allegro* phrases and long-held groupings in Cunningham's style trace durational measures. The variety of movement components (*any* movement—found, indeterminate, chance-derived—can serve as dance material) permits the eye choice—and allows the choreographer to dramatize the distance he can place between surface decoration and rhythmic ground. The dancers interpret their assigned material for the audience, adding to the mix their inevitably more "conventionalized" versions of Cunningham's unconventional dance ideas. The dancer's virtuosity must therefore be an "intellectual" one. The dance material is held in evidently raw form long enough so that the choreographer can work quasi-musical processes of manipulation (canon, retrograde, inversion, etc.) upon it and so the evidence of those processes can be partially seen, thus adding the pleasure of analysis to the display, the audience recognizing the basic materials but glimpsing their preparation prior to final compositional shaping.

All of these categories of innovation are minor matters, of course, in comparison to other, more substantive areas of dance opened up by a durational approach to rhythm: qualities of attack, preparation, transition, phrasing, etc. In fact, it is easier to give credence to the presence of something like a durational rhythm in Cunningham's dance than to the claim for a general "baroque" esthetic of developmental variation. If it is true, for example, that Cunningham works free variations on his dance themes, what is fascinating is the nature of those themes; the resultant floridity in the dance facture would be on an inevitably lower level of interest. In fact, if there is a theme-and-variation process going on, what does it consist of? In other words, what are Cunningham's dance equivalents of music's harmonic and contrapuntal devices? Does his dance *plastique* really read as such a device, as I have suggested it may? Is it possible that Cunningham's idea of variation technique only "turns the ground"—allowing another process of variation to occur in performance? If so, what are the conditions of Cunningham performance that allow a further analysis? Such questions do not have easy answers, but they identify living areas of Cunningham's dance thought in a way that restatements of the publicized Cunningham-Cage general esthetic no longer do. If Cunningham's dances "develop"—generate themselves from within—in ways that are different from the dances of other choreographers, I suspect the difference may derive from an approach as basic as Cunningham's durational rhythm.

All the usual critical and theoretical approaches to Cunningham's dance don't really carry us very far. If we admit the presence of a durational emphasis in Cunningham's dance rhythm, however, some things can be said. The Cunningham dancer must confront certain challenges. The dancers must generally "hide" the initiation that gets them into a dance phrase, much as dancers trained in ballet must cover their preparation. I suspect this is Cunningham's way of fighting the complacency that a durational approach to rhythm could precipitate. The performer must negotiate the long and short lengths in the dance rhythm, using the persistence of the durational units and the allowed extent of Cunningham's (often discontinuous) phrases. The metrical lengths thus expose a dancer to immediate challenges that accentual rhythms do not. The phrases require a light, tensionless hand to keep them transparent, while the dancer simultaneously profiles and inflects them, even in their sometime brevity. The Cunningham phrase has these features: it expands outward from within, floated by the durational quantities; and it is pressured toward succinct statement from without because of the self-consciously "structural" emphasis. The dancers must avoid both complacency and busywork. They cannot "ride" the indications of an accentual dance rhythm as ballet or tap dancers can. They choose actively. An accentual dance rhythm allows the performer to pick from among arranged highlights. The durational approach of Cunningham forces regularity of choice, and the soloists' accents seem their own in their performance weight. The danger in performing Cunningham is that the dancers may project an overwilled, premeditated lifelessness. The accentual approach, on the other hand, makes spontaneity crucial, and its danger for the performer is mindless joyriding.

In the Events context of presentation, Cunningham's dance materials must stand up to any variety of sound matrices thrown at them. When excerpts from several works in the current Cunningham repertory are olioed across the length of an Event, the durational rhythm presents nary a jarring splice between works of very different technical requirements and atmospheres. An Event is a sign on a large scale that Cunningham's dance rhythm has a weight, a momentum, and an homogeneity. The juxtaposition of excerpts from several works sometimes allows an Event more contrast within an evening than individual Cunningham works sometimes offer, between one another and within themselves. When this happens, I think it is because of Cunningham's tenacity in holding to his rhythmic approach.

There is a paradox in a dance esthetic that asks us to concentrate *only* on the surface of the spectacle while simultaneously exploiting a tension between an underlying organizational principle and the richly elaborated surface. One reason commentators seize on a "baroque" approach to Cunningham is that the idea posits a prior identification of thematic material while converting the dance surface into so much brilliant ornamentation or choreographic improvisation. It is possible that Cunningham's actual thematic materials require a less complacent approach for their identification, and that the progress of his dance conducts itself—sustains itself—in a fashion that goes beyond conventional ideas of variation technique. Not only is it difficult to extend the "baroque" analogy from the musical and plastic arts to Cunningham's dance style without falling into a critical impression, but the attempt reminds us of the very different matrix from which Cage and Cunningham derive their thematic materials.[6] For example, Cage conceives of musical duration in an absolutely temporal sense; in contrast, Virgil Thomson conceives of a "quantitative" metric as in complicity with a received musical tradition. Cunningham may insist upon his choreographic absolutes as well, and such an insistence renders thematic identification in his dances a challenge for critical analysis. The idea of a "baroque" esthetic requires that thematic materials be precisely identified. An analyst of dance rhythm—Kenneth King, for example—could make a catalog of Cunningham's durational metric values and his characteristic surface formulas for elaboration. Such an approach would have definite interest. But I'm not sure that such an analysis is more than a beginning.

Early Cunningham gained some of its initial shock from confronting the audience with the durational approach. As patterns and formulas in his repertory accumulated, the surface of Cunningham dance gained in its ability to guide the performer and the viewer in the perception of the rhythmical ideas, and that surface has at length acquired a quasi-accentual aspect. Early Cunningham dancers could appear innovative from the "perversity" of an "antidance" (because anti-accentual) approach. The later Cunningham dancers join a developed metrical idiom, so they must reinvent for the new audience something like that original shock. Today's dancers must first sustain their phrase length, then create as thickly encrusted and detailed a surface profile as they can, while never abandoning their obligation to reassert the deeper controls of durational periods. The dancers must navigate between surface and ground. In this sense, time and change have themselves allowed one level in Cunningham's dance that might be described as "baroque." In *Torse* and *Rebus*, the original cast performed full-out on the heavily stressed surface patterns; there was no time to play them off against the durational ground. The result was as close as Cunningham has come to bombast.

This play of surface and ground may be the best (because overriding) example in Cunningham's style of what French estheticians on the left like to think of as his nonhierarchical, "open," expository achievement—in which both foreground and background, and, indeed, all framing devices, are confessed as distinct and nonillusionary tools, and each compositional element is used as just one more auxiliary (and thus uncoercive) control. Indeed, a durational rhythm itself would serve—in its implications—as a framing device, a principal background for exquisitely chosen choreographic elements. But a rhythm is a useful tool for a dancemaker only in its hold on his imagination, and a good new Cunningham dance is a world of hierarchical movement discriminations. *Phrases* (1984; New York premiere March 5, 1985), his best new piece since *Fractions* (1977–78), reminds us of what Cunningham basics are meant to accomplish. *Phrases* has all the weight we expect in Cunningham's temporal world. It's a fully stated piece, unlike *Native Green* (1985) and *Doubles* (1984), which clip their feathers close. *Phrases* thus has time to unfurl a range of "structural" bracketings, types of rhythmic organization. The largesse of invention begs the question of an easy tag—"baroque" doesn't quite fit. And the durational approach gives us again the sometime pathos of the Cunningham spectacle, the dancers' details absorbed, swallowed in the context, and yet regularly, almost defiantly, reiterated. *Phrases* is an update of one of those ensemble works of the seventies—*Landrover, Rebus, Torse*—but warmed and individualized. The choreographer himself visits his creatures in one of those cameo roles he makes for himself, the ghostly super of the co-op. David Bradshaw's costumes head toward basic blacks and whites and then veer toward the original ochres just before the end. And Cunningham has arranged one of his surefire endings—the stage darkening and swept by vigilant patrols.

But the dance details are fresh and almost impossible to categorize as one watches. Their play is too agile and their deployment too flexed. The dance figures—reversed, echoed, refracted, time-delayed—question the eyes' ability to bracket a "phrase." Thus, we look even more closely, only to discover the parodic elements within the bracketings: for example, the quoted *balancés* of Cunningham and Cathy Kerr during their *entrée*. The quotes are yet another fantastication, a witty reference this time to classical ideas of phrasing.

The overlapped bracketings force our gaze within and without simultaneously. Without: to that extraordinary mixture of quotidian gesture with heroic image everywhere in Cunningham, as, for example, in Robert Swinston's winged entrance across the back of the stage with three attendant women, or Chris Komar's and Karen Fink's *pas de bourrée* progress across the back with changing arm positions. Within: the accentual surprises and virtuoso initiations, as in Swinston's pivot leaps when he first appears in white or in Alan Good's jumps just before he is joined by Kerr toward the end. It is this double vision that permits Cunningham his boldest ploys—surprising interruptions and resumptions of his line of thought.

In *Phrases*, the line is both finer and larger than any one of its signs. The durational rhythm is part of the *bas relief* of the Cunningham style: it aids in the release of the dance details even as it holds them. Thus, embellishment itself becomes context. We sense that the dance idea's full statement is withheld so as not to overapproximate its locus. The individual vibrato of the piece (an aural effect, as well as visual, given the percussiveness of the Cunningham style) pulls us in. *Phrases* has the characteristics of all of Cunningham's best work: a natural calm, an acclimated alertness, a deepening of rhythmic thought, and a resultant iridescence.

Phrases escapes the principal danger in a durational metric from a compositional point of view—a "materialism" of dance facture, a lack of skepticism toward the produced surface of the dance. For example, ballet choreographers who employ a durational component in their work—I am thinking of Jerome Robbins and Eliot Feld—sometimes allow their materials to harden into phrasal units intractable to variation or regeneration. Cunningham, on the other hand, maintains a critical attitude toward the durational metric. His dance, as in *Phrases,* is something more than an illustration of methodology or a certification of craft. The surface of his dance is often closer to a balletic surface than is the work of many "classical" choreographers. Perhaps this explains American Ballet Theatre's fascination with that surface.

Cunningham's durational dance rhythm suggests a more methodical, strategically held esthetic than can be usefully admitted by those who advertise Cunningham dance. Actually, I suspect that Cunningham's conception of dance rhythm is a means whereby he can subject his materials to regular observation, to inspection—i.e., that it is a precompositional laboratory technique out of which the specifics of individual works are allowed to develop. The master's secret is less in his use of a type of rhythm than in the quality of his inspection of materials. The other reason that apologists for the Cunningham style may not have found it useful to discuss this aspect of Cunningham's dance is that a theory of his rhythm would posit a dependence on musical sources and analogies (Bach, swing, Cage) that would be at variance with Cunningham's stated goal of making dance independent of all such immediate and "authoritarian" controls. To suggest that durational or quantitative rhythm is at the base of the Cunningham esthetic makes the master seem subject to the laws of fashion in the arts (for example, the same laws that linked up the Bach revival around 1900 with the primitivistic experiments of Picasso and Nijinsky, that early conjunction of experimental tastes in advance of the thirties' back-to-Bach movement). After all, the Duchampian esthetic of Cage and Cunningham is supposed to exist outside of history, beyond strict influence and any fashion. Merce of Egypt, indeed. But a thinking audience may have to risk that kind of misprision in order to rescue Cunningham from the boutique sensibility of the eighties.

From the evidence of its influence, Cunningham's durational orientation appeals to today's neophyte choreographer as sheer availability, dance matter conveniently cleansed of ostentatious stylistic reference, solid enough to cry out for shaping, roomy enough to allow for performance choices freed from conventional ideas of formula or drama. For the young, the style is risky business for fun and profit. In its most profligate examples, Cunningham's extended academy (all those choreographers who have danced with his company and then left to choreograph, and all those choreographers—many more—who borrow ideas from his example) is capable of producing just as much second-rate dance as any other school; but the antisentimentality of Cunningham's method helps accustom young choreographers to their own way of moving. What is then done with the discovered individuality is dependent on choices that the young must manage beyond the help of any master. The elements of Cunningham's style trigger free-thinking dancers and galvanize potential dancemakers. The approach does not guarantee anything beyond such instigation.

Graduates of the Cunningham academy cover the earth, and the colonialization has partially come about because of the concentration in Cunningham's recent works on ensemble over soloist roles. Dancers come into the company, stay for a year or two, and then graduate to form companies of their own around the globe. In Cunningham's current company, the relationship of soloist to ensemble is discussed only intermittently in new additions to the repertory, and often with the choreographer taking the solo roles. Dancers seldom "move up"; there is no "up" in the avant-garde. But they may not also in any observable sense become more *themselves* in interesting and new ways as we watch them season after season. (That this situation exists within companies—Tharp's is another one—which claim a "radical" esthetic and which presumably attempt a regular radical redefinition of concepts like "role" and "characterization" is something of a paradox.) A dance experimentalist can devote decades to an ensemble style and the examination of its "impersonal" energies without ever attaining that higher impersonality that regularly produces soloists. As a result, ambitious dancers in such companies eventually strike out on their own and make "radical" dances for themselves, spawning yet another generation of dance makers. (Modern-dance history reads like self-preservation by other means.) In this way, too, Cunningham's approach to dance rhythm has become an aspect of dance language propagated throughout the West.

Notes

1. Quoted in Paul Griffiths, *Cage* (New York: Oxford University Press, 1981), 11.
2. John Cage, Notes on *First Construction (in Metal)* (1934), in the album booklet for George Avakian's recording *The 25-Year Retrospective Concert of the Music of John Cage*, recorded in performance at Town Hall, New York, 15 May 1958. (The 1959 album has recently been reissued.)
3. In a 1950 review, Virgil Thomson described Cage's structural rhythm this way: "John Cage employs a numerical ratio in any piece between the phrase, the period, and the whole, the phrase occupying a time measure which is the square root of the whole time and the periods occupying times proportional to those of the different rhythmic motifs within the phrase. This procedure, though it allows for asymmetry within the phrase and period, produces a

tight symmetry in the whole composition. . . ." Quoted from "Atonality Today," originally published in the *New York Herald Tribune*, 5 February 1950; reprinted in *A Virgil Thomson Reader* (New York: E.P. Dutton, 1981), 340.

4. John Cage, "Experimental Music," *The Score and I.M.A. Magazine*, 12 (June 1955): 65–68. Reprinted in John Cage, *Silence: Lectures and Writings by John Cage* (Middletown, CT: Wesleyan University Press, 1973), 15.

5. See "Swing Music" and "Swing Again" in Virgil Thomson, *A Virgil Thomson Reader* (New York: E.P. Dutton, 1981), 28–32 and 33–37. The essays were first published in *Modern Music* in 1936 and 1938.

6. See Earle Brown's comments on "proportional" or "nonmetric" musical notation in relation to Cunningham's dance, in "The Forming of an Aesthetic: Merce Cunningham and John Cage," *Ballet Review*, XIII/3 (Fall 1985). Brown's Cunningham pioneers a metrically unconventional or nonmetrical rhythm. From that perspective, my analysis (which sees Cunningham's dance rhythm resolving itself into durational periods beyond whatever "unconventionality" it attains) would be retardative.

Alastair Macaulay

THE MERCE EXPERIENCE (1988)

The story is told that an eminent figure in the dance world recently wrote to Merce Cunningham politely asking him to send, for reference purposes, a brief résumé of what he had done "since leaving Martha." Well, Cunningham left the Martha Graham company in 1945. This summer will mark thirty-five years of his own company's existence—over half his life. This (and much more) is history—isn't it?

In March, Cunningham presented at the Joyce Theatre the longest season of repertory he has ever given in New York: seven performances a week, four weeks, thirteen works. This is the most sustained exposure to his work that any city has had since that surprising season in London in 1964, when a week's visit was so warmly acclaimed that it was turned into a month's stay.

Twenty-four years later, a month of Merce no longer provokes astonished hosannas or outraged jeers. He is simply a landmark. Has something been lost in the process? No doubt. I never saw Carolyn Brown, Viola Farber, or other Cunningham dancers of that generation perform onstage, and I'm prepared to accept that, with their departure, a certain greatness vanished from the face of the world—just as I do when thinking of other dancers I never saw, like Violette Verdy and Edward Villella. And it is possible, I suppose, to see the revivals of *RainForest* (1968) and *Septet* (1953) mainly as ghost-town ballets. But Cunningham's recent repertory is no decaying museum or academic exercise ground, and his dancers aren't machines or clones. Far from it. Technique in Cunningham performance today is highly accomplished, and almost every iota of it is dissolved into style. Each of the men has registered as a character for

173

some time; in recent seasons, the women have begun to follow suit, although some of them some of the time still like to maintain a good-girl impersonality. A few newcomers in the past couple of years, such as Dennis O'Connor and Larissa McGoldrick, have at once made an explosive, eccentric impact on the repertory; and the newest girl, Kimberly Bartosik, dances as if her whole life had been invested in joining this company. Experienced performers like Alan Good, Robert Swinston, Victoria Finlayson, and Kristy Santimyer project their own imaginative spell in all they do.

So when at other performances in March several New York dancegoers told me without any very good reason that they "didn't make it to Merce this season," I was stumped. ("I can't stand him" would have been reason enough.) Even in a city with the dance abundance of New York, a month of this repertory is too rich to be overlooked. What greater choreographers are active today? And what choreographer is in finer harmony with his present gathering of dancers?

During the eighties, it is time to say, Cunningham's choreography has shown a fresh, autumnal wisdom—whether tragic (*Quartet* [1982]), idyllic (*Pictures* [1984]), lyrical (*Doubles* [1984]), bleak (*Shards* [1987]), or all these things by turns (*Fabrications* [1987]). It would be wrong to assume that just because Cunningham is no longer a revolutionary his work has had its day. Actually, most years of this decade have given us at least one new masterpiece; 1987, for instance, produced *Shards, Fabrications,* and the stage version of *Points in Space.* By such standards, 1988's new items—*Eleven,* in its world premiere; *Carousal* (1987), new to New York; the *RainForest* revival—should make the Joyce weeks rank as small beer. True, *RainForest* is part of Cunningham's legend (even if its most famed component is its Warhol decor: the billowing array of helium-filled silver pillows—they're both floating foliage and swaying undergrowth). It's still an arrestingly conceived work, its dances constructed largely of nonacademic material and marked by a subdued, feral quality. At the opening-night performance, it struck me as more subdued than feral—undernuanced. Even those pillows were well behaved. Not surprisingly, the revival elicited murmurs of nostalgia: "Helium isn't what it was when we were what we were," and so on. As for the premieres, *Carousal* was a patchwork of convivial episodes; incidentally fascinating, it was flimsy over all. *Eleven,* which contained variations on the choreographic forms Cunningham has been employing in recent years, and which in other circumstances might have emerged as an elegant work, was crippled by its score and its costumes.

And yet it was an enthralling season. The Merce experience remains—the Merce experience, that is, as it has come to be in the mid-eighties. The greatest pleasure of these seasons lies not in the premieres or the golden oldies but in one's gradual immersion in those dancers, those dances, and those things which run deepest in his work: the unique stillnesses and distances and perspectives onstage; the odd, flat, natural rhythms; the countless resonances and ambiguities of each piece.

The finest Merce experience I have ever had was in Montreal in 1985, with a triple bill of *Inlets 2* (1983), *Doubles,* and *Pictures.* Yes, three idylls: it was like going from the countryside of Bohemia to the Forest of Arden and then on to Prospero's isle. No other choreographer in history could have brought it off. All three works were to be seen at the Joyce this year, albeit on different programs. In *Inlets 2,* one of Cunningham's most hushed nature studies, I cherish the long-held Seurat poses in profile, the echoes of Nijinsky's *Faune* choreography they suggest, and the way they realize Edwin Denby's point about *Faune* that "the space between the figures becomes a firm body of air, a lucid statement of relationship, in the way intervening space does in the modern academy of Cézanne, Seurat, and Picasso." Above all, the work shows how those flat rhythms of Cunningham dance can catch the very essence of animal life: I see birds floating, taking wing, hovering, resettling; rodents scuttling and then freezing. This evocation of fauna, which Cunningham can reinforce in some dances with unspecific pictorial suggestions (hands held like paws, as in *RainForest;* the curve of a back; the angle of a haunch; the arch of a neck), is achieved primarily through timing. And it is part of his poetic genius that he can convey all this while employing in other works the most purely academic vocabulary. In *Points in Space* an ensemble of women, all facing the same way to concentrate on the rigors of stationary adagio, will suddenly change tempo and travel across the stage: something has disturbed this flock. In *Doubles* there is a web of rhythm: it is the most lyrically buoyant work in the repertory. The two women who walk around the stage's perimeter for long spells, and off into the wings and on again as if they'd never been absent, are all tender, quiet, calm legato. The other dancers have a much wider range of accent, and the solos appear peacefully full of human self-contradictions. *Pictures,* with its miraculous tableaux of dancers linked in horizontal lines, its many serene slow variations on walking, presents dancers in an unaffected, rapt state of grace. Each dancer establishes a single tempo upon entrance and maintains it for a long span of time.

Some Cunningham works seem deliberately to splice material from two or more others. *Shards* grafts the stillnesses and concentration of *Inlets 2* onto the racked, dark urgency of *Quartet.* What seems at first to be a nature study is punctuated by contained violence. Tension builds. No one communicates. *Fabrications* evokes phrases and motifs from numerous other works from the repertory, past and present, and assembles them into a broad canvas unlike anything else this choreographer has made.

There are many things in Cunningham's work that have long reminded me of Chekhov: the poignant overlap of several different narrative threads, the variety of material within any one character's solo, the contrast of fluent lyricism and blunt prosiness as a natural condition of human existence. *Fabrications* is his most thoroughly Chekhovian work, and it is like another Chekhovian dance work, by Frederick Ashton: it's Merce's *Enigma Variations—*

rich in brief, telling incidents and in dramatic ironies. The work is studded with short duets in which couple after couple demonstrate their own species of cooperation and mutual absorption. Each duet counts powerfully, and even more moving is the way the duets are set apart from the ensembles that are the work's basic orchestration. Toward the end, Cunningham brings six couples on together in a ring, all performing the same few charged phrases of supported adagio. But there is no sense of completion in this—partly because you can't quite forget the fleeting glimpses you've had of soloists distanced from the main action, among them that old man who has bumbled from time to time across the stage. The score, by Emanuel Dimas de Melo Pimenta, seems to augment the fluctuations of feeling and immediacy in the work, and helps you to sense that this is one man's memory of a society and intimacies gone by.

In no other choreographer's repertory is stasis so expressive. Dancers standing still, dancers maintaining cool balance without a tremor, tableaux of stationary dancers supported or unsupported: these are basic Cunningham fare, and *Septet* reveals that they have been since at least 1953. In a central passage of this work, we see a row of three male-female couples. As the Satie music proceeds, each woman hangs on her partner, and each is motionless in a different bleak pose: individual urgency preserved in amber. Cunningham went on to invent variations on this theme. How many straight lines, horizontal or diagonal, has he made out of three pairs, each carved in a different stationary position? And always the eye is rewarded as it takes in the geometrical intricacy and organizational wit of the tableau. But in the context of *Septet* the image has a peculiar force: it reminds me, curiously, less of other Cunningham works than of a dance for the two secondary couples late in Balanchine's Robert Schumann ballet, where each women rests or presses upon her partner in one still pose after another. In *Septet,* it reinforces the point of a note that Cunningham used to publish in the programs between 1955 and 1964—that the ballet's subject "is Eros," and its occurrence "is at the intersection of joy and sorrow." (Cunningham was right, however, not to use that note in the eighties revival. We can see now how very many things *Septet* is "about"—not least, ballet tradition and Merce's individual talent.)

Cunningham's work reminds me of many things just because it is about people dancing and because of its catholic notion of what dancing can include. Watching the delicious opening duet (or double solo) of *Carousal,* I recalled Denby's words about certain Balanchine ballets: "What an extraordinary absence of prejudice as to what is proper in classicism these odd works show." Chris Komar and Dennis O'Connor—left and right of center, respectively—execute two different solos that return at different points to the same motif, a very Cunningham pattern of high-plucked, treading footwork that gets them nowhere in particular. Doing it, they resemble wading birds, or Wilis in *Giselle.* But each solo contains what dance analysts would call "movement information" of a completely distinct kind. Sometimes the distinction is in a minor detail. Each man retreats into a striking fourth position, leans backward, chest spread proudly, and looks over his shoulder: it's angled so that whereas Komar looks away from us, tossing his head back, right out of sight, as if in despair, O'Connor turns his face to us with a touch of self-glamorizing nonchalance. What a neatly odd couple (Komar has been in the company fourteen years longer than O'Connor; both are blond and of a height), and what a neatly odd split-focus duet (O'Connor's section contains falls, rolls, and hops that are nothing like Komar's). If only *Carousal* were that *neatly* odd throughout. Instead, it's a list of communal vignettes that don't cohere. We never recapture the taut rhythm of the opening.

Eleven, of course, is a right little tease. After all, we knew where we were with *Septet*, which is for six dancers, and with *Quartet*, for five. But *Eleven* has *eleven* dancers, and occasionally they're all onstage together. The Master must mean *something* by this, but I missed it. Fending off the wretched music, as I tried to do at a second performance, I isolated several new aspects of movement information. In particular, the duets here are different. Throughout the eighties, Cunningham's duets have tended to follow the rules of ice dancing; no high lifts and not more than a yard or so between male and female. But here are couples addressing each other with the whole width of the stage between them, sometimes even along a diagonal bisected by another couple's duet. There are further points to admire, not least a rather Ashtonian trio for two men and a woman, in which Patricia Lent's line as she is lifted by Robert Swinston is echoed by the stationary Alan Good. But to what end? Robert Ashley's score is Cunningham's most intrusive to date. Two metrical monologues, chanted in contrasting Japanese and American accents, that turn out to be a dialogue of sorts taken from a scene in a post-mod, sci-fi soap opera, whose metres may at times be related to the choreography . . . And, yes, while I was trying not to listen, whole sections of Cunningham invention went in one eye and out the other.

Would that I could say the same of the designs. The company's design department has for almost four years been in the undistinguished hands of William Anastasi and Dove Bradshaw. At their undistinguished best (*Native Green* [1985], not seen this season; the videodance original of *Points in Space* [1986]; the *Shards* costumes), they seem to design with at least a backward glance at the more striking work of their predecessors. Thank heaven, there were no backdrops for *Carousal* or *Eleven*. The *Eleven* costumes, and the backdrops for *Grange Eve* (1986), *Fabrications*, and *Shards*, suggest little Abstract Expressionist sketches blown up and thrown onto the stage like custard pies. The baggy costumes used in *Fabrications*, *Grange Eve*, and *Carousal* are appropriate to those works' moods. Even so, all of them lack any theatrical dimension, and the specific characteristics of each are so unmemorable that the dancers seem to be dressed in rehearsal kit, waiting until the next Mark Lancaster comes along to array them in impeccable combinations of Cézanne colors.

It is still an unwritten law of Cunningham dance theatre that he, in his very late sixties, should appear in one work per evening. And the works he uses for this purpose—*Quartet, Pictures, Grange Eve, Fabrications*—compose a repertory. To enjoy watching him is to enjoy the pleasure of ruins—the way we enjoy the artistry of those singers who committed their singing to the earliest 78s when they were long past their vocal prime. It would be courteous to say, as Herman Klein said of Adelina Patti's recordings, that you are observing the *beaux restes* of great singing, but, really, Cunningham's aren't very *beaux*. And there isn't a lot left he can do. Few things are simpler for a dancer than to rise from a kneeling position. When Cunningham does it in *Fabrications*, however, he steadies himself with one hand during the first part of the maneuver. Yet he does it with exactly the same timing at every performance. The precise spontaneity is endearing. It reminds me of Ralph Richardson's performance, at a similar age, in a William Douglas Home play I have otherwise forgotten, in which he made something touchingly hilarious out of slowly bending his knees and solemnly preparing to sit on a lawn. Cunningham is growing old—publicly, ungracefully, disarmingly.

Nancy Dalva

THE WAY OF MERCE (1992)

"Chance is the dogma, but look deeper."

Carolyn Brown[1]

". . . if the dancer dances, *everything is there. The meaning is there if that's what you want."*

Merce Cunningham[2]

Starting nearly fifty years ago, Merce Cunningham began to change the way people dance and the way people see dancing in the same way that Picasso and the cubists changed the way people painted and the way people saw painting.

He took dance apart and put it back together again, leaving out all but the most essential. He stripped dance of conventional narrative; he ordered it by chance procedures; he conceived it without music and without decor. He took it out of the proscenium (but later put it back) and exploded the stage picture into fragments. He made the viewer the *auteur*. The great irony of all this is that only a great storyteller possessed of extraordinary intrinsic musicality could have stripped away so much and be left with more. Cunningham is able to separate dance from its traditional trappings not because dance does not need them, but because dance—at least in his hands—already has them.

There has been a lot said about Merce Cunningham and John Cage and their working method—most of it said by neither of them. But of all of the odd things people have thought about Cunningham's dances over the years, the oddest—including the notion that the dances are in part or whole improvisational—have arisen from his use of chance, the most confusing element of the

Cunningham-Cage dogma. To some, its use seems flaky. To others, it implies a certain haphazardness, the evidence of the dances notwithstanding.

Cunningham uses chance, in some form, at some point (but not the same point) or points in the making of every dance. While the habit may have been inspired originally by Cage and Marcel Duchamp—friend to both Cage and Cunningham—two reasons (other than a playful disposition) for its continuance suggest themselves: first, that Cunningham either does not like to make or at times cannot easily make choices; second, that Cunningham is intentionally—if minimally—depersonalizing his work in order to open it out to the individual viewer.

When in some small way the choices made in making a dance are made, not by the choreographer, but by an impersonal agent, or fate, the viewers are temporarily freed from the tyranny of the artist's vision, and released into their own. In other words, the use of chance gets Cunningham out of the dance and lets us in, just as he has let musicians into the pit to do what they will, and let various artists and designers superimpose their work on his own.

According to the dogma, these artists and their work stand independent of the choreography. But where a trinity is proposed—dance, music, decor— we, the audience, experience unity. Only by extricating a dance from its decor and score will we learn its own story and hear its own music. To see it separately is to see it the way Cunningham made it and probably still sees it. (The way to do this sounds like instructions for meditating; you just concentrate on the dance and let everything else fall away.)

With few (and these are wonderful) exceptions, Cunningham's dances look best with the simplest settings and costumes, and it is arguably in the area of decor that the Cunningham repertory has been most often hoist by the Cage-Cunningham petard. Their gospel—separation of choreographer, composer, and designer—has indeed yielded much that is splendid, antic, and beautiful over the years, but also much that is not. Among the artists who have designed for the company are, in chronological order,[3] Remy Charlip, Robert Rauschenberg, Frank Stella, Jasper Johns, Andy Warhol, Robert Morris, Bruce Nauman, Mark Lancaster, and Morris Graves. Inevitably, each colored the work he decorated, some more indelibly than others. (Think of Rauschenberg's decor for *Antic Meet* [1958], *Winterbranch* [1964], and *Travelogue* [1977]; Johns's for *Walkaround Time* [1968] and *Exchange* [1978]; Warhol's for *RainForest* [1968]; Lancaster's for *Sounddance* [1975] and *Neighbors* [1991]; Graves's for *Inlets* [1977].) Since 1984, Dove Bradshaw and William Anastasi have served as the company's artistic advisors.

Because we see their work not merely along with but actually on top of Cunningham's, there is a frequent assumption that these artists (however various) and Cunningham share an esthetic. Actually, Cunningham's painterly motivation, as it were, is much closer to that of the early cubists. Duchamp, whose famous nude always seems to have descended from a landing on which Picasso's *Demoiselles d'Avignon* are standing, is his link to them—in fact, *Walkaround Time* is an explicit tribute to Duchamp, with Cunningham dancing a variant of *Nude Descending a Staircase*. Their shared vision has something to do with *breaking things up*—whether the planes of the face or the increments of the dance phrase. It also involves a passion for showing all the sides of a thing at once.

Fragmentation, collage, simultaneity—these are also the concerns of modern literature, where language itself breaks down, and the characteristic gesture is erasure.[4] One finds such things in Cunningham's choreography; one finds them in a good deal of our poetry, starting with T. S. Eliot; and one finds them in James Joyce, whose work is read aloud daily[5] by Cage.

At least four titles of Cunningham's dances (*In the Name of the Holocaust* [1943] and *Tossed as it is Untroubled* [1944],[6] early solos; and *Sounddance* [1975][7] and *Roaratorio* [1984]) come from Joyce. How much more of his imagery and in fact his method are Joycean is a fascinating, and open, question. The importance of the everyday and a genius for epiphany are but two of the correspondences. But, at the least, Cunningham has clued us into his affinity, indicated the kind of associative narrative and diction to which he is drawn, and placed himself squarely within the Joycean tradition. This is very far from being within the esthetic of his most prominent artist collaborators. Cunningham's work is neither abstract nor expressionist. As he says:

> I have many references, many images, so in that sense I have no images. Because I could just as well substitute one image for another, in the Joycean sense of there being not *a* symbol but multiple [symbols]—one thing can build on another, or you can suddenly have something—the same thing— being something else. . . . That seems to me the way life is anyway.

Just as the overlapping of dance and decor has led to certain assumptions about Cunningham's dances, so—conversely—has the separation of dance and music. The dogma has given rise to the notion that the dances are somehow unmusical, or lacking music.

In performance, Cunningham's dances usually are accompanied by live music, occasionally by silence. Sometimes (as with the denser scores of David Tudor) the music is a kind of painful aural fog that forces the viewer to concentrate on the dance the way dusk makes a driver concentrate on the road. Sometimes (as with Cage's accompaniment for *Duets* [1980] and Tudor's for *Exchange*) the sound seems to support the dance. Occasionally, the sound suggests natural environments—watery, crickety—and occasionally it is so loony and deracinated that it diminishes one's experience of the dance. But, whatever it is, it is not the music of the dance, merely the music that happens at the same time.

The dance's music can be seen but not heard, except in the footfalls of the dancers and their breathing. The dance's music is its rhythm. Perhaps the easiest place to see Cunningham rhythm is his unison sections, and the easiest place to find such sections is in the early video works choreographed first for camera, then transferred to the stage. Here one finds the dancers disposed in squads. To see one squad opposed against another is to see two unisons at once: basic Cunningham counterpoint.

Always—in stage, on film, in videos, and in rehearsal—the dancers seem to be dancing *to* something—keeping up with it, slowing down to it—their phrasing exquisite and driven. By what? By the sound—or the memory—of Cunningham's own snapping and clapping. Merce Cunningham works with a stopwatch. He is the White Rabbit ("I'm late! I'm late!") of choreographers, and in his own way the most musical of all. One could see this when he revived *Septet,* made in 1953 to Erik Satie's *Trois Morceaux en Forme de Poire.* To see *Septet* is to realize that, for Cunningham, working to music must be like turning on the radio when the record player is already on. It interferes with music he already hears.

Using a plot would interfere with Cunningham's storytelling in a similar way. It is here that the dogma is most pernicious: that the dances have no obvious narratives or superimposed mood has led to the notion that they tell no stories. Further, this lack of invented roles and moods has led some viewers to find the performers impersonal. The exact opposite is true. The work is in fact personality-driven, for what could be more personal, more transparent, than dancers who are always performing as themselves? Cunningham himself has said:

> The idea of personality not being there isn't true simply because when the dancers do it, they in doing it take it on—it's like a second skin.

If there has been a general trend in Cunningham criticism in the last decade, it has in fact been a movement away from calling the dances "abstract." Today, the critically correct position is to call them "dramatic," in recognition of their inherent theatricality. Cunningham himself, in conversation about his work, often talks about "the theater"[8] instead of "the dance." Generally speaking, when people write about the dramatic aspect of these dances, they are referring either to the actorly aspect of Cunningham's own performances, or to the overall tone of a piece—its lightness, or darkness. As Noël Carroll and Sally Banes wrote in 1983 in *Ballet Review,* "We don't paraphrase his dances into propositions about the nature of art . . . nor do we take them to be alchemical allegories."[9]

Maybe not, but there is nothing in the dances that deters this. Actually, Cunningham himself looks more and more woolly and wizardly every year. Where he used to look like Prospero, he now looks like Lear or, in his lighthearted moments, a sort of dotty Merlin. Of all the choreographers who have taken to the American stage, he's the one who'd look right at home with an owl on his shoulder. In the current repertory, the dances in which he performs lend themselves the most easily to story telling. They are also instantly dramatic: the contrast between Cunningham and his company is a bold one.

When Cunningham is in a dance, it tends to be "about" him; his presence evokes metaphor, story, association. By instinct, by position, and by the circumstance of his age, he plays a role. Here is neither a young dancer, pretending for the sake of a role to be young, nor an old dancer, pretending for the sake of the spotlight to be young. Cunningham has become his own subject—no matter what he does, the mere fact of his doing it is dramatic, his very presence a *memento mori*. Increasingly, as the years have passed, Cunningham has cast himself as odd man out. At least fifteen years ago, he began to set himself apart from the company, often taking the role of an on-stage director, genially scurrying about disposing his dancers.

Lately, he has been placing himself differently, furtively. Often the dancers seem to avoid, ignore, or suffer him. In *Gallopade* (1981), ostensibly a children's romp, he cannot keep up, and the dancers play games without him. The dance—one of several portrait-of-the-artist dances—can be read as the story of a dancing life, telling what it is like to dance and then not to dance, and showing what Cunningham's dances will look like without him.

There are five dancers in *Quartet* (1982), and Cunningham is clearly the one uncounted. This work finds its parallels in the many ballets in which a figure representing death comes between two lovers, but here Cunningham is separated from his partner by a figure representing youth. In the spring 1991 season at City Center, it was David Kulick (a very handsome young dancer) who separated him from Helen Barrow (a great beauty who is the company's senior female). When Cunningham stands between Kulick and Barrow and waves his arms in protest, your heart breaks for him. He is on stage with four dancers, but he is alone.

Cunningham uses the age-youth contrast to different effect in *Pictures* (1984), a series of frozen, floodlit groupings, with dramatic lighting that tends to obscure its lovely transitions. Cunningham enters the scene upstage, part way through the dance, but he lets us know that he stands at its figurative center. At the end, he stands alone on stage with Patricia Lent (in 1984 his newest dancer), holding her in his arms, so that they suggest a Pietà. Will she die, the image asks, grow old and stop dancing (here the same thing as dying), leave him (like Carolyn Brown, Sandra Neels, Viola Farber, Valda Setterfield, Karole Armitage, Meg Harper, and all the others)? Will she leave him, and will he carry on? After you've seen *Pictures* a few times, the whole dance builds towards the final moment.

More and more these days, this is what Cunningham's dances seem to be about: means of support; community. In a sense, it is what they have always been about. Just as, in a sense, all great dance works take dance itself as their subject matter,[10] Cunningham takes his company as his subject matter in all of his dances. He himself has said that *RainForest*, one of his great nature studies, "suggests a little community of six people."[11]

If in earlier works the Cunningham community was one of equals, lately the choreographer has been testing the dynamics of a much more various group of sixteen, expressing the adjustments and subtle shifts within the company by opposing different styles of movement. As Cunningham expresses it:

> Drama is simply opposition—one thinks of good opposed to bad, or one kind of thing opposed to something else. That makes drama. . . . If you do a light movement and then you do a strong movement, you have a kind of opposition. Or if you have one person going one way and somebody else going another way, you have a kind of . . . opposition. And if at the same time they're doing different kinds of movement—or if they go at each other with different kinds of movement—that seems to me to give a kind of drama without making any issue about it.

Recently, this use of opposing forces has yielded works strongly connected thematically, but telling different tales. They are about dancers and dancing, but also about the natural world, wooded and swampy, microscopic and macroscopic; about the phenomenon and structure of chaos;[12] about the cosmos; about himself; and about us.

In both *Five Stone Wind* (1988) and *Neighbors* (1991), an isolated movement style is transmitted from one group of dancers to another, becoming a shared style. In each case, newcomers on the scene attract (or infect) dancers whose presence is already strongly established. The fifty-minute *Five Stone Wind* is a full-company work. Here is one element—wind, or air—or at any rate one *style*—anthropomorphised in three or four skittering and scintillating sprites, fast, sharp, clear, and precise. They blow through a community of grave and relatively slow movers, and gradually prove contagious: they change the way the community moves—and thus, in Cunningham terms, the way that community *is*.

Neighbors tells a similar story on a smaller scale, employing three couples. The dance looks like a John Updike story acted out by a *commedia dell'arte* troupe. The most fun occurs when the women get together without the men—another style contrast—and perform a Cunningham take on vogueing, his equivalent of gossiping and trying on hats. A waltz (originally for Finlayson and Lent) is particularly pleasurable; I see it as a tribute to the female knack for intimacy.

There have also been dances about *not* sharing, about inviolable stylistic isolation—for example, *Shards* (1987), where single figures are immobilized; and *Field and Figures* (1989), where four stylistic groups intersect without connecting.

Field and Figures is Merce Cunningham's *Four Temperaments*. But because he is not Balanchine but Cunningham, these are not "The Four Ts," but "The Four Es": earth, wind, fire, and water. It is a dance with a very clear scheme—

once you filter out the terrific distraction of the vastly irritating Duchamp-based read-aloud score (Ivan Tcherepnin's *The Creative Act*) and recover from the shock of Kristin Jones and Andrew Ginzel's futuristic set (banded and spangled grey backdrop, laser-beam-like red stabile, revolving bronze pendant, *Star Trek* lighting).

The fourteen dancers in the piece are divided into four companies. They rarely meet. On those occasions when they do, the interaction is more in the nature of a collision than a collusion. There is not exchange of styles. That we have been looking at four different dances happening in the same space becomes especially clear later. After *Field and Figures*, one is primed to notice that Cunningham usually has used a single style in a dance.

Cunningham made *Neighbors* over a long period of time during which he was also learning to use a computer program as a choreographic device, and there are certain postural correspondences between it and *Trackers*, the other new dance of the 1991 season—but that's the only affinity, besides the subject matter: community again. Here, the choreographer is concerned literally and figuratively with support systems.

Trackers is a large work that takes place against a dense dark drop, the dancers in designer Dove Bradshaw's brightly fashionable versions of their studio garb. (Imagine a tropical fish tank.) The choreography employs some atypical group lifts (a body raised between parallel lines of dancers; a person hoisted up out of a knot of dancers) and some straightforward calisthenics (a backbend and a cartwheel) more typical of Paul Taylor than of Cunningham. At the center of the dance is an actual plot-in-a-nutshell: Chris Komar, the company's senior dancer (now old enough to be the father of the youngest in the company, just as Cunningham might be her grandfather), lies alone on the floor. The rest of the dancers (except Cunningham) perform a combination on the other side of the stage. Komar seems unable to rise, but they travel across the stage in unison to collect him, and he gets up and dances on.

As does Cunningham, who in *Trackers* actually performs with a portable *barre*. While some see it as a walker, I see it simply as his daily partner, here revealed on stage. His routine probably is not much different from what he does everyday, but onstage the *barre* becomes a narrative element he puts to tragicomic use. It supports Cunningham but it also separates him from the dancers.

The work's most sustained image is a tableau that moves across the stage, Cunningham clumping along with his *barre* at the rear as a dancer (in the first performances his youngest dancer, Emily Navar; currently, Patricia Lent) is borne aloft at the front. Dancers providing the kind of daily support they give each other both physically and emotionally, or something more? It was possible to look at the stage and see the dead raised up, to see the company carrying Navar as Cunningham had earlier carried Lent in *Pictures*. But whatever else one saw, there was Cunningham, proceeding in all grimness and gaiety, doing what he always does. If ever there was a performance that said, "I can't go on, I'll go on," this was it.

Notes

1. Panel discussion moderated by David Vaughan as part of "Merce Cunningham and the New Dance," presented by the State University of New York's Programs in the Arts, 1987.
2. Unless otherwise noted, all Cunningham quotations are from an interview published as "The I Ching and Me" in *Dance Magazine* in March 1988. This particular quotation comes from an article published in *The Daily Texan* on February 14, 1977.
3. Through December 1984, all dates are from David Vaughan's chronological list of Merce Cunningham's choreographies published at the end of *The Dancer and the Dance, Merce Cunningham in Conversation with Jacqueline Lesschaeve.* New York and London: Marion Boyars, 1985.
4. Cunningham's investigative use of contemporary technologies—including the computer (which breaks information down into "bytes") and film and video shooting and editing techniques and devices—is a logical extension of his concerns with aleatory procedures, fragmentation, multiplicitous points of view, and erasure.
5. William Anastasi, personal communication.
6. Lesschaeve, *op. cit.*, 83
7. *Ibid.*, 119.
8. For example, in the article "The I Ching and Me," *op. cit.*
9. Carroll, Noël, and Sally Banes, "Cunningham and Duchamp," *Ballet Review* XI/2 (Summer 1983).
10. This idea was discussed by dance critic Arlene Croce in a conversation about *Le Sacre du Printemps* following the Joffrey Ballet's revival of the ballet broadcast on WNYC-FM's afternoon program called "Around New York."
11. Lesschaeve, *op. cit.*, 114.
12. The connections between Cunningham's work (and the Cunningham-Cage philosophy) and contemporary physics are many, and apparent even to the lay reader. For recent relevant articles on "chaotic systems" see *Science News* 139 (1991): 60, 70, 148, 182, 248; 140 (1991): 59, 200, 229, 239, 282.

Gymnasium Event #1, Queensborough Community College, 3 April 1968.
Photo © James Klosty, courtesy Cunningham Dance Foundation.

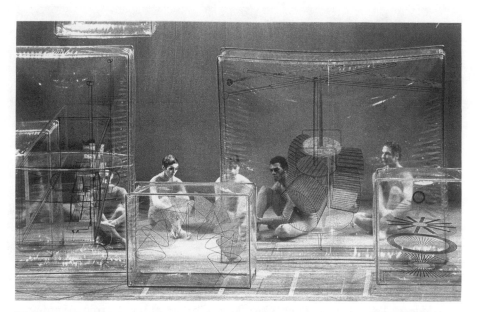

Walkaround Time, 1968. L to r: Carolyn Brown, Valda Setterfield, Meg
Harper, Gus Solomons jr, Merce Cunningham. Photo by Oscar Bailey,
courtesy Cunningham Dance Foundation.

Canfield, 1969. Photo © James Klosty, courtesy Cunningham Dance Foundation.

Sounddance, 1975. L to r: Ellen Cornfield, Chris Komar, Karole Armitage, Louise Burns, Rob Remley, Merce Cunningham.
Photo © 1992 Johan Elbers.

Squaregame, 1976. Karole Armitage and Merce Cunningham. Photo by Charles Atlas, courtesy Cunningham Dance Foundation.

Travelogue, 18 January 1977, premier performance at the Minskoff Theater, New York. Photo © Jack Vartoogian.

Tango, 1978. Photo by Nathaniel Tileston, courtesy Cunningham Dance Foundation.

Galopede, 1982. L to r: Merce Cunningham, Rob Remley, Judy Lazaroff, Robert Swinston. Photo © 1992 Johan Elbers.

Phrases, 1985. Merce Cunningham and Catherine Kerr. Photo © Tom Brazil.

Points in Space, 1986. L to r: Chris Komar, Robert Swinston, Karen Radford. Photo by Robert Hill for the BBC, courtesy Cunningham Dance Foundation.

Roaratorio, 1986. L to r: Megan Walker, Alan Good, Catherine Kerr, Merce Cunningham, Rob Remley, Dennis O'Connor, Kristy Santimyer. Photo © Tom Brazil.

Fabrications, 1987. L to r: Alan Good, Chris Komar, Merce Cunningham. Photo © Jack Vartoogian.

Grand Central Event, 9 October 1987. L to r: Helen Barrow, Merce Cunningham, Dennis O'Connor. Photo © Tom Brazil.

Merce Cunningham, John Cage, and company, 1988. L to r: Victoria Finlayson, Catherine Kerr, Dennis O'Connor, Alan Good, Megan Walker, Patricia Lent. Photo © Jack Mitchell.

Trackers, 1991. L to r: Michael Cole, Merce Cunningham, Carol Teitelbaum, Robert Wood, Emily Navar (in the air). Photo © 1992 Johan Elbers.

Kenneth King

SPACE DANCE AND THE GALACTIC MATRIX: MERCE CUNNINGHAM, AN APPRECIATION (1991)

Merce Cunningham is our first Space Dancer. His galaxy of dances has expanded the parameters and horizons of modern dance, heralding the post-modern. Our conceptions of space, its boundaries and reality, and his radical ideas about time and structuration (through his lifelong collaboration with John Cage) have challenged the givens of our perception, and our presuppositions about the art of the dance.

Merce is the Einstein of modern dance. More than anyone, he has found **mind** in dance. Merce dances the **idea**; his **systems dances** are kinetically animated treatises (videotexts, now, too!) that are cognitive and hyperdimensional. In fact, Merce Cunningham has been the singular most revolutionary (i.e. transformative) modern artist (and the most advanced choreographer on the planet) whose dance combines, extends, and breaks the codes of both modern dance and ballet. So after nearly twenty-five years of watching his work—a great pleasure—one feels prompted by the impossible to sketch an Appreciation.

Merce Cunningham is a man who obviously likes to muse on many things at once; his dancing, and the diversity of his large repertoire, roams and *ranges* over immense distances and galactic terrains. His own dancing is always characterized by a certain, ineffable, fleeting touch, his fingers are always probing and slightly vibrating, then reaching, letting the whole body sluice its

187

way deliciously through space with an elfin musicality. An uncanny, visceral awareness permeates the registers of his physicality; his head is sensor and antenna—a bristling punctuation underscores all the ways his movement pulses create dynamic surprises, unusual placements, and wonderfully unexpected linkages. Legs and lines strike in sharp, clear distinction, both severing and opening space, moment, mind. Here, too, to appreciate his dances, we need the words of Gaston Bachelard: *". . . they must be lived in their poetic immensity."*[1]

Merce's body was the first to **systemically** synthesize ballet and modern dance to find all the multiplex ways the contracting and rotating spine could work with and against the mechanics of the legs to create planar shifts and **axial** transformations, and the first to register the **digital pulse,** coincidentally, around 1950, at the time when TVs were entering every household. (The digital pulse links *three* contracting spinal and thoracic zones in the lower, middle, and upper spine. And: when you pulse, contract, **and** rotate the spine's *"geomimetric"* facings, you get the metatheoremics of robotics! Merce's dance is already a kind of futuristic Artificial Intelligence with a concrete, cogent reflexivity of kinetic possibilities. So there!) It was the **digital pulse** that enabled him to transform the frequencies of his choreography, and extend the synchronicity of multiple temporal modalities.

Merce is **pure** semiotics—before they became an international intellectual practice and enterprise! Codes, signals, and signs provide the **multi**lectic of Merce's **modus kinecti!** Merce Cunningham's dances realize William James's prophetic projection of contemporary words and ideas like **digital, field, event, import** (instead of meaning as literality), and kinetic pluralism—cornerstones of essential Cunningham which take on new meanings, and—treatises. (James was working with these ideas *before* Einstein, and **before** the 1890 publication of *The Principles of Psychology.* Imagine William James watching Merce and company! His scientific eye, pragmatic sensibility, and seminal modernism would be delightfully challenged.) Merce realized the digital *kinetrics* of structural relativities; actually, **schematologies** of relativities which underlie the structurations of his dances, the animation of a stage **continuum,** and the hyperdimensionality of the body through extended, high-frequency, spatial ambients. (His dances *also* generate vectorially circuited biospheres, motoric continuums, and kinetic (e)ideograms.)

I first saw Merce Cunningham and Dance Company in *Variations V,* a multimedia extravaganza-spectacle at Lincoln Center in 1965, with music by John Cage and David Tudor (the floor had been miked to incorporate the sound made by the dancers' feet as a compositional component) and multimedia by Stan VanDerBeek (film) and Nam June Paik (TV images). During the latter part of the sixties and early seventies, I saw several of Cunningham's seasons at the Brooklyn Academy of Music which featured such works as *Antic Meet* (1958), *Nocturnes* (1956), *Winterbranch* (1964), *Crises* (1960; a revival, with

Viola Farber), *Summerspace* (1958), *Canfield* (1969), *Signals* (1970), *Scramble* (1967), *Walkaround Time* (1968), *TV Rerun* (1972), *Objects* (1970), *RainForest* (1968), *Tread* (1970), *Place* (1966), *Second Hand* (1970), *Borst Park* (1972), and *Landrover* (1972), among others.

By this time, Merce's work had already sparked a controversy of misappropriated critical response. Critics—surprised or bewildered by the shift to unconventionally formal, discontinuously lyrical priorities, and the patent lack of emotive, romantic, literary, or psychological supports—called his work "non-referential." How could an avant-garde dancer be a non-referential lyricist?!

What Merce Cunningham actually discovered of course was **how** movement of whatever mode or register can create its *own contexts* and, further, how those contexts can flexibly shift the focus, perspective(s), and dimensionalities within the internal logi(isti)cs and cohesiveness of a dance. (The **form** of a dance depends on the accountability of its **structures**.)

The critics' "non-referential" disclaimer sabotaged recognizing the wider esthetic and structural processes of composition, the registers of abstraction, the expanded conceptual permutations of form, and their semiotic transformations. (We've had descriptive journalistic criticism instead of dance literature; Merce, though, is worthy of a Paul Valéry, Maurice Merleau-Ponty, or a Jacques Derrida.) I have always been interested in the reflexivity of his dances and movement invention (their *modus operandi*)—how they kinetically mirror the rigorous principles of their deployment, and their uncanny intellection that makes them scrupulously fascinating. In terms of spatial plasticity, sculpture is probably the closest art to dance, with and without analogies. Merce *sculpts* space by attending to the multiplex details of each individual figure in the rapid continuum transformations within the ongoing intricacies of his ensemble.

Merce Cunningham has scored still *another* first, which is probably already taken for granted—he's the first choreographer to forge, develop, and exemplify **synergetics** in the dancing body, creating "**geokinenometrics**" or *multilexical* structural architectonics. His repertory is a parallel galactic shorthand, whose comprehensive functionalities are (meta)theoretically mirrored and exposited in R. Buckminster Fuller's two-volume source primer, and *magnum opus, Synergetics,* a monumental superlogical systemicity of numerically ordered entries spanning technological, engineering, and mathematical disciplines, somewhat recollecting the unique logistical, typological ordering of Wittgenstein's *Tractatus Logico-Philosophicus*, but whose seminal interdisciplinary typographizing comes **after** technology, electronics, and atom smashing. The transactions between processes and system are the techno(onto)logical horizon of the arts and sciences. That a multiplicity of rhythmicized structures can create interactive continuums, that dance steps can **synergize** to raise the frequency of the dancing body, and that a heightened body frequency can process several streams of *digitation*—information—and cognition **is** *Merce's* invention.

The origin of both the synergetics of the movement, and the structural fusion of modern dance and ballet, undoubtedly have their roots in the formative development of his early work, around 1952, that began at Black Mountain College (the celebrated experimental school that initiated an entire modern-art movement, where John Cage staged the first "happening"), where Merce met Bucky, and where both initially collaborated. Two of Merce's first, most dedicated, and special dancers, Carolyn Brown and Viola Farber, brought a unique set of complementary talents and originary contrasts that synergized the combined stylistics of those two predominant dance forms. The balletic polarity can be traced to the immaculate artistry of Carolyn Brown; her pristine classical precision, and the beautiful, lyrical ideality of her placement and being, heightened the modernist impulse. Viola Farber, on the other hand, was quixotically quirkier—like silly putty with surefire hyperplex instincts, and with an angular, wiry, and sinuously off-centered flexibility. Merce, of course, magically merged both sets of qualities in his own dancing and in the later development of his company.

Cunningham's field-continuums (**"Events"**) developed in the late 1960s as a free-wielding, more flexible (and economic) repertory format, synchronistically recombining sections of dances, collaging excerpts and activities, thus merging disparate materials while also permuting new structural variables (also creating omnitopologies [Fuller's word]), paralleling the "open systems" of microbiologists. Though the structuralities of his dances are always clearly delineated, delimited, and pluralistic, ply and play with multiple modes (and codes) of patterning and configuration, their form always remains open, and open to further horizons of possibilities. (Of course Merce's dances all coordinate synchronistic factors and structures, **but** within the cohesion of a specific work; Events span and interconnect the broad range of *all* his works.) In fact, Merce Cunningham's dances are virtual and systemic *treatises*—he's gone the furthest in carrying abstraction of form, its temporal and spatializing processes and presentations, to new, all-inclusive thresholds.

How movement is form, filament, and function of **space** is Merce's unique praxis and insight. In her great three-volume book, *Mind: An Essay on Human Feeling*, Susanne K. Langer says: "The problems of abstraction in art have never been philosophically surveyed and analyzed."[2] Just as John Cage's sonic experiments might be said to explore physiognomic hearing (and neuroacoustics), Merce's dancing celebrates a kinesthetically active physiognomic seeing. (Also: a *kinelexically* active seeing, or the way we *read* different, simultaneous kinetic orders of movement, motion, and animation.) His calibrated choreographies might well exemplify Edmund Husserl's conceptual term—**kinemathics**—the mathematical components of (con)figurated kinetics, or, **kinetrics**—as (meta)*systems* of topologically transactive kinetic possibilities.

Over the years, part of the reflective pleasure of watching Cunningham's dances has been trying to puzzle out their "genealogies"—their seeming "family resemblances"—how they relate to, reflex with, grow out of, or from, previous works, or share an adjacency with them, but it is always in a new vein, not just additively. Right away, one differentiates the serious from the humorous pieces. *Antic Meet, Borst Park, Roadrunners* (1979), and *Grange Eve* (1986), with its whimsical, offbeat vaudevillian trappings, are hilarious, absurdist spoofs—dance farces.

The serious dances in turn are of two basic kinds: either systems-oriented, like *Canfield, Torse* (1976), *Landrover,* and *Fractions* (1977), or dramatic dances, such as *Winterbranch, Quartet* (1982) *RainForest,* and *Points in Space* (1986). (*Winterbranch* is a stark apocalyptic work; *Canfield,* based supposedly, at least in title, on a kind of solitaire, was an early, perhaps the first, evening-length **systems dance** with a mysterious floating light sculpture/decor by Robert Morris that slowly transversed the foreground of the stage casting an imposing, stark shadow along the backdrop during its elongated passage. *Canfield* might well have been the turning-point between repertory and the development of Events. *Canfield* was a muted, somber, **existential** dance whose extended *duration* seemed to forge a new programmatic continuum. Perhaps that dance stylistically shares a "family resemblance" with highly rigorous, dramatically portending works like *Exchange* [1978]. Two other full-length works that preceded *Canfield* and *Landrover* were *Variations V* and *Walkaround Time.*)

Signals dates back to 1970, made before *Landrover,* but I believe both occurred around the same time that the systems choreography we now associate as staple Cunningham was inaugurated. *Signals* is episodic; it begins with an intriguing trio of two men and a woman. One man maneuvers a magic wand or long stick to energize and define the sharp spaces between their bodies. There are specific sections: solos, trios, duets, etc., and at various times during its performance, non-active dancers sit on a few folding chairs placed in an upstage corner.

Landrover is much more spatial; it spans a huge, implicit expanse. It is one work that cogently clarifies the dialectic of bodies and space, geometry and geography. The ground of one's body geometry is anchored by the vertical axis of the spine, which can reposition the use of one's weight and balance, and the ways vectors and lines are coordinated from the dancer's visceral center, creating (omni)directionality, and the complex, vertiginous contours of projected, virtual space. "Geography" refers to the spatial implementation of patterns in typographizing space, and their patterned extendabilities.

In a conversation in his studio, when asked about *Landrover,* Merce Cunningham said that the idea occurred to him because of all the company's travels; he wondered how a dance might appear if the background, or scenery, were always changing. (A landrover, of course, is a kind of caravan vehicle. In one of Merce's early videos, *Blue Studio: Five Segments* [1975], made with videographer Charles Atlas, computerized editing allowed Merce to create five separate interactive dancing selves, *and* dance on a road with a continuously moving landscape.)

What connects *Signals* and *Landrover* are unique passages in which a group of five or more dancers start flush in a line, suddenly begin travelling forward, seemingly toppling and spilling, then suddenly veering tangentially on spiky and fragmented vectors so that it appears as if they had actually detached the spindle or "handlebar" of the diagonal, a seemingly fixed and unmovable staple of stage space, and were able to move and deploy it in various, sharply diverging directions, folding and redoubling their patterned excursions back into the accreting, ongoing momentum. The effect astounds, and tackles one of the first esthetic items commonly cited as Cunninghamesque—fragmentation.

The modes of fragmentation that Merce Cunningham's dances exercise as virtual, compositional devices celebrate and recircuit a wider perceptual phenomenon. These **discontinuous** ways of structuring discrete units, phrases, and overlapping steps, bodies, and juxtaposable materials developed from Merce's insistence **NOT** to dance on the musical beat (although the dancers do use precision counting), and not to choreograph to the specifics of a score. This enables any given dance to have a compositional autonomy, and the potential to be danced to different scores, as happens in "Events," when only selections from repertory are assembled using chance methods for a given occasion.

But first, where does our notion of fragmentation come from? Undoubtedly from the excess of impressions, the fitful complexity of our technological world, and the contents of our media-magnified world that splinter our reality and our ability to attend simultaneously to multiply interactive phenomena and foci.

In Merce's dances, abstraction and kinesthesia are expanded by the fragmentation of several vying foci, which he has been able to use as a kind of esthetic coup. Instead of splintering his dances' materials, or one's perception of them, fragmentation is transformed by Merce's *oeuvre* and actually becomes a unique holistic pivot—a perceptually assimilative device that allows the eye to take in greater, more inclusive, and multiple ranges of (overlapping) details, and how the parts (whether individual dancers or different ensemble sections) resonate or coalesce together on stage, or in the mind's eye. Cunningham uses fragmentation in reverse flow, to great advantage and catalytic effect, to expand the options of his movement manifold, as a kind of compositional electron microscope.

For example, a hilarious trio in *Borst Park* (a spoof **of a** spoof!) features two men and a woman carrying out a purposefully intricate, craftily engineered virtuosity—holding, chaining, and interchanging hands and limbs while enacting a complicated exchange of weight, balance, and precision partnering—

still managing to tie them up in knots (also spoofing Balanchine)—**while at the same time** linking together pieces of phrases—almost like pieces of a quilt that are kinetically fractured—not only in their timing, but in their multiplex spatial deployments, their junctures, and anglings. A new dynamic unity always emerged, a kind of seeming kinetic paradox.

Fragmentation as a psychological state short-circuits clarity of perception, but as an objectifying mode of organization in the dances, it **implements** an expanded perception and clarity. In psychological reality, fragmentation splinters the conscious field; in Merce's dances, it **reunifies** the elements and eidetic (perceptual) factors. But fragmentation, referring to the **processings** of multiply interactive structures, speeds the informational relays of the dance materials, just as video accelerates the velocity of kinetically processed bytes. In addition, used as a group compositional tool, fragmentation discontinuously layers subgroupings and overlaps ensemble structures in multiply, and integrally ingenious, ways, helps eradicate hierarchical structurings (everyone in the company is a virtuoso anyway), and becomes a discontinuous harmonic, or *systems tonic.*

Placed in its historical frame of reference, this seems even more astounding. That is, Merce Cunningham follows Martha Graham, with whom he performed in the early years of his career. Only, instead of heavy, linear plots with formidable characters and libidinous, psychological motives, Merce was the first to present animated **figures** in a **discontinuous field,** forging an esthetics of abstraction whose formal parameters recontextuated the dramatic dynamic and reconstituted the threatricalizing thread of the modern impulse. Merce broke, or opened, the expressionistic mold—structuralities with discontinuous and asynchronous cadences and punctuations that open other body vistas and space scapes. (Theater is often situated in specific locations, but this is less so in dance. And, with regard to minimalism, Merce unloaded the representationally symbolic cargo beforehand; **being** emerges instead of characters, **patterns** instead of plots.) The idea of a **field,** and the field as a negotiable, *open* continuum of discrete, albeit interactive **events,** of course, belongs to relativity theory, though, as aforementioned, William James used these terms with their emerging modernist denotations almost a century earlier. But in dance, during the late forties and fifties, it was still a revolutionary change after decades of inveterate emotionalism and overspent, narrative catharsis.

It was probably during the late 1970s that I began wondering . . . imagining what William James would think and say about Merce's dances! I imagined James as a virtual reference in order to reappraise, reposition, or question my own perspective. William James, of course, had forged a completely modern sensibility well before the 20th century officially arrived, and his encyclopedic two volumes on psychology, as well as his wide-ranging philosophical acumen and contribution, did more than any other American thinker to catalyze a genuine interdisciplinary momentum.

(We know James championed a no-nonsense, concrete, everyday lexicality, but some fancy literary equipment is necessary too; Merce is our cosmic ornithologist, plotting complex flights with fleet feet. So, when watching a Cunningham performance, I often imagine William James in his **own** private balcony box delightfully bewildered, puzzled, and thrilled about what he sees, testing and inquiring as to just **what** can be said: how movement reflexes [a phenomenological] intentionality, how codes inform the dances' underlying structural permutabilities, the compositional complexities of a movement field, the dynamics of the discontinuous, especially with regard to aligning divergent **processes,** and synergizing systematic elements and rhythms, the margins of indeterminism [and the "margins" of movement and visibility: eidos and gestalt], digital geomimetrics, multidimensionality, would be some of the esthetic issues and "problems" that surely would fascinate him.)*

Of course it is well-known that Merce Cunningham utilizes chance operations to overcome the personalisms of decision-making, following John Cage's practice. Very simply put, chance is an objectifying means to remove motives and egos from dance making, and is the means to break the given, temporal logic or structure of a phrase, and the expectations of movement's order and sequence. Chance too covers many methods of composition, and enables Merce to play with the blind spot of the eye, the visual tricks that accrue as the eye sweeps and scans the performance and space of any given dance, and the cognitive manifold that switches between perception and apperception, processing and entraining the bundles of after-images. (Its logistics still baffle experts and audiences alike.) The point is that **intentional** structures (Husserl, again) superseded "motivated," psychological, and emotive movement, and prepared the field so that discrete and fragmented dance materials could discontinuously **but** formalistically collage space and bodies, thus moving all their (implicit) kinetic imageries and registers past their usual frames of reference, generating a palpable plurality of meanings, or polysemia.

Synchronicity and chance create an unusual spontaneity in the performance of the entire repertory, which can also be deceiving; some viewers are fooled into thinking that the dances are improvised, and one might say that Merce is so adept that he can **simulate** the look of an improvised spontaneity, but, of course, the simulacrum he's tapped into is the synchronicity of multiple *digital* rhythms. (This simulacrum points in the direction of dancers' true freedom and artistic autonomy, by giving the **semblance** of navigating through space on their own

---

*Several words need careful, topical clarification: **eidetic, mimetic,** and **kinetic.** The eidetic (from the Greek word *eidos*) refers to the clarity of prehending the visual, virtual, mental contours and factorealities of phenomena. The mimetic originated with language (and art), and refers to the animation of the elemental factors and action(s) of the processes underlying (linguistic) perception, and, with regard to dance, suggests all the ways signals and signs (con)figure in the perceptual field. Kinetics refers to motion and movement factorealities; kinetrics to the system(at)ic interfaces of movements and structures. Kinesthesia is a separate sense matrix, the total sensibility that apprehends all the orders of motion perception. *Kinelexia* refers to the modes and codes of how movement gradients and a dance's intraleveraged structural plays are "read."

decisions.) Synchronicity involves the parallel and/or concurrent synchronization of diverse rhythms, melodic, and motific elements; the results of the (intra)coordinated cycles and unexpected linkages of steps and structures are always surprising. Maybe even more than being the master structuralist, Merce is the multiplex *structurations* expert, since the decentralization of the spatial focus recircuits the given, hierarchical conditioning of our organized perceptual habits. In Merce's dances, synchronicity makes for **systemicity,** the concatenation of pluralistic, multiplex details and overlapping visual scanning reflexes deployed through formal contexts and their implicitly resonating, virtualized registers. *Systemicity*, as the axial interconnectedness of movement systems, makes Merce one of the first true choreographers!

A constant dialectical interplay between an individual dancer and the interpression of ensemble configurations informs the orchestration of each work. A quick, ready analogy for structural transformations, rules, and transpositions of choreographic operations is computer games, which depend on the constant **digitality** of recomposable configurations. It's the p(l)ace(s) between patterns, pathways, and passages that locate(s) the pluriverse's pluralistic diversity, and the cosmic intervallics, of his compositions.

Instead of stories, **placements** make **relations** between bodies, and steps register, cohere, and have import; instead of psychology, a dancing calculus; instead of motivation, **intentionality;** instead of an ego, a field. And though the essential key is structurality, Merce's dances always exemplify dramatic ideas, as in *RainForest* where he seems to be a paternalistic, or strong authoritative figure in the midst of a charged and restless drama, or perhaps a general or leader in *Exchange* (1978), and a totemic guardian, spirit, or near invisible ancestor in *Quartet* (1982). Instead of adumbrating actual locations, Merce's dances seem to inhabit and celebrate **scapes;** *Rebus* (1975), for example, seems to occur in a classroom as the matrix or ground for the variety of the dancers' work routines—but in a **dream** classroom with surrealistic dislocations and lyrical relocations of space, that continually recontext the dancers' festive contestings. The viewers' "problem" is apperceiving the riddle of the dance's patterns, rhythms, pulses, and structural juxtapositions; the axial axiomat(h)ics of the rotating spine and configurative logics, and the planar concentration of pulses, reveal the daily ritualizing processes, different dancerly endeavors, and company interactions. (There's a modern metal clothes rack in the upper left stage corner covered with appropriately concealing garments that Merce periodically disappears behind, changes, and reemerges from, and in one sequence—his "dakini" solo—he is hidden behind a clover clump of four dancers who splay and fall to the floor revealing Merce in a svelte red unitard, very whimsically and dramatically plying tiny, quizzically meticulous details and gestic changes!) *Rebus* is a dance of red, sensual, with richly textured, sharp, and quixotically punctuated dynamics and hyperspatialized **qualities,** which the steps serve to generate and heighten.

The compositional shift is thus from psychological motivation to field theory; that is, what makes a dance have its emotive impact and coherence are the resonances of its structuralities, which creates multiply layered, interacting, and suggestively **sign**ifying linkages. The formalist esthetic therefore refers to the systems, modes, and registers of structuralities. How multiple logics thread, filter, and inform his work—**synergetics**—has a double (to be explained later) double connection with his friend and fellow globe-travelling genius, R. Buckminster Fuller. Merce uses a *double* **double** syncopation as a digital counterpoint (i.e., a double pulse) to create great synchronistic effects (and in terms of temporal dimensionalities, the digital pulse coordinates both the continuous and discontinuous, and the symmetrical and asymmetrical— and *both* at the same time). **Merce is the dancing dymaxion body!**

In a typically fast Cunningham dance, the signs and signals transpire at a rapid, fluent, and profuse pace in high mimetic interface. If semiotics were to move through and include dance and kinelexical analyses in its methodology repertoires, then Merce would be its very best exemplar. How a dance builds up a kinelexic systemicity by concatenating structuralities—alignments of kinetic grammatologies of signs, signals, impulses, flexions, vectorialities, (con)figurations, etc.—is dance's semiotic component. Sight is constantly irrupted, interrupted, and refocused to (re)integrate the discrete relationships of wholes/parts, and their intricate, mimetically fluent registers. Viewers must swivel their heads to scan any number of rapidly changing stage zones and (overlapping) space scapes, then in apperception or mind's eye, (re)assemble the pictures, impulses, and eidetic transformations, *so that signals thrown and sprung as signs are not always localizable or (re)cognizable as signs*, but *are* so by default or *de facto* proximation. A group of signals may also act as a sign (or sign proxy), without actually being so *per se*, and the hyperfluent accumulation of passages, phrases, and structures also generates other **orders** of signs (from signal valences) as shifts between metrics and measurement ply the continuous **and** discontinuous. The semiotic puzzle is comprised of interacting kinetic layers having mimetically *sprung* "quantum indexes"—coefficients and exponentials of movement registers built up by accreting and concatenating weaves of gradients, and codes whose transparencies enable one to glimpse the genetic (then **galactic**) matrix. The galactic matrix is thus the reflexive *continuum* of micro-macro scalar transformations that "protoportionally" (inter)connect and interprocess the kinetic/kinelexic grammarizing, typologies, and axes of the figurative/configurative structurations. (Dances like *Torse, Changing Steps* [1975], *Landrover,* and *Channels/Inserts* [1981], and of course Events, which collage and interleve repertory excerpts into new compositive performance formats, weave complex and dense typographies that eloquently shift scope and scale.)

One of Merce's biggest **conceptual** breakthroughs is the awareness that a full field of feeling and perception *will* emerge if the dancers consistently follow the formal plottings of the dances, and Merce's plottings amount to fourth-dimensional calculi and advanced systems engineering! By the mid- to late 1970s, works like *Torse, Fractions,* and *Locale* (1979) featured high-energy, detail-dense, *systems* explorations.

Torse, for example, is a kinetic (and philosophical) motion treatise (and pure, reflexive, kinetic polemic) on all the ways the rotations and torquing of torso, spine, and joints can realign the segmented, isomorphic articulations and ro-torized, planarized (re)facings of the body. (In fact, body isomorphisms are **tropisms** in Merce's work.) This dance is thorough in the spatial diversity of its rigorously paced, geometric choreographic variations, and rhythmically placed and spaced (re)combinations. This evening-length work (often performed in separate sections), to a spare, electronic score by Maryanne Amacher, systematically explicates the methodically and concretely graphed permutations of its multiplex spatial deployments: rotating, highly alert, antennae-like spines; swivelling torsos torquing and tilting; high attenuated leg extensions; brisk, sharp, pivoting jumps; a full field of intricate spatial patternings; and omnitropic, overlapping group configurations.

The (analogical) key to these "genealogical" space tracings involves different orders of **typographizing**—steps, structures, stage zones, and modes of configuration, all suggestively interactional as well. This is where the ontology of the dance differentiates regions, realms, and domains—real and virtual, actual and transcendental, natural and supernatural. The spaces of the dances sometimes imply specific places and locations: *RainForest*'s title is self-referential, and Andy Warhol's enigmatic decor of floating silver pillows, gives a sense of intensity (heat) and atmospheric suspension (cold); *Rebus* may take place in a dream classroom; *Sounddance* (1975) creates a highly active, dynamic realm both primordial and ritualistic but also amazingly futuristic and otherworldly; *Arcade*'s (1985) ambient suggests both a Spartan ruin or reexcavated archaic site; *Roaratorio* (1983) is a bright dancing (Irish) circus; *Fabrications* (1987) might be a galactic ceremony taking place, if the backdrop is the indicator, in either (or both) a giant machine, or in the magnified thoracic bone of a huge dinosaurial ancestor; and works such as *Fractions* and *Locale* celebrate non-(site) specific, but open, or unnameable realms, regions, or domains. Rather than archetypes, spirits, sprites, and angels, we see highly animated, implicitly expressive kinetic figurations in informationally abstract modes that liberate us from the literality and nomenclature of species-specific mythologies. (Merce's dancers might well be beings from other orders or higher dimensions. And *this* facticity: archetypes naturally and plastically emerge in the body's movement stream, whether the dance is formal and/or abstract.)

Walkaround Time featured an extraordinary kind of double collaboration with Jasper Johns who designed the figuratively translucent set, one of Merce's most intricate, adapted from Marcel Duchamp's celebrated classic, the "Large Glass," by transposing the design of the original composition, with its complex axial and planar spirals and paramechanic insignia, onto transparent plastic cubes of varying sizes that the dancers moved behind and around. The choreography discontinuously combined activities with informally overlapping episodes; it was also balletically leggy and elongated, and cut through space punctuated with sharp falls, structural foils, and stillpoints—moments and figures frozen in the shifting panoply of sections and activities. (Even the intermission was a programmatic part of the dance, in which the dancers, in rehearsal attire, or dressed in slippers and protective clothing, went through their usually unseen offstage rituals.) This dance thus accentuated and intensified the perception of multiply contexted, diagrammatic zones and cubistic planes in space—human beings interacting with space and structures, and **space** itself . . . empty, but an entity nonetheless.

The space around the dance(s) is also important, sometimes, as important as the dance, since it sets off its virtuality and presentational foci. Works like *Squaregame* (1976) point this up by removing all the backdrops and side-stage curtains, revealing a naked backstage area with pipes and ropes, and by using a pristine white floor cloth to accentuate the dance's centered spatial placement. The dancers, in sporty pastel garments (by Mark Lancaster), periodically pass, toss, lounge by (and, in Merce's case, humorously hides behind) duck white canvas gym bags (the large kind used in football scrimmage), while moving through complex, athletically bounding ensemble subgroupings that mix and merge. The energy and excitement of the work are additionally punctuated by the extra margins of space that further set off the totality of all its interlacing rhythms and mimetic details.

This kind of extended and suspended placement of the dance moved all the way toward a *galactic* realization when the company performed a week of Events at the 66th Street Armory on Park Avenue in New York City in June 1983. The spectacularly vaulted spatial expanse, as large as a city block and several stories high, architechtonically advanced the space-age dimensions and volumetrics of Merce Cunningham's work. The "off-stage" margins of the performance space (in full view) were active, dynamic ingredients in seeing and recycling the virtual **tao**tality (and the perceiver's scan patterns) of his work, letting us see how the dancers exit and make off-stage transitions. (The margins of the performance space are akin to the peripheral field of vision where, according to Marshall McLuhan, we *field* new information.)

There's an anecdote in John Cage's book *Silence* about Merce and space—as if his studio were analogous to the confines of a backyard, a bound and limited space, but one that opens onto the unbound if every inch is carefully utilized—a marvelous metaphor for the tending and expansion of space. In *The Poetics of Space,* Gaston Bachelard considers how (the creation of) a site can both condense quanta of detail, then open out on immensity. The esthetics of expansion and contraction of space and the dialectics of qualities, contrasts of scale, and the tensities that support it, are topics that Susanne K. Langer treats in "A Chapter on Abstraction" in the first volume of *Mind: An Essay on Human Feeling*.

* * * *

One of the most magical moments I've ever witnessed in Cunningham's work is the solo finale to *Place* (1966), which I saw at the Brooklyn Academy of Music. A dramatic, existential dance with a patch-like constructivist rear-wall set made out of a white, lattice-like grid with attached, corrugated designs (and highly contrasted, zone-shifting lighting) by Beverly Emmons, this dramatic group dance created quite some controversy. It generated rumors that Merce was "alienated" from the company; he became a decentralized solo figure, very much in the back, making lone, mysterious moves, suggestive gestures, and aloof connections whenever he entered or passed through the dance, sometimes creating an unusual contrast by his presence or placement, sometimes instigating or dispersing relationships, other times gently touching a group of dancers, tapping them on the shoulder with a benign shrug as if to say "enough"—as if paternity or authority could be dispensed with.

At the very end of the dance, on an empty stage, he came all the way downstage alone, suddenly holding a sack, which was done so quickly the viewer had no idea where it had come from, and somehow, again without seeing how, he managed to climb into it—the lights were already beginning to fade and all this happened very rapidly—as he rolled on the floor upstage toward darkness and the void, the sack just up to his chest, his eyes beady and urgent, his sense of imminent disappearance interrupted by the falling curtain. Surely this is a moment Samuel Beckett would have cherished—archly existential, also profoundly and magically mysterious.

* * * *

Torse was both a systematic **and** *systemic* breakthrough. Systematic because the carefully calculated progressions of the repetition variations of the steps and sections of the dance were mathematically plotted and spatialized. (In interviews, Merce explained that he used the ancient Chinese book of wisdom, the *I Ching*, with its sixty-four hexagrams, to map out the work's spatiality, to organize the dance's internal structure, and to typographize the ensemble sections.) *Systemic* because the repetition variations further heightened the accreting and fractionating mimetic "integers" and dynamic "coefficients" of the seriated steps and structures, their plastic transformations and themic permutations. The staggered temporal modalities recombined (often in one's afterimagings while watching, or remembering), then concatenated, both in the branchings of their transassociative eidetic suggestions, and in terms of their actual **quantum** impact on perception. The continually transformative structurations options, codes, borders, and parameters of Merce's dance are analogous to differential equations that charter the way systems continually change, permute, and transmute, not without reference (and relevance, too) to the linguists' "deep grammar," transformational rules, and synergy underlying language. (After I saw *Torse* during Merce's January 1977 Broadway season I told him in great excitement that, there's ballet, modern dance, Cunningham technique, **and now** *Torse*, meaning one could derive *several* parallel systems and branching techniques from its extended principles, structural premises, and *grammatological* parameters.)

Axiologies are about the multiple coordination of structural matrices and configurative alignments; *galactic space is* **superaxialized** *space*. (Axiology: the term is from Husserl's *Ideas*.) The intricate structurations of configurative possibilities **axialize** both the stage space and the deportment of each dancer, just as the vertical axis and upright deportment of the spine (and gravity) anchor the body's weight placement(s) in space. Axiologies also refer to the mimetic alignments of perspectiv(iti)es of a dance, and their temporal dimensionalities.

The axial (and axiotropic) possibilities of the moving spine have greatly extended the balletic innovation in Merce's dances, and those include (again, in *Torse*) rotating, curving, tilting, and dipping, and the incremental vectors that fall between, out of, and intersect different turnout and rotary vectors. *Merce's choreography can fractionate each and every plane of body and space.* The spine can swivel and rotate against the direction and movements of the legs, in vectorial opposition, and it can also curve or contract in the process. Tilting is lateral—the sideways springing, leaning, and off-centered shifting of the body alignment and weight—a kind of windmilling of the frontal upright. Dipping actually plays with scooping out space on different planes and axes by using the curvilinear **gradients** of gravity to accent the fall, swoop, or drop of the body. (Gradients refer to scalar and proportionalities ratios.) When any of these axial moves are performed against fairly basic balletic leg movements, the result is surprising and thrilling because multiply intersecting lines, physicalized vectors, and planes animate the mimetic coefficients of the dynamic image, and emphasize the vertical displacement of the zones of the body: close to the earth, then midbody and overhead, immediately suggesting a palette of vastly different (and interactive) realms and domains.

In 1977, the Cunningham company used three cameras to film *Torse* (Merce was one of the cameramen), and around 1980 there was a private showing projected simultaneously on two adjacent screens at the Bruno Walter Auditorium at Lincoln Center (private, because funds for rights and salaries couldn't be met and the film had to go into the Dance Collection's archives at the Library for the Performing Arts). Several simultaneously potent foci are a natural presentational (and democratic) format for Merce, as opposed to the monocentralized, authoritarian focus of the ballet, TV, or single screen. The film of *Torse* is one of the furthest experiments of dancefilm, and it's unfortunate that at this time it cannot have wider viewings. Also, being a film, it reiterates the unusual perceptual puzzles—two screens, multiple foci, overlapping structures, and frame switching—that also inform all the ranges of Merce's stage experiments.

In 1974, when Merce moved into his Westbeth studio (which had been Bell Labs' **top secret** telecommunications/technology research center during World War II, *and* the room where the **first** television was demonstrated!), he made a video and dance of the same title. Since then, he has continued his extensive experimentation with video. Videography telescopes, encapsulates, and can accelerate time and perception; what takes ten seconds to see on stage takes only two to three seconds on video. Dancers are creatures of the mirror—that's how they learn and see; video is a kind of electronic mirror, and provides other, immediate feedbacks and compositional perspectives of a dance. Several dances, such as *Channels/Inserts* and *Points in Space* (1986), were first made for video, then reworked for the stage, because of the specific spatial confines that videography necessarily imposes. This is revealed in the video of *Locale*, a highly active, synergistic dance with dense, intricate, and constantly changing ensemble configurations. *Locale* is a *digital* dancing calculus (still in repertory) that hyperanimates spatial, spinal, and compositional axialities, eideticizing the virtual centers of focus and propulsion, with rapid detail realigning the perspectivities of its corporeal geometricities, then by frequency-pulse transformations, creating a dense dancing systemicity. This is evidenced in the video *Roamin' I* (1979) made of the making of Locale (also by Charles Atlas), an experiment in (meta)videography where a second set of cameras documents how the main cameras, rigged on ropes and pulleys, were also able to swing and travel, providing another reflexively kinelexic element. The potentially programmatic synchronicities of eye and camera, bodies, field, and **digitized** space(s) really require a separate essay; what needs noting here is that video introduces other compositionally interactive processes that can inform both the choreography, staging, and the "read" of a dance.

Video makes the mirror electronic, and is a concretely reflexive tool for choreographers and dancers to join inner and outer, providing immediate feedbacks; it also has phenomenological correlations. As Maurice Merleau-Ponty described it:

> More completely than lights, shadows, and reflections, the mirror image anticipates, within things, the labor of vision. Like all other technical objects, such as signs and tools, the mirror arises upon the open circuit [that goes] from seeing body to visible body. Every technique is a "technique of the body." A technique outlines and amplifies the metaphysical structure of our flesh. The mirror appears because I am seeing-visible, because there is a reflexivity of the sensible; the mirror translates and reproduces that reflexivity . . . The mirror's ghost lies outside my body, and by the same token my own body's "invisibility" can invest the other bodies I see. Hence my body can assume segments derived from the body of another, just as my substance passes into them; man is mirror for man. The

mirror itself is the instrument of a universal magic that changes things into a spectacle, spectacles into things, myself into another and another into myself . . ."[3]

*   *   *   *

If *Torse* and *Fractions* are advanced field theory, then *Sounddance* is **quantum mechanics!** Though it's impossible and ludicrous to even attempt to have a "favorite" Cunningham dance, *Sounddance* still seems to be in, and have, a category all its own. Choreographed in 1975, the program quotes a concisely ironic Joycean citation: "In the buggunning is the woid, and in the muddle the sounddance" (also cited in Norman O. Brown's *Closing Time*). *Sounddance* was made during the period of Merce's *very* high energy space dances; **very** stretched, driven, and electric!

The curtain rises on an empty stage. Mark Lancaster designed the white costumes, decor, and lighting. Upstage, a bare pipe used for hanging scenery has been lowered halfway and remains in full view; from it is suspended a kind of white canvas material slit in the middle, as an opening. The set reminded me of a (cosmic) magician's cabinet, or possibly a **solar** tabernacle. David Tudor composed an absolutely magnificent, intergalactic score, *Toneburst*, whose powerful acoustic volumetrics amplified the electrochromatic profiles of chordal strings, sounding like cosmically magnified celery fibers being stripped, and their overtone clusters split apart—like popcorn!—heavy crackling and galactic sounding interference creating immense reverberations, sonic blasts, and (implicit) stellar spaces. (David Tudor is due special credit; his amazing, powerful compositions are more space-age and futurological than the other composers, and his music perfectly synchronizes acoustic volumetrics with the kinetic amplitudes and precise sculptural architechtonics of Merce's dances.)

In the beginning, Merce is propelled out of the cleft in the fabric; the momentum, and its bristling, charged dynamic, suggest that he has been thrust into *this* space from an unknown source, realm, or dimension. From the very beginning of the dance until the very end a **tremendous** vibration is palpable. (It's a genuine gooseflesh experience!)

The dancers enter one at a time, but almost horrifically because the energy is so mighty it's all they can do to manage. They skitter, tilt, lurch, careen. Perhaps Meg Harper or Ellen Cornfield enters first, the other(s) shortly afterwards. Then, after the full company has assembled, bodies bolt to the floor, bound back, then are buffeted, thrown, tossed; they're rhythmically jittery and spastic, but always **dynamimetically** fluid. (Rhythm and dynamic have their own elusive musicological counterpoints and differentials; rhythm refers of course to all the metered, metrical, and cadential portionments of musical time; dynamic is more elusive—a kind of **tonus** that modulates and is modulated by the temporal unitizing of rhythms.)

Toward the beginning, Merce grabs the hand of one dancer—as if to rescue and steady her quivering impulsiveness—as her feet bleat, knead, and strike rapidly against the floor. The movements were not only extremely fast, dexterously flexed, and articulate, but their vectors slice across all seeming directions liberating untold stores of energy. The dance was sinuous, non-stop, and elastic—bouncing, hopping, and *popping,* too—it **exploded! This dance was from another universe!** Its design suggested both an archaic as well as futuristic dimension. The group choreography fluidically linked tensegrity structuralities so that vectors (equi)calibrated and supported unusually tensile body volleys at high kinetic momentum whose interface included split-second, acrobatic finesse: dancers lifted, carried, swept, and tossed. The dance seemed to split apart the movement matrices that held it together, and the impulses that figurated (and fragmented) the intricate phrases, and their dynamics played with atomizing the rhythmicity of the passages of the movement, perhaps, by analogy, the way James Joyce put morphemics and syntax into his holy atomic cyclotron in *Finnegans Wake.*

Sounddance reminded me of the restless tremors of an acid trip—a certain abrasive, **t-h-r-o-w-n** dynamic, and sprung propulsion **vigorously** hyperanimated each dancer. As they converged, a manic edge, thrilling and apocalyptic, scattered the impulses of their movements in bounding waves that surged and swept fluidly and propulsively across the stage. *Sounddance* broke open the codes of movement, spilling the complex dynamic ingredients and valences, balletic and modern—even the codes of Merce's oeuvre, too. This dance could also be seen as a celebration of electricity, cosmic electricity . . . or solar fire. Movement **can** release the energy of the cellular, genetic, and phonemic.

At the climax, Merce performed an absolutely amazing series of rapid, high-frequency, covertly suggestive hieratic gestures, his legs in parallel position, his torso smoothly spiralling and rotating with great forceful pulses that fluently rippled across the body while arms, then hands, unfurled imprecating and magical gestures with a secret, liquid virtuosity, and supreme mythic amplitude, supreme gestures, **Mahamudras,** fingers in ecstatic release, causing currents and shudders. Though hyperanimated and magically manic, there was a bristling ecstasy too, the way Walt Whitman might celebrate the **body electric** if plugged *directly* into a lightbulb or turbine!

This dance also seemed to have both a cosmic and Buddhist reference. The cleft in the drop cloth suggested a cavernous, primordial source, cosmogonic metaphor, too—the void behind the origin of the world (also womb-like). One Buddhist tenet is that sound and vibration precede creation; sound thus is anterior to, and originates before, image and appearance. It suggests the way creation spins and sp(l)its out its individuated particulars. The dance's overriding dramatic edge was apocalyptic because of the intense, loud, highly condensed, physicalized acoustic energy. There was something anxious, urgent, and sonically shattering—here Merce **is** the wizard of the galactic matrix—perhaps, ideally, foreshadowing the futuric merger of the step with higher neurotropic processes that Susanne Langer adumbrates at the very end of the third volume of *Mind: An Essay on Human Feeling*. (Galactic space is neither inner nor outer, objective nor subjective, a paralogical shift has occurred). Like Nikola Tesla (to whom Merce dedicated *Canfield* in 1969), who was photographed at the World's Fair early in this century, sitting nonchalantly inside a huge, high-frequency dynamo in an electrically charged field rife with crackling bolts and flying sparks all around him, Merce inhabits **kinetically** accelerated electromagnetic realms. (When I first saw *Sounddance* I remember telling him that it is very definitely the *first* **intergalactic** dance; maybe it's from Jupiter! It realizes a higher frequency, futuristic and higher dimensional ambience, and reveals an exciting transcendental realm quite unlike any other ballet or dance I've ever witnessed.)

Sounddance might also take place in a wind tunnel, or in a twilight realm between worlds, or between the interstices of dimensions. Toward the end there is another palpable dynamic transformation, as the dancers are "pulled" singly backwards and out of the space, disappearing one by one into the slit in the rear canopy, and the momentum builds further until Merce is left alone, and, as the final ante builds, he's spun and pivoted upstage. Just as he is about to crash into the cleft, the stage curtain comes down leaving the audience drenched in vibration, before they're on their feet screaming! Maybe it was at the last performance of the work when I overhead a woman behind me say to her companion: "**That** was supernatural!"

*   *   *   *

These descriptions are not just the dances' meanings, nor only this writer's interpretations, but rather the explicit, denotative structures, the trails and tracers of images and imageries, that sweep across the resolution screen of one's watching dancing (a new epistemic). Merce is fond of saying in interviews that he begins a dance alone in a studio, by taking a step. He insists his business is just to make the movement, **but** movement *does* transmit imageries, reflexes the wor(l)d and our experience, suggesting correspondences and analogies. How or why there are images in the mind, or, sometimes several simultaneous streams of movement imagery in a dance, has been deemed complex and unknown (cf. Susanne K. Langer in *Philosophical Sketches*).

Merce's **systems dances** of the late sixties and seventies were complex works transformative of every artistic factor, including our perception, and whose import extends through realms other than dance too. Merce's dances and **dancing** *are* metaphysical, and he has written that dance is the natural double for metaphysical problems and paradoxes. Merce is a man who has danced **beyond** shadow and double. An **otherness** always informs the grain and gain of his work. (Merce has often expressed his admiration for Fred Astaire, notably on his Guggenheim application in 1951. Everything is metaphysical, one can claim. Though both are incomparable, in spite of all the high-scale, commercial production values in Astaire's movies, *Merce* is the more classical, metaphysical, contemplative, and intellectual innovator.)

For Merce, the galactic matrix means operating at ontothetic space scales equilibrating higher frequency phases of being. In Buckminster Fuller's words:

> But frequency, as a word key to a functional concept, never relates to the word one because frequency obviously involves some plurality of events . . .[4]
>
> The physical Universe is an aggregate of frequencies. . . . The different frequencies of one element's set produce unique cyclic-frequency interactions whose resonances are similar to musical chords . . . The human senses are able to tune in no more than one-millionth of the total known frequency range limits of the presently known electromagnetic spectrum.[5]

From Buckminster Fuller's far-ranging chapter, **Conceptuality** in *Synergetics* (Volume I):

> Frequency is plural unity. Frequency is multicyclic fractionation of unity. A minimum of two cycles is essential to frequency fractionation. Frequency means a discrete plurality of cycles within a given greater cyclic increment.[6]
>
> Science has not found any continuous surfaces, solids, straight lines, or infinitely extensible, nonclosed-system planes.[7]

Then: omnitopology, vector equilibrium, pattern integrities, all-space filling, axes of symmetry (and asymmetry), isotropic vector matrices, discontinuous compression have *concrete* parallel extensions in Merce's galaxy of dances:

> All of our vision operates as an omnidirectional TV set, and there is no way to escape it. . . . But all vision actually operates inside the brain in organic, neuron-transistored TV sets. . . . All we do is deal in brain images.[8]

Merce's work inaugurated the modernist-dance focus on structure and system. The chapters in *Synergetics* on structure, system, and conceptuality in their entirety have a direct relevance, with far too many passages than can be cited here. For example:

> A structure is a self-stabilizing energy-event complex.[9]
>
> Constellar means an aggregation of enduring, cosmically isolated, locally co-occurring events dynamically maintaining their interpositioning.[10]
>
> It is a tendency for patterns either to repeat themselves locally or for their parts to separate out to join singly or severally with other patterns to form new constellations.[11]
>
> A system is a closed configuration of vectors. It is a pattern of forces constituting a geometrical integrity that returns upon itself in a plurality of directions. . . . Systems have an electable plurality of view-induced polarities.[12]
>
> Planet Earth is a system. You are a system.[13]

Systems can spin. There is at least one axis of rotation of any system.[14]
Systems can orbit. Systems can contract and expand. They can torque;
they can turn inside out; and they can interprecess their parts.[15]

There is another great 20th-century philosopher who most certainly would
have had a unique insight and appreciation of Merce Cunningham. That thinker,
who shares a profound ontopoetic kinship with Paul Valéry and is the heir to the
philosophical legacy of Henri Bergson, is Maurice Merleau-Ponty, whose ontothetic analyses of the facticity of physicality and corporality advanced the
phenomenological researches of the human body more than any of his predecessors. Merce in turn has forged an active phenomenology of the dancing body
that cerebrates and **calibrates** the multiplistic interprecession of sights, signs,
events, perspectivities, rhythms, and dimensionalities that reflexively mirror the
cogent, (para)systemic dance of perception (i.e. the totality of a dance is more
than its steps and structures). To quote Merleau-Ponty:

> . . . that body which is an intertwining of vision and movement . . . it is just
> as true that vision is attached to movement . . . the visible world and the
> world of my motor projects are each total parts of the same Being. . . . My
> movement is . . . the natural consequence and maturation of my vision. I
> say of a thing that it is moved; but my body moves itself, my movement
> deploys itself. . . . The enigma is that my body simultaneously sees and is
> seen . . . it sees itself seeing; it touches itself touching . . . the world is made
> of the same stuff as the body.[16]

Merce's dances celebrate the paradox of simplicity and complexity; any
movement can be interesting, revealing, effective, if it is structured and rooted
in a clear kinetic context—even if, or when, arrived at by chance. "Why worry
about structure, it is always there," John Cage reminds us parenthetically in
Silence.

The temporal invention of Merce's choreography is an intricate subject.
Not dancing on the metrical beat, and not having his dances be dependent on
music, were a watershed for Merce. Merce has proven that the autonomy of
dance from music is a necessary liberty. In early interviews, John Cage, when
discussing his studies with Arnold Schoenberg, explains why he had no
interest in, and wanted to dispense with, harmony. Harmony, of course,
supplies the flowing rhythmic coordinations of passages and movement, and
figures differently as a compositional factor in dancemaking. Unlike Cage,
Merce's dances are exemplary for their harmonics, meaning kinetically balanced tonics—of qualities, motor impulses, the flow of signs, rhythms, structural conjunctions, feelings, etc. Merce works with a synchronistic open
form—graphs of structural possibilities—but, unlike Cage, whose scores involve improvised decision-making by the performers, once dice, or chance
procedures, determine the sequences of a dance, the structure is set. (Supposedly the "fork in the road" was the celebrated 1963 UCLA performance that

Carolyn Brown has written about in Jim Klosty's photo and essay book, *Merce Cunningham*, that was one of the only, early occasions where the dancers could decide in performance variations to which the repertory could be subjected.) In composition workshops, and in his company, dancers have to be able to **know** how to kinetically measure time, which they learn by using stop-watches. But time can also be filled, measured, or used *without* being **metered.** Chance is another means to (ap)portion the temporal. Some works that celebrate multiplicity, like *Canfield, Landrover, Walkaround Time,* and *Torse,* involve an extended duration, and blur and suspend the accountability of a linear, sequence-specific response. Others seem to condense and encapsulate discrete and overlapping times, so that complex, synchronistic weaves of action, occurrence, and occasion play and ply a plurality of temporal **registers** (*Sounddance, Locale,* and *Changing Steps*).

Merce's biography *is* the landscape of his dances. (Someone has to write about Merce and John Cage and their biographical connections. Their long collaboration and the development of Merce's company provided Cage with an ongoing platform and laboratory; how the spectrum of his musical works and how his collaborations with Merce unite and diverge from his entire opus would make a very timely essay.) At the end of his solo, *Loops* (1971), which also concluded *Changing Steps,* Merce's lithe, supple hand gestures dramatically grab the air, twist, and feistily pull invisibles into his center, condensing and wrapping up the entire, formidable energy and **landscape** of the performance.

*   *   *   *

The dancer is **not** separate from the dance—motion is all-enveloping and transactional. Merce's dancers, always immaculately rehearsed, bring exemplary brio and style to the works they perform. The fact that the whole company is a collection of virtuosi (listed alphabetically) is taken for granted. So it seems natural in trying to recollect the specifics of a given dance to realize that the particular qualities are inseparable from what the dancers bring to their parts. In 1984, Merce choreographed *Doubles* for his lifetime-achievement award given by the Samuel Scripps Foundation at The American Dance Festival at Duke University in Durham, North Carolina. *Doubles,* a work for eight, was choreographed separately on two different groups of his company, to account for the structural variances and differences that each cast would bring to the work. Supposedly the parallel choreographies between the casts weren't rigid, and Merce worked with each separately, so steps *and* interpretations would vary. (This suggested the possible occasion for both groups to perform the work simultaneously, one behind the other, at a space site like New York's immense Park Avenue Armory on 66th Street.)

Merce's work is always new, always different, **always** challenging. And you have to puzzle it out—that's an invitation! I remember meeting the celebrated dance critic and poet Edwin Denby in 1983, after an Event, in the very back of the balcony at City Center in New York City, which we again agreed *is* the best location from which to watch dance (because **that's** where the eyes can **see** the *dynamic* image [Susanne Langer has clarified and differentiated the actual image from the dynamic image, which is the virtualized realization of all its projected qualities and elements.]). Upon attempting to recollect the totality of any given work, all the parts jangle in the mind's eye and in the reflex and challenge of (re)collecting them. I was surprised when Edwin, who had seen Merce's performances decades longer than I had, confessed that he, too, could not always identify the specific dances that are excerpted during an Event. Sections usually performed to a given score may be seen against another, in silence, and/or vice versa. This is always a puzzle, because the sections, dynamics, structures, and "takes" can be (or seem) easily recontexted.

*   *   *   *

In the summer of 1966, I studied with Merce at his studio, then on Sixth Avenue and 14th Street on the top floor of a building formerly used, shared (and found for him) by Julian and Judith Malina Beck of The Living Theater. During this time I learned his basic exercises, which I continue to do this day. Merce's technique is a kind of yoga that ingeniously combines modern dance and ballet in a new key.

The first surprise in technique class is the use of parallel legs, which ballet never uses, and that is actually quite difficult at first. This makes three physical feats, and demands, possible. First, it enables the dancers to work on their turnout, by pulling up from the inside of their thighs to connect and control the legs from the abdomen and high in the hips. Secondly, it enables the dancers to align the two (often nonsymmetrical) sides of their spine, which controls their whole body weight/axis from the top of the hips, and to isolate the segmented zones of the back so as to be able to drop their weight into the floor while **lifting** up their carriage and varying the back's modes of deportment. This gives dancers an extra spatial mobility to rapidly change tempi and direction. Thirdly, it secures the torso by isolating the hips to further enable a fluent series of segmented, isomorphic contractions and rotations of the spine so as to easily coordinate off-balance and decentered movement sequences.

Merce has always stood out from his company for his pliancy and plasticity of expression, his mimetic virtuosity, and his ability to transform expression into a new performative style. Merce is a great actor and comic, and in works like *Antic Meet, Borst Park, Roadrunners,* and *Grange Eve* the wizened vaudevillian emerges around the corners and edges.

In 1966, Merce gave one of his rare lectures at the 92nd Street Y (one of the mainstays of modern-dance concerts in the fifties and sixties). And though it was years before the popularization of video, there was a monitor in the lobby for latecomers enabling them to see Merce on stage in the process of his program. He began at a microphone with a modest but informative commentary, then turned on a tape recorder so his lecture could continue while he moved out onto the stage to perform solos that demonstrated some of the different structural and compositional problems he had set for himself. The dialectic of words and movement was tremendously insightful, revealing the careful methods and transformative processes Merce had discovered, and, in an indirect way, offered a performative solution to the bicameral mind-body linkage. Though the compositional factors always proceed from a formal concern, the dramatic contours, kinetic colors, and kinesthetic harmonics are always evident. Merce is clearly a man who *thinks* with his (whole) body.

* * * *

And, one shouldn't overlook the fact that the discovery and articulation of the dancing body in the late 20th century might not have proceeded without all the parallel, complex, and generative processes of language and language researches—linguistics, semantics, logical analysis, semiotics, structural and post-structuralism, etc. And though dance is a non-discursive art, learning it requires constant explanation for even the subtlest changes and qualities. The generation of sounds, words, memory icons, then phrases and syntax involves the constant concatenation and syntheses of neurotropic processes that constantly mix and merge the kinesiology of signals and signs in high interface, that are also the components of thinking. From William James's psychology, to Ernst Cassirer's study of symbolic forms, to Ludwig Wittgenstein's logical analyses, to Roland Barthes's awareness that language and the body are two of the (combined) fertile frontiers even as this century lurches toward completion, remind us that though dance is a non-discursive art, (formally) independent of semantic meaning, it **does reflect** the **tao**tality of experience. That dance is a language is already a moot point. Merce shies away from language and explanation, so it is easy to dismiss just how **axial** the interaction and parallel developments of language and dance **are.**

I've left the dance that initially had the biggest impact to last—*How to Pass, Kick, Fall and Run* (1965)—which dramatized the potency of a text for dance accompaniment. It was a fun piece, deceptively engaging, that collaged activities interseamed (it seemed) with a complex mixing principle at its center. John Cage began by popping a bottle of champagne that instantly caused the audience to rally to a convivial, party-like, celebratory atmosphere. The piece was accompanied by him reading a chance-ordered, musicologically metered medley of stories and anecdotes with purposeful, pregnant pauses, and which provided a bubbly and often ridiculous textual and **theatrical** counterpoint to the dance. But it was the syntactical, rhythmic, gestic, and kinetic **correlations** that lifted the dance out of the realm of the symbolic into a new domain of the concrete, giving new meanings to *meaning* as the **contexture** of a continuum—interprocessed processings threading activities and coincidences in wry, witty juxta- and super-impositions. The reverberations, articulations, and punctuations of the interlaced, cadential weaves between language and dance theatricalized the mercurial, often rapid shifts of contexts. Words build up other sonic-acoustic registers, references, and resonations, and are thus another (meta)musicological phenomena, providing a highly kinetic companionship. It's exactly what fascinates me to this day—two parallel and coconcurrent or **compossible** (Merleau-Ponty's word after Husserl) **processes** to bridge the brain's bicameral, hemitropic *dialexis*, to multiswitch its usually one-sided attunement(s).

Merce's dances are an emblematic reinforcement of futurity's presence; he is more than a choreographer of open spaces and galactic ranges; his high frequency works are also energy experiments that reveal new frontiers of frequency and registers of bioenergetic potential (realized) on a grand scale, ranking with such pioneers as Nikola Tesla and Wilhelm Reich. The **tao**tality of his work bridges East and West, activity and stillness. His work has taught us to **read** multiple kinelexic spectrums of movement. "Yes, truly we dream while reading,"[17] Gaston Bachelard reminds us, and we also dream while calmly and attentively watching dance (the mimetic having its source in the onieric).

*   *   *   *

Here are some brief, fragmentary recollections of memorable individual dancers' exceptional performances to help spark other organizational and mnemonic links.

I remember Carolyn Brown—fluid, mercurial, sleek, and fleet, always *tensile* too, in giving movement its due, its full body (not setting it up, as Merce sometimes does!) in *Winterbranch, Walkaround Time, Second Hand*, and *Tread* (the dance with huge industrial fans blowing full tilt on stage—*and* three more dances, too, to write about!).

I remember Viola Farber's languishing leggy hyperplex—purposely off-balanced stumbling, jangling, and gangling, with a wonderful hyperextendability—then punctuated by an arrested stillness; suddenly, astonishingly, one saw that space *too* has nerve(s)! In *Crises* (revived at the Brooklyn Academy of Music in 1969), she and Merce performed a duet connected at the hips by an enormous elastic band.

I remember Patricia Lent (1986) at the City Center Theater, and Catherine Kerr (1988) at the Joyce Theater performing the long, immaculate opening solo in *Doubles*. Patricia Lent often reminded me of Merce, the way she would lunge on the diagonal, her arms cleanly etching the surrounding air while inscribing arcs, punctuating her body moves through space with an exciting exactitude, and moving so that each point contrasted with every other point or body part; also her perfectly controlled, difficult, and sustained balances on one leg.

I remember Cathy Kerr in *Arcade* (1986) in what seemed to be a lead role (usually anathema for Merce) dancing with both detached, cool, yet fervent, intense finesse, like an Amazon or Egyptian priestess or regal statuary!

I remember Louise Burns, perky and quirky, and so resilient with refreshing athletic prowess in *Torse, Rebus, Duets*, and other works, busily brushing her feet, turning the tendu into an exotic item belying her thrill with a brisk attack and beaming smile.

I remember Chris Komar in *Torse* with Merce's mercurial, faun-like aware-ness amplifying his incredibly articulate performance of precise jumps, sharp, immaculate phrasing and delivery, at one moment reminding me of Thornton Wilder's *Our Town* in a wistful solo while the rest of the dancers were frozen in space with their backs to the audience (recalling Emily's death scene). I remem-ber Alan Good and Megan Walker in the opening duet of *Coast Zone* (1983) in a kind of purely sculptural epiphany; their pristine partnering making the eye dart and swim in an effort to savor the *deliciousness* of their intricately shared, omnidirectional exchange.

I remember seeing at least eight performances of *Exchange* with severe, dark costumes and decor by Jasper Johns, and music by David Tudor, one of the most exciting and complex of all of Merce's dances; each viewing made me certain that either new sections had been added, or that it was impossible to perceive in its totality. It is a streamlined, subtly ritualized work that Merce created—like a kind of general, leader, or guardian; the work seemed to speak to the dark, uncertain dangers we are all facing, at times as if during a storm, with upheaval or war reverberating in the distance. (Thinking back on it now, it's a dance rich with duets and double exchanges, with a multiplicity of kinetic and dynamic logics and interactive, configuratively interpenetrating struc-tures, though formal and abstract, actuating complex transformations, with many mysterious meanings and dimensions.)

I remember the company's opening night on Broadway (January 1977) when *Travelogue* was premiered with playful pastel silk drops and a mobile train of children's chairs and desks on a roll-on platform by Robert Rauschen-berg pulled on at the beginning of the dance, and naturally, a terrific, poignant solo by Merce tilting with windmill arms and flexed feet, Chaplinesque. I remember Merce's careful hand-to-mouth silent scream in *Scramble*, a bright, modern, full-company work with pastel-colored screens on wheels by Frank Stella, that somewhat resembled, and that could be moved like, tennis ac-coutrements, which were rearranged for the various sections.

I remember *Roaratorio* kicking off the Next Wave Festival at the Brooklyn Academy of Music in 1987, Merce's spectacle of an Irish circus with a densely multilayered, wildly cacophonous score by John Cage that combined site-specific sounds, music, and bagpipes from Joyce's Dublin, with text weaves derived and transposed from *Finnegans Wake*. It was preceded by *Inlets 2* (1983), a gorgeous, truly **pure** dance that was totally complete and that could have been an evening-in-itself—very sculptural in the way it released the integrity, grain, and tones of motion, and their inhering sets of qualities. (Supposedly a "pure" dance is a contradiction of terms, possibly akin to the Buddhist "subject"—which doesn't exist!)

I remember the delightfully goofy finale to *Borst Park* performed on the stage of the Opera House of the Brooklyn Academy of Music, with the musicians featured on stage; at the end, the dancers attempt to serve a picnic; a red-checkered tablecloth is laid down, but quickly begins *moving* across the stage as the gregarious gaggle of dancers gambols and scrambles to follow it, *and* **as** a RUBBER CHICKEN is pulled out of a wicker picnic basket and tossed on it, while the curtain is falling (with the audience falling out of their seats laughing!).

I remember Merce downstage in his Westbeth New York studio (with a glorious aerial view of the sparkling nightlit megacity below) around 1980 very close to the audience in an Event performing an excerpt from *Landrover* with arms outstretched, flicking and rotating, making powerful, outwardly directed gestures and zapping me in the front line of focus. I remember Merce at the end of *Changing Steps* performing his *Loops* solo—reaching, grabbing, and pulling invisibles out of the air with a very uncanny, magical finesse. I remember the March 17, 1982 (to be precise) Event on a Thursday night at City Center that was also very magical—the stage suddenly became empty (after an excerpt from *Winterbranch*). There was a huge, unrecognizable door covering the entire rear wall; when it was unexpectedly thrown open it revealed a massive, cavernous backstage area, Merce was standing there alone. It sent a charge surging through the whole audience. I remember Merce's (animal) *Solo* that began with him upstage in profile walking *en passé* as if he were approaching the void (the left side of the stage being much darker) then turning, and, in the course of the dance, animals appeared—suddenly an iguana or lizard, serpentine and aquatic, as he snakily shifted his hips while the tongue flickered, then later on the floor making circular, preening-like feline hand (or paw) movements around his head like an endearingly furry mammal. I remember the last performance of *Sounddance* (at City Center) as the audience immediately rose, stood, stomped, applauded, hooted, cheered, bravo'd— whistling, screaming—**SHRIEKING!**

to be continued . . .

NOTE: Special Thanks to Majorie Gamso, Anne Lall, Mary Lisa Burns, and Ted Marks for their editorial suggestions and corrections.

Notes

1. Gaston Bachelard, *The Poetics of Space* (Boston: Beacon Press, 1969), 210.
2. Susanne K. Langer, *Mind: An Essay on Human Feeling* (Baltimore, MD: The Johns Hopkins Press, 1967), I:153.
3. Maurice Merleau-Ponty, "Eye and Mind," in *The Primacy of Perception* (Evanston, IL: Northwestern University Press, 1964), 168.
4. R. Buckminster Fuller, *Synergetics* (New York: MacMillan, 1975), 153.
5. Ibid., 249.
6. Ibid., 250, entry 515.30.
7. Ibid., 614.

 8. Ibid., 440, sections 801.21/22.
 9. Ibid., 314, entry 600.02.
10. Ibid., entry 600.04.
11. Ibid., entry 601.01.
12. Ibid., 97, entry 400.09.
13. Ibid., 102, entry 400.47.
14. Ibid., entry 400.60.
15. Ibid., entry 400.61.
16. Merleau-Ponty, "Eye and Mind," 162–63.
17. Bachelard, *The Poetics of Space*, 162.

CHRONOLOGY OF WORKS BY MERCE CUNNINGHAM

As of July 1992

Compiled by David Vaughan

MCDC = Merce Cunningham [and] Dance Company
NYCB = New York City Ballet
ABT = American Ballet Theatre
GRCOP = Groupe de Recherche Chorégraphique de l'Opéra de Paris
All solos danced by Merce Cunningham unless otherwise stated

TITLE	MUSIC	DESIGN	DANCERS	PLACE/DATE OF FIRST PERFORMANCE
Seeds of Brightness (Choreographed with Jean Erdman)	Norman Lloyd	Charlotte Trowbridge	Merce Cunningham Jean Erdman	Bennington, VT; 1 Aug 1942
Credo in Us (Choreographed with Jean Erdman)	John Cage	Charlotte Trowbridge	Merce Cunningham Jean Erdman	Bennington, VT; 1 Aug 1942
Renaissance Testimonials	Maxwell Powers	Charlotte Trowbridge	Solo	Bennington, VT; 1 Aug 1942
Ad Lib (Choreographed with Jean Erdman)	Gregory Tucker (John Cage 1943)	Charlotte Trowbridge	Merce Cunningham Jean Erdman	Bennington, VT; 1 Aug 1942
Totem Ancestor	John Cage	Charlotte Trowbridge	Solo	New York, NY; 20 Oct 1942
In the Name of the Holocaust	John Cage	Merce Cunningham	Solo	Chicago, IL; 14 Feb 1943
Shimmera	John Cage	Merce Cunningham	Solo	Chicago, IL; 14 Feb 1943
The Wind Remains (*Zarzuela* in one act after Federico Garcia Lorca)	Paul Bowles	Oliver Smith Kermit Love	Merce Cunningham Jean Erdman et al	New York, NY; 30 Mar 1943
Triple-Paced	John Cage	Merce Cunningham	Solo	New York, NY; 5 Apr 1944
Root of an Unfocus	John Cage	Merce Cunningham	Solo	New York, NY; 5 Apr 1944
Tossed as it is Untroubled	John Cage	Merce Cunningham	Solo	New York, NY; 5 Apr 1944

TITLE	MUSIC	DESIGN	DANCERS	PLACE/DATE OF FIRST PERFORMANCE
The Unavailable Memory Of	John Cage	Merce Cunningham	Solo	New York, NY; 5 Apr 1944
Spontaneous Earth	John Cage	Merce Cunningham	Solo	New York, NY; 5 Apr 1944
Four Walls (A Dance Play by Merce Cunningham)	John Cage	Arch Lauterer	Merce Cunningham Julie Harris et al	Steamboat Springs, CO; 22 Aug 1944
Idyllic Song	Erik Satie arr. John Cage	Merce Cunningham	Solo	Richmond, VA; 20 Nov 1944
Mystericus Adventure	John Cage	after David Hare	Solo	New York, NY; 9 Jan 1945
Experiences	John Cage Livingston Gearhart	Merce Cunningham	Solo	New York, NY; 9 Jan 1945
The Encounter	John Cage	Merce Cunningham	Solo	New York, NY; 12 May 1946
Invocation to Vahakn	Alan Hovhaness	Merce Cunningham	Solo	New York, NY; 12 May 1946
Fast Blues	Baby Dodds	Merce Cunningham	Solo	New York, NY; 12 May 1946
The Princess Zondilda and Her Entourage	Alexei Haieff	Merce Cunningham	Merce Cunningham Virginia Bosler Katherine Litz	New York, NY; 12 May 1946
The Seasons	John Cage	Isamu Noguchi	1 Ballet Society with Merce Cunningham 2 NYCB	New York, NY; 18 May 1947 New York, NY; 14 Jan 1949
The Open Road	Lou Harrison	Merce Cunningham	Solo	New York, NY; 14 Dec 1947
Dromenon	John Cage	Sonja Sekula Merce Cunningham	Merce Cunningham and group	New York, NY; 14 Dec 1947
Dream	John Cage	Merce Cunningham	Solo	Columbia, MO; 8 May 1948

TITLE	MUSIC	DESIGN	DANCERS	PLACE/DATE OF FIRST PERFORMANCE
The Ruse of Medusa (a lyric comedy by Erik Satie, translated by M. C. Richards, directed by Arthur Penn)	Erik Satie	Willem and Elaine de Kooning Mary Outten	Merce Cunningham et al	Black Mountain, NC; 14 Aug 1948
A Diversion (also given in quartet and solo versions)	John Cage	Mary Outten Merce Cunningham	Merce Cunningham Sara Hamill Louise Lippold	Black Mountain, NC; 20 Aug 1948
Orestes	John Cage	Merce Cunningham	Solo	Black Mountain, NC; 20 Aug 1948
The Monkey Dances (from *The Ruse of Medusa*)	Erik Satie	Mary Outten Richard Lippold Merce Cunningham	Solo	Black Mountain, NC; 20 Aug 1948
Effusions avant l'heure (later called Games; Trio)	John Cage		Merce Cunningham Tanaquil LeClerq Betty Nichols	Paris, France; summer 1949
Amores	John Cage		Tanaquil LeClerq Merce Cunningham	Paris, France; summer 1949
Duet			Betty Nichols Milorad Miskovitch	Paris, France; summer 1949
Two Step	Erik Satie	Merce Cunningham	Solo	New York, NY; 18 Dec 1949
Pool of Darkness	Ben Weber	Merce Cunningham	Merce Cunningham Dorothy Berea Mili Churchill Anneliese Widman	New York, NY; 15 Jan 1950
Before Dawn		Merce Cunningham	Solo	New York, NY; 15 Jan 1950

TITLE	MUSIC	DESIGN	DANCERS	PLACE/DATE OF FIRST PERFORMANCE
Waltz	Erik Satie		1 Student group 2 Solo	Baton Rouge, LA; 27 June 1950 New York, NY; 24 Nov 1950
Rag-Time Parade	Erik Satie		1 Student group 2 MCDC	Baton Rouge, LA; 27 June 1950 New York, NY; 24 Nov 1950
Waltz	Erik Satie		Solo	New York, NY; 24 Nov 1950
Sixteen Dances for Soloist and Company of Three	John Cage	Eleanor de Vito John Cage Remy Charlip Merce Cunningham	Merce Cunningham Dorothy Berea Mili Churchill Anneliese Widman	Millbrook, NY; 17 Jan 1951
Variation	Morton Feldman	Merce Cunningham	Solo	Seattle, WA; 12 Apr 1951
Boy Who Wanted to be a Bird			Solo	Martha's Vineyard, MA; Summer 1951
Suite of Six Short Dances	Recorder pieces arr. W. P. Jennerjahn		Solo	Black Mountain, NC; Spring 1952
Excerpts from *Symphonie pour un homme seul*	Pierre Schaeffer with Pierre Henry		1 Merce Cunningham & group 2 MCDC (under the title *Collage*)	Waltham, MA; 14 June 1952 Black Mountain, NC; 21 Aug 1953
Les Noces	Igor Stravinsky	Howard Bay	Merce Cunningham Natanya Neumann and group	Waltham, MA; 14 June 1952

TITLE	MUSIC	DESIGN	DANCERS	PLACE/DATE OF FIRST PERFORMANCE
Theatre Piece (arranged by John Cage, poetry by Charles Olson and M. C. Richards, film by Nicholas Cernovitch)	David Tudor	Robert Rauschenberg	Merce Cunningham	Black Mountain, NC; Summer 1952
Suite by Chance	Christian Wolff	Remy Charlip	MCDC	Urbana, IL; 24 Mar 1953
Solo Suite in Space and Time	John Cage	Merce Cunningham	Solo	Baton Rouge, LA; 23 June 1953
Demonstration Piece			Student group	Baton Rouge, LA; 23 June 1953
Epilogue	Erik Satie		Student group	Baton Rouge, LA; 23 June 1953
Banjo	Louis Moreau Gottschalk	Remy Charlip	MCDC	Black Mountain, NC; 21 Aug 1953
Dime a Dance	19th century piano music selected by David Tudor	Remy Charlip	MCDC	Black Mountain, NC; 22 Aug 1953
Septet	Erik Satie	Remy Charlip	1 MCDC	Black Mountain, NC; 22 Aug 1953
			2 Rambert Dance Co	Glasgow, Scotland; 20 Nov 1987
			3 Pacific Northwest Ballet	Seattle, WA; 15 Nov 1989
			4 Repertory Dance Theatre	Salt Lake City, UT; 9 March 1991
Untitled Solo	Christian Wolff	Merce Cunningham	Solo	Black Mountain, NC; 22 Aug 1953

TITLE	MUSIC	DESIGN	DANCERS	PLACE/DATE OF FIRST PERFORMANCE
Fragments	Pierre Boulez	Remy Charlip	MCDC	New York, NY; 30 Dec 1953
Minutiae	John Cage	Robert Rauschenberg Remy Charlip	MCDC	Brooklyn, NY; 8 Dec 1954
Springweather and People	Earle Brown	Remy Charlip (Robert Rauschenberg, 1957)	MCDC	Annandale-on-Hudson, NY; 24 May 1955
Galaxy	Earle Brown	Remy Charlip	MCDC	South Bend, IN; 18 May 1956
Lavish Escapade	Christian Wolff	Merce Cunningham	Solo	South Bend, IN; 18 May 1956
Suite for Five in Space and Time (later called Suite for Five)	John Cage	Robert Rauschenberg	MCDC	South Bend, IN; 18 May 1956
Nocturnes	Erik Satie	Robert Rauschenberg	MCDC	Lee, MA; 11 July 1956
Labyrinthian Dances	Josef Matthias Hauer	Robert Rauschenberg	MCDC	Brooklyn, NY; 30 Nov 1957
Changeling	Christian Wolff	Robert Rauschenberg	Solo	Brooklyn, NY; 30 Nov 1957
Picnic Polka	Louis Moreau Gottschalk	Remy Charlip	MCDC	Brooklyn, NY; 30 Nov 1957
Collage III	Pierre Schaeffer with Pierre Henry		Solo	Pittsburgh, PA; 21 May 1958
Antic Meet	John Cage	Robert Rauschenberg	MCDC	New London, CT; 14 Aug 1958

TITLE	MUSIC	DESIGN	DANCERS	PLACE/DATE OF FIRST PERFORMANCE
Summerspace	Morton Feldman	Robert Rauschenberg	1 MCDC 2 NYCB 3 Cullbergbaletten 4 Boston Ballet 5 Théâtre du Silence	New London, CT; 17 Aug 1958 New York, NY; 14 April 1966 Stockholm, Sweden; 5 Oct 1967 Boston, MA; 7 Nov 1974 La Rochelle, France; 29 Oct 1976
Night Wandering	Bo Nilsson	Nicholas Cernovitch (Robert Rauschenberg 1963)	1 Merce Cunningham Carolyn Brown 2 5 by 2 Plus	Stockholm, Sweden; 5 Oct 1958 Anchorage, AL; 3 Sept 1977
From the Poems of White Stone	Chou Wen-Chung poems by Chiang Kuei	Robert Rauschenberg	MCDC	Urbana, IL; 14 Mar 1959
Gambit for Dancers and Orchestra	Ben Johnston	Robert Rauschenberg	MCDC	Urbana, IL; 14 Mar 1959
Rune	Christian Wolff	Robert Rauschenberg (Mark Lancaster, 1982)	MCDC	New London, CT; 14 Aug 1959
Theatre Piece	John Cage	Robert Rauschenberg	Merce Cunningham Carolyn Brown	New York, NY; 7 Mar 1960
Crises	Conlon Nancarrow	Robert Rauschenberg	MCDC	New London, CT; 19 Aug 1960
Hands Birds	Earle Brown	Robert Rauschenberg	Carolyn Brown	Venice, Italy; 24 Sept 1960
Waka	Toshi Ichiyanagi	Robert Rauschenberg	Carolyn Brown	Venice, Italy; 24 Sept 1960
Music Walk with Dancers	John Cage	Robert Rauschenberg	Merce Cunningham Carolyn Brown	Venice, Italy; 24 Sept 1960

TITLE	MUSIC	DESIGN	DANCERS	PLACE/DATE OF FIRST PERFORMANCE
Suite de Danses a work for television, directed by John Mercure	Serge Garrant	Jasper Johns	MCDC	CBC-TV, Montreal, Canada; 9 July 1961
Aeon	John Cage	Robert Rauschenberg	MCDC	Montreal, Canada; 5 Aug 1961
Field Dances	John Cage	Robert Rauschenberg (Remy Charlip, 1967)	MCDC	Los Angeles, CA; 17 July 1963
Story	Toshi Ichiyanagi	Robert Rauschenberg	MCDC	Los Angeles, CA; 24 July 1963
Open Session	Merce Cunningham	Merce Cunningham	Solo	Hartford, CT; 19 Mar 1964
Paired	John Cage	Robert Rauschenberg	Merce Cunningham Viola Farber	Hartford, CT; 21 Mar 1964
Winterbranch	La Monte Young	Robert Rauschenberg	1 MCDC 2 Boston Ballet	Hartford, CT; 21 Mar 1964 Boston, MA; 7 Nov 1974
Cross Currents	Conlon Nancarrow arr. John Cage (John Cage, Oct 1964)	Merce Cunningham	1 MCDC 2 US Terpsichore 3 Werkcentrum Dans	London, UK; 31 July 1964 New York, NY; 3 Oct 1980 Rotterdam, The Netherlands; 19 Sept 1984
Variations V	John Cage	Film: Stan VanDerBeek TV images: Nam June Paik	MCDC	New York, NY; 23 July 1965
How to Pass, Kick, Fall and Run	John Cage		MCDC	Chicago, IL; 24 Nov 1965
Place	Gordon Mumma	Beverly Emmons	MCDC	Saint-Paul de Vence, France; 6 Aug 1966
Scramble	Toshi Ichiyanagi	Frank Stella	MCDC	Chicago, IL; 25 July 1967

222 *Chronology of Works by Merce Cunningham*

TITLE	MUSIC	DESIGN	DANCERS	PLACE/DATE OF FIRST PERFORMANCE
RainForest	David Tudor	Andy Warhol	MCDC	Buffalo, NY; 9 Mar 1968
Walkaround Time	David Behrman	after Marcel Duchamp	MCDC	Buffalo, NY; 10 Mar 1968
Assemblage a film for television directed by Richard Moore	John Cage David Tudor Gordon Mumma		MCDC	KQED-TV, San Francisco, CA; Oct–Nov 1968
Canfield	Pauline Oliveros	Robert Morris	MCDC	Rochester, NY; 4 Mar 1969
Tread	Christian Wolff	Bruce Nauman	MCDC	Brooklyn, NY; 5 Jan 1970
Second Hand	John Cage	Jasper Johns	MCDC	Brooklyn, NY; 8 Jan 1970
Signals	David Tudor Gordon Mumma John Cage	Richard Nelson Merce Cunningham	1 MCDC 2 Ohio Ballet	Paris, France; 5 June 1970 Akron, OH; 20 Feb 1981
Objects	Alvin Lucier	Neil Jenney	MCDC	Brooklyn, NY; 10 Nov 1970
Loops	Gordon Mumma	Jasper Johns	Solo	New York, NY; 3 Dec 1971
Landrover	Jasper Johns Gordon Mumma David Tudor	Jasper Johns	MCDC	Brooklyn, NY; 1 Feb 1972
TV Rerun	Gordon Mumma	Jasper Johns	MCDC	Brooklyn, NY; 2 Feb 1972
Borst Park	Christian Wolff	The Company	MCDC	Brooklyn, NY; 8 Feb 1972
Un Jour ou deux	John Cage	Jasper Johns	Paris Opéra Ballet	Paris, France; 6 Nov 1973
Westbeth a work for video directed by Charles Atlas and Merce Cunningham	John Cage	Mark Lancaster	MCDC	New York, NY; fall 1974
Exercise Piece		Mark Lancaster	MCDC	New York, NY; 14 Feb 1975

TITLE	MUSIC	DESIGN	DANCERS	PLACE/DATE OF FIRST PERFORMANCE
Changing Steps	John Cage	Charles Atlas (Mark Lancaster, 1978)	1 MCDC 2 Théâtre du Silence 3 Purchase Dance Corps	Detroit, MI; 7 Mar 1975 Paris, France; 17 April 1979 Purchase, NY; 2 April 1987
Video version directed by Elliot Caplan and Merce Cunningham				October 1989
Rebus	David Behrman	Mark Lancaster	MCDC	Detroit, MI; 8 Mar 1975
Solo	John Cage	Sonja Sekula	Solo	Detroit, MI; 8 Mar 1975
Sounddance	David Tudor	Mark Lancaster	MCDC	Detroit, MI; 8 Mar 1975
Blue Studio: Five Segments videotape by Merce Cunningham and Charles Atlas			Solo	WNET, New York, NY; Oct 1975
Torse	Maryanne Amacher	Mark Lancaster	MCDC	Princeton, NJ; 15 Jan 1976
Squaregame	Takehisa Kosugi	Mark Lancaster	MCDC	Adelaide, Australia; 24 Mar 1976
Video version, Squaregame Video, directed by Charles Atlas			MCDC	New York, NY; 1976
Video Triangle part of Event for Television, directed by Merrill Brockway	David Tudor	Mark Lancaster	MCDC	WNET, New York, NY; Nov 1976
Travelogue	John Cage	Robert Rauschenberg	MCDC	New York, NY; 18 Jan 1977
Inlets	John Cage	Morris Graves	MCDC	Seattle, WA; 10 Sept 1977
Fractions videodance directed by Charles Atlas and Merce Cunningham	Jon Gibson	Mark Lancaster	MCDC stage version	New York, NY; Nov/Dec 1977 Boston, MA; 26 Feb 1978
Exercise Piece I			MCDC	New York, NY; 25 Mar 1978

TITLE	MUSIC	DESIGN	DANCERS	PLACE/DATE OF FIRST PERFORMANCE
Exercise Piece II	John Cage	Mark Lancaster	MCDC	Toronto, Ontario; 18 Aug 1978
Exchange	David Tudor	Jasper Johns	MCDC	New York, NY; 27 Sept 1978
Tango	John Cage	Mark Lancaster	Solo	New York, NY; 5 Oct 1978
Locale filmdance directed by Charles Atlas and Merce Cunningham	Takehisa Kosugi	Charles Atlas	MCDC stage version	New York, NY; Jan/Feb 1979 Paris, France; 9 Oct 1979
Roadrunners	Yasunao Tone	Mark Lancaster	MCDC	Durham, NC; 19 July 1979
Exercise Piece III	John Cage	Mark Lancaster	MCDC	New York, NY; 23 Feb 1980
Duets	John Cage	Mark Lancaster	1 MCDC 2 ABT	New York, NY; 26 Feb 1980 New York, NY; 18 May 1982
Fielding Sixes	John Cage	Monika Fulleman (William Anastasi, 1986) Mark Lancaster for Ballet Rambert	1 MCDC 2 Ballet Rambert	London, UK; 30 June 1980 Manchester, UK; 11 Feb 1983
Channels/Inserts filmdance directed by Charles Atlas and Merce Cunningham	David Tudor	Charles Atlas	MCDC stage version	New York, NY; Jan 1981 New York, NY; 24 Mar 1981
10's with Shoes	Martin Kalve	Mark Lancaster	MCDC	New York, NY; 17 Mar 1981
Gallopade	Takehisa Kosugi	Mark Lancaster	MCDC	London, UK; 10 June 1981
Trails	John Cage	Mark Lancaster	MCDC	New York, NY; 16 Mar 1982
Quartet	David Tudor	Mark Lancaster	MCDC	Paris, France; 27 Oct 1982

TITLE	MUSIC	DESIGN	DANCERS	PLACE/DATE OF FIRST PERFORMANCE
Coast Zone filmdance directed by Charles Atlas and Merce Cunningham	Larry Austin	Mark Lancaster / Charles Atlas	MCDC / stage version	New York, NY; Jan 1983 / New York, NY; 18 Mar 1983
Inlets 2	John Cage	Mark Lancaster	1 MCDC / 2 GRCOP / 3 Concert Dance Co. of Boston / 4 Sharir Dance Co. / 5 Rotterdamse Dansgroep / 6 Charleroi/Danses	Lille, France; 26 Oct 1983 / Paris, France; 3 Dec 1983 / Cambridge, MA; 13 Apr 1986 / Austin, TX; 11 Mar 1988 / Rotterdam, The Netherlands; 9 Feb 1991 / Charleroi, Belgium; 13 Dec 1991
Roaratorio	John Cage	Mark Lancaster	MCDC	Lille, France; 26 Oct 1983
Pictures	David Behrman	Mark Lancaster	MCDC	New York, NY; 6 Mar 1984
Doubles	Takehisa Kosugi	Mark Lancaster	1 MCDC / 2 Rambert Dance Co.	Durham, NC; 27 June 1984 / Birmingham, UK; 30 Jan 1990
Phrases	David Tudor	William Anastasi / Dove Bradshaw	MCDC	Angers, France; 7 Dec 1984
Deli Commedia videodance directed by Elliot Caplan	Pat Richter	Dove Bradshaw	Student group	New York, NY; Jan 1985
Native Green	John King	William Anastasi	MCDC	New York, NY; 12 Mar 1985
Arcade	John Cage	Dove Bradshaw	1 Pennsylvania Ballet / 2 MCDC	Philadelphia, PA; 11 Sept 1985 / Philadelphia, PA; 14 Nov 1985

TITLE	MUSIC	DESIGN	DANCERS	PLACE/DATE OF FIRST PERFORMANCE
Grange Eve	Takehisa Kosugi	William Anastasi	MCDC	New York, NY; 18 Mar 1986
Points in Space videodance directed by Elliot Caplan and Merce Cunningham	John Cage	William Anastasi	MCDC stage version 1 MCDC 2 Paris Opéra Ballet	London, UK; May 1986 New York, NY; 10 Mar 1987 Paris, France; 6 Jun 1990
Fabrications	Emanuel Dimas de Melo Pimenta	Dove Bradshaw	MCDC	Minneapolis, MN; 21 Feb 1987
Shards	David Tudor	William Anastasi	MCDC	New York, NY; 4 Mar 1987
Carousal	Takehisa Kosugi	Dove Bradshaw	MCDC	Lee, MA; 18 Aug 1987
Eleven	Robert Ashley	William Anastasi	MCDC	New York, NY; 9 Mar 1988
Five Stone	John Cage David Tudor	Mark Lancaster	MCDC	Berlin, Germany; 16 June 1988
Five Stone Wind	John Cage Takehisa Kosugi David Tudor	Mark Lancaster	MCDC	Avignon, France; 30 July 1988
Cargo X	Takehisa Kosugi	Dove Bradshaw	MCDC	Austin, TX; 27 Jan 1989
Field and Figures	Ivan Tcherepnin	Kristin Jones Andrew Ginzel	MCDC	Minneapolis, MN; 17 Feb 1989
August Pace	Michael Pugliese	Sergei Bugaev (Afrika)	1 MCDC 2 Paris Opéra Ballet (excerpts)	Berkeley, CA; 22 Sept 1989 Paris, France; 23 Oct 1990
Inventions	John Cage	Carl Kielblock	MCDC	Berkeley, CA; 23 Sept 1989
Polarity	David Tudor	Bill Anastasi Merce Cunningham Carl Kielblock	MCDC	New York, NY; 20 Mar 1990

TITLE	MUSIC	DESIGN	DANCERS	PLACE/DATE OF FIRST PERFORMANCE
Neighbors	Takehisa Kosugi	Mark Lancaster	MCDC	New York, NY; 13 Mar 1991
Trackers	Emanuel Dimas de Melo Pimenta	Dove Bradshaw	MCDC	New York, NY; 19 Mar 1991
Beach Birds	John Cage	Marsha Skinner	MCDC	Zurich, Switzerland; 20 June 1991
Film version, *Beach Birds for Camera*, directed by Elliot Caplan			MCDC	New York, NY; Dec 1991
Loosestrife	Michael Pugliese	Carl Kielblock	MCDC	Paris, France; 10 Sept 1991
Change of Address	Walter Zimmerman	Marsha Skinner	MCDC	Austin, TX; 31 Jan 1992
Touchbase	Michael Pugliese	Mark Lancaster	Rambert Dance Co.	London, UK; 20 June 1992

SELECT BIBLIOGRAPHY
OF CUNNINGHAM CRITICISM

Adam, Judy, ed. *Dancers on a Plane/Cage Cunningham Johns*. NY: Alfred A. Knopf, 1990.

Brown, Carolyn. "On Chance." *Ballet Review* II/2 (Summer 1968).

Carroll, Noël, and Sally Banes. "Cunningham and Duchamp." *Ballet Review* XI/2 (Summer 1983).

Cohen, Selma Jeanne. "Avant-Garde Choreography." In *The Dance Has Many Faces*, 3rd. ed., ed. Walter Sorell. Pennington, NJ: a cappella books, 1992.

————, ed. "Time to Walk in Space: Essays, Stories and Remarks." Contributions by Clive Barnes, Carolyn Brown, John Cage, Arlene Croce, Merce Cunningham, Edwin Denby, Jill Johnston, David Vaughan. *Dance Perspectives* 34 (Summer 1968).

Copeland, Roger. "The Politics of Perception." In *What Is Dance?*, ed. Roger Copeland and Marshall Cohen. NY: Oxford University Press, 1983.

Croce, Arlene. "Notes on a Natural Man." *The New Yorker* (7 February 1977).

————. "Crises." *The New Yorker* (3 April 1989).

Cunningham, Merce. "The Function of a Technique for Dance." In *The Dance Has Many Faces*, 1st. ed., ed. Walter Sorell. Cleveland: World Publishers, 1951.

————. *Changes: Notes on Choreography*, ed. Frances Starr. NY: Something Else Press, 1968.

————. "Choreography and the Dancer." In *The Creative Experience*, ed. Stanley Rosner and Lawrence E. Abt. NY: Grossman Publications, 1970.

———. "The Impermanent Art." In *Esthetics Contemporary*, ed. Richard Kostelanetz. Buffalo, NY: Prometheus, 1978, 1989.

———. "You Have to Love Dancing to Stick To It." In *The Vision of Modern Dance*, ed. Jean Morrison Brown. Princeton, NJ: Princeton Book Co., 1979.

Finkel, Anita. "Kristy's Red Hair." *The New Dance Review* (July/August 1989).

Fleming, Bruce. "Thoroughly Modernist Merce." *Washington Dance View* (Autumn 1989).

Goldner, Nancy. "Cunningham Diary." *Bennington Review* (Sept. 1978).

Greskovic, Robert. "Cunningham as Sculptor." *Ballet Review* XI/4 (Winter 1984).

Grossman, Peter Z. "Talking with Merce Cunningham about Video." *Dance Scope* XIII/2–3 (Winter–Spring 1979).

Gubernatis, Raphael de. *Cunningham.* Arles and Paris: Editions Bernard Coutaz, 1990.

Harris, Dale. "Merce Cunningham." In *Contemporary Dance*, ed. Anne Livet. NY: Abbeville, 1978.

Johnston, Jill. "Modern Dance." In *The New American Arts*, ed. Richard Kostelanetz. NY: Horizon, 1965.

———. "To Whom It May Concern." In *Marmalade Me.* NY: E. P. Dutton, 1971.

———. "Jigs, Japes, and Joyce." *Art in America* (January 1987).

Jowitt, Deborah. *The Dance in Mind.* Boston: David Godine, 1985.

———. "Illusion of Choice—Acceptance of Chance." In *Time and the Dancing Image.* NY: William Morrow, 1988.

Klosty, James, ed. *Merce Cunningham.* NY: Saturday Review Press, 1975 (reprint, NY: Limelight, 1987).

Kostelanetz, Richard. *The Theatre of Mixed Means.* NY: Dial, 1968.

———. "Modern Dance." In *Metamorphosis in the Arts.* Brooklyn, NY: Assembling, 1981.

———. "Dance." In *Conversations with Cage.* NY: Limelight, 1988.

———. "Cunningham/Cage." In *On Innovative Music(ian)s.* NY: Limelight, 1989.

———. "Merce Cunningham." In *On Innovative Art(ist)s.* Jefferson, NC: McFarland, 1992.

Lesschaeve, Jacqueline. *The Dancer and the Dance: Merce Cunningham in Conversation with Jacqueline Lesschaeve.* NY: Marion Boyars, 1985.

Lorber, Richard. "From Cimabue to Cunningham." *Millennium Film Journal* (Fall–Winter 1981/82).

Macaulay, Alastair. "On the Clouds." *The Dancing Times* (August 1985).

———. "Found in Space." *The Dancing Times* (September 1987).

———. "Happy Hooligan." *The New Yorker* (27 April 1992).

Mazo, Joseph. "Merce Cunningham: Multiple Choice." In *Prime Movers: The Makers of Modern Dance in America.* Princeton, NJ: Princeton Book Co., 1984.

McDonagh, Don. *The Rise and Fall and Rise of Modern Dance.* Rev. ed. Pennington, NJ: a cappella books, 1990.

Reynolds, Nancy. "Chance is a Nickname for Providence." *Dance Magazine* (July 1990).

Schöning, Klaus, ed. *Roaratorio*. Konigstein, Germany: Athenäum, 1985.

Siegel, Marcia B. "Summerspace and Winterbranch," "Septet." In *The Shapes of Change: Images of American Dance*. NY: Henry Holt, 1980.

———. "Repertory in Spite of Itself." *Hudson Review* (Summer 1985).

Snell, Michael (pseud.). "Cunningham and His Critics." *Ballet Review* III/6 (1971).

Tomkins, Calvin. *The Bride and the Bachelors: Five Masters of the Avant-Garde*. Rev. ed. NY: Viking Press, 1968.

Vaughan, David. *Diaghilev/Cunningham*. Hempstead, NY: Hofstra University, 1974.

———. "Ashton versus Cunningham?" *Dancing Times* (July–August 1979).

———. "Merce Cunningham: Origins and Influences." *Dance Theatre Journal* I/1 (Spring 1983).

———. "Cunningham, Cage and Joyce: 'This long awaited messiah of roaratorios.' " *Choreography & Dance* I/4 (1992).

CONTRIBUTORS NOTES

JACK ANDERSON (b. 1935) has authored eight books of poetry and seven of dance history and criticism. He is a dance critic for *The New York Times,* coeditor of *Dance Chronicle,* and New York correspondent for *The Dancing Times* of London. He has taught dance history and criticism around the world.

CAROLYN BROWN (b. 1927) was a founding member of the Merce Cunningham Dance Company, originating many roles during her tenure from 1952–1972. She is currently writing her memoirs.

EARLE BROWN (b. 1926) is an internationally acclaimed composer. Influenced by avant-garde artists of the fifties, Brown developed new notation and scoring methods, and originated "open form" compositions that allowed for individual improvisation.

JOHN CAGE (1912–1992) was a distinguished American avant-garde composer. Along with Merce Cunningham, whom he first met in 1938 when he was teaching at the Cornish School in Seattle where Cunningham was a student, he has championed radically alternate methods of composition. He has been the music director of the Cunningham company since its inception in 1953.

REMY CHARLIP (b. 1929) is a choreographer, dancer, theater and film director, painter, designer, teacher, playwright, songwriter, and author of over two dozen children's books. While a member of the Cunningham company, Charlip designed sets and costumes for several dances, as well as performing in them. He has performed worldwide as a soloist and leader of his International All-star Dance Company.

ARLENE CROCE was the founding editor of *Ballet Review* from 1965–1978, and has served as dance critic of *The New Yorker* since 1974. Her dance writings have been collected in *Afterimages* (1977), *Going to the Dance* (1982), and *Sight Lines* (1987).

MERCE CUNNINGHAM (b. 1919) is one of America's greatest dancer/choreographers. His work has influenced countless new artists and dancemakers.

NANCY DALVA is a senior editor at *Dance Magazine.*

DON DANIELS is presently an associate editor of *Ballet Review*.

EDWIN DENBY (1903–1983) was, in his time, commonly acknowledged to be the dean of American dance critics. His complete dance writings were collected in 1987 and published by Alfred A. Knopf; his *Complete Poems* was published in 1986.

DOUGLAS DUNN (b. 1942) performed with Merce Cunningham from 1969 to 1973. He was a founding member and performer with Grand Union in the seventies. He currently leads his own company, choreographs, and performs as a soloist.

VIOLA FARBER (b. 1931) danced with the Cunningham company from 1953 to 1965, returning temporarily in 1970. She currently teaches dance at Sarah Lawrence College.

BARBARA FROST graduated in 1948 from Vassar College, whose alumni office lost track of her in the mid-1980s.

JILL JOHNSTON was the dance critic at *The Village Voice* in the 1960s; some of these reviews were collected in *Marmalade Me* (1971). She is currently writing a multivolumed autobiography that includes *Mother Bound* (1983).

KENNETH KING is a dancer/choreographer and writer, and Artistic Director of Kenneth King & Dancers/Company. He has been called an inventor and philosopher because of the diversity of his "transmedia" experiments and interdisciplinary explorations that combine dance, voices/texts, music, and technology. His prose and poetry have appeared in many magazines and anthologies.

RICHARD KOSTELANETZ (b. 1940) has written and edited scores of books of and about contemporary literature and art, including *Conversing with Cage* (1988) and *On Innovative Music(ian)s* (1989). As a composer, he has received annual Standards Awards from ASCAP; as a media artist, he has received grants and residencies for his work in radio, video, holography, and film. His visual art has been exhibited around the world. He lives in New York City.

ALASTAIR MACAULAY reviews dance, music, and theater for *The Financial Times* of London. During the 1988–89 season and again in 1992, he was guest-critic at *The New Yorker*. He founded *Dance Theatre Journal* in 1983. A collection of his writings on Frederick Ashton appeared in 1988.

DON MCDONAGH (b. 1932) has authored several books on dance, including *Martha Graham* (1973), *The Complete Guide to Modern Dance* (1977), and *The Rise and Fall and Rise of Modern Dance* (1990). He is currently the managing editor of *Ballet Review*.

WILFRID MELLERS, some time professor of music at the University of York, England, has authored many books about classic and contemporary music.

FRANK O'HARA (1926–1966) was a distinguished American poet and art historian and critic, whose work has been widely published.

STEVE PAXTON (b. 1939) performed with the Cunningham company from 1961 to 1965. He was one of the founding members of the Judson Dance Theater in 1962. He has performed and taught contact improvisation internationally. Winner of numerous awards and grants, he is currently a contributing editor to *Contact Quarterly*.

VALDA SETTERFIELD danced in the Cunningham company from 1964 to 1974. She continues to perform with her husband, dancer/choreographer David Gordon.

SYBIL SHEARER (b. circa 1918) was a distinguished dancer with the Humphrey-Weidman company, before making her solo debut in New York in 1941. Since the mid-forties, she has danced, taught, and choreographed in Chicago. She is currently Chicago correspondent for *Ballet Review*.

MARCIA B. SIEGEL (b. 1932) has collected her fugitive dance reviews in four books: *At the Vanishing Point* (1972), *Watching the Dance Go By* (1977), *The Shapes of Change: Images of American Dance* (1979), and *The Tail of the Dragon* (1991). She is also the author of *Days on Earth* (1988), a biography of Doris Humphrey. Dance critic for *The Hudson Review*, she teaches in the Performance Studies Department at New York University.

MARIANNE PREGER SIMON is now a psychotherapist in private practice in Whately, MA. She danced in Cunningham's first company from 1952 to 1958, and was the first dance critic for *The Village Voice*.

STEPHEN SMOLIAR began publishing dance criticism while finishing his doctorate in Applied Mathematics at MIT in 1971. He has since been involved in artificial intelligence research with particular attention to the application of technology to music. He has also composed music for dance and currently is review editor for *Artificial Intelligence*.

GUS SOLOMONS JR (b. circa 1940) danced with Cunningham from 1965 to 1968. He now directs his own dance company, for which he choreographs and performs, in addition to writing on dance.

CALVIN TOMKINS is a staff writer at *The New Yorker*. His classic profile of Cunningham was reprinted in the revised edition of his book *The Bride and the Bachelors* (1968).

DAVID VAUGHAN (b. 1924), born in London, England, has lived in New York since 1950 and has been associated with the Merce Cunningham Dance Company in various capacities since the 1960s, presently as its archivist. He has written *Frederick Ashton and His Ballets* (1976).

JAMES WARING (1922–1975) was a noted American dancer, choreographer, and teacher. A student of Cunningham's, he ran his own company from 1949–1966, while also choreographing for other leading international dance companies.

INDEX

All works otherwise unattributed are by Merce Cunningham.

ballet influences on works of, 117, 118; classicism of, 129; collaborations with other artists, 44–47, 96, 180–81; dance choreography of the eighties, 174; dance classes of, 121, 123, 208; durational dance rhythm of, 170–71; educational background of, 26; fragmentation in the dances of, 192–93; humor in the dances of, 26; in Martha Graham company, 117; increasing speed of pieces of, 115; independence of choreography, sound, and design, 67; influence of John Cage on, 48–49; influence of New York school of artists on, 45–46; influence of modern dance on, 117; influence on modern dance of, 72, 171, 179, 187; influence on performance art, 47; life of, 1–2; "lighter" versus "darker" works of, 72–73; misapprehension by critics of, 189; musical accompaniment to the dances of, 74–75, 76; 1966 lecture-demonstration at the 92nd Street Y, 206–9; "noise" in the dances of, 71; performances in the early 1960s, 15–17; position in twentieth-century dance of, 131; relation of choreography to music and decor, 126; relation to his dancers, 60, 104–7, 110, 113, 118–19, 126–27; relation with Marcel Duchamp, 67–68; relinquishing roles to younger dancers, 130–31; revivals of choreography of, 127, 128; rhythmic structure of dances of, 163–64, 165, 166–68; sense of community in the dances of, 183–84; solo dancing of, 27–30, 61, 114; spontaneity in the dances of, 51–52; stillness in the work of, 119; "stories" of dances of, 30; structural qualities of dances of, 64; theatricality of the dances of, 182–83; theories of space and time in modern dance, 37–39; timing in the dances of, 62–63; treatment of stage by, 129; unison dancing in the choreography of, 107–8; use of chance as working method, 179–80; use of music to accompany dances of, 181–82; use of stopwatch in rehearsing choreography, 56–57; videodances of, 19, 151–55, 156–59, 201

Cunningham Dance Company: changes in, 115–17, 124–25; early years of, 54, 101–02; individual quality of dancers in, 104

Cunningham Dance Studio, 2

Cunningham technique, 119, 122; changes in, 122–23; compared to ballet, 128

D

Dadaists, 59

Dalva, Nancy, 131

Dance Observer, 60

Dance Perspectives, issue on Cunningham, 79, 94

Dance Theater of Harlem, 17

Dance: "open-form," 51–52; relation of music to, 72

Dances Before the Wall (Waring), 58

Dark Meadow (Graham), 26

de Kooning, Elaine, 67

de Kooning, Willem, 67

Deaths and Entrances (Graham), 23

December 1952 (E. Brown), 52

Denby, Edwin, 175, 176; reaction to a Cunningham Event, 207–8

Denishawn, 132

Derrida, Jacques, 189

Designs, for Cunningham's dances, 177–78

Diaghilev, Serge, 66, 67

Digital pulse, in the work of Merce Cunningham, 188

Dinosaur Parts (Farber), 134

Diversion, A, 29, 54

Doubles, 169, 174, 175, 207, 210

Duchamp, Marcel, 43, 46, 67, 68, 69, 70, 85, 166, 180, 197

Duets; 181, 210; American Ballet Theatre production of, 160–61, 164–65